Artificial Intelligence

Ian Pratt

Department of Computer Science
University of Manchester

MACMILLAN

First published 1994 by
THE MACMILLAN PRESS LTD
Houndmills, Basingstoke, Hampshire RG21 2XS
and London
Companies and representatives
throughout the world

ISBN 0-333-59755-9

A catalogue record for this book is available
from the British Library.

Printed and bound in Great Britain by
Mackays of Chatham PLC, Chatham, Kent

Contents

Preface

A rough definition of artificial intelligence might be: the enterprise of programming computers to reason. For instance, an intelligent computer interface would be one which reasoned about its user's commands so as to interpret them sensibly and flexibly; and an intelligent robot would be one which could reason about novel ways to carry out its tasks in a changing environment. Indeed, is hard to see what intelligence without reasoning could be, and hard to see how, in practice, an artificial device could be made to reason without being controlled by some sort of computer.

As such, AI is, and needs to be, a highly technical discipline. It traffics in symbols and formulae, logics and computer languages, theorems and algorithms. Computers brook no vagueness or hand waving: the theory of reasoning required by AI must therefore be a theory more precise and detailed than any that has gone before. Yet it would be a mistake to think that AI is a discipline concerned primarily with computers. For what makes AI so challenging (and at the same time so fascinating) has less to do with the computers in which it hopes one day to produce intelligence, than with the mystery of what, exactly, the intelligence it hopes to produce in them *is*. That is, the problems of AI are not primarily computing problems (hardware or software), but problems concerning what it is for a device to reason. And the most valuable contributions made by AI are not primarily contributions to computing technology, but the precise expression of insights into the very nature of thought itself.

Thus, a textbook on AI should have two main aims: first, to explain the technical details behind the most important advances in the subject, and second, to explain the essential insights into the nature of thought which they express. These are the aims of this book.

The material presented in the following pages derives from courses given at the University of Manchester (both at undergraduate- and MSc-level) and at the Universität Hildesheim. It is designed primarily for university courses in AI which aim to take the student to a level where a large proportion of articles in the journal *Artificial Intelligence* are accessible. The book is thus suitable for AI courses from the 2nd year onwards (for students specializing in AI) up to master's level (for students encountering AI for the first time). Thus, this book covers material at a greater level of sophistication than is normal for AI textbooks. At the same time, the book is self-contained in that it presupposes only a minimal background in mathematics and computing. In particular, the appendix contains a tutorial introduction to logic.

Each chapter contains suggestions for further reading, and there is a selection of exercises which vary from the routine to the very challenging. No reliance is made on any specific programming language, although some exercises concern computer implementations of algorithms discussed in the text. Chapters 1–6 form the core of the book, and are best tackled in order; chapters 7–10, by contrast, are more independent, and readers may choose to skip one or more of them. Having gone rather deeper into many issues than other currently available AI textbooks, I have had to be more selective in the topics covered. My response has been to ignore natural language processing, computer vision and motor control. The justification for this selection is purely pragmatic. The omitted topics rely on specialized background knowledge in linguistics or applied mathematics, and are, I believe, best treated in specialist books.

Finally, I have a number of acknowledgements to make. My stay in Hildesheim, where I was privileged to teach some of this material, was made possible by a grant from the *Deutscher Akademischer Austauschdienst*, as well as by the efforts of various members of staff there. Much of the writing was done during sabbatical leave from Manchester at the *Max Planck Institut für Informatik* in Saarbrücken. I am indebted to the Department of Computer Science at Manchester University, to the Royal Society for funding this sabbatical, and of course to my erstwhile colleagues in Saarbrücken for their overwhelming hospitality and friendliness. In addition, progress on this book was aided by a research grant from the Joint Councils' Research Initiative in Cognitive Science, no. SPG 8920254. I wish also to express my gratitude to the following individuals for their help: John Stobo, David Brée, Jens Dörpmund, Detlev Fehrer, Chiara Menchini, Luoping Xu, Jeff Paris, Andrzej Glowinski, Ivan Leudar and Vaughan Marks. Finally, I would like to thank my long-suffering students, both in the UK and in Germany, for being so patient while I was trying out a variety of ideas on them, only some of which I have thought it wise to print.

1 What is Artificial Intelligence?

1.1 Introduction

Imagine you are at home, sitting in an armchair, when you notice that it is uncomfortably hot. You walk over to the central heating control and look at the thermometer. "30°C," it says. You turn the temperature control knob down a few notches and return to your seat, confident that the temperature will fall. Now consider things from the thermostat's point of view. It had been set to keep the heating at 30°C, and was busily switching the heaters on or off depending on whether the thermometer registered less than or more than 30°C. After you turn it down a couple of notches, it does exactly the same thing but for some lower temperature.

In some respects, you and the thermostat have much in common. The thermostat is set to a temperature which it is its job to maintain. It is so wired-up to the thermometer and the heating system that a drop in temperature below the set level causes the heating to come on, and a rise above that level causes the heating to go off. You too might be said to want to maintain a certain level of comfort regarding how hot or cold you feel (this in turn may depend on a number of factors). You are so wired-up that if you become uncomfortably cold, you turn the heating control knob up a few notches; and if you become uncomfortably hot, you turn it down.

So much for the similarities between you and the thermostat; now for a crucial difference. Although both the thermostat and you react to changes in temperature so as to control them, only you have any idea of what you are doing, and why you are doing it. You *want* to make things cooler, *believe* that turning the heating down has this effect, and *infer* or *decide* that the thing to do is to operate the appropriate control. But the thermostat (according to conventional wisdom) does not *want* or *believe* or *infer* or *decide* anything: it just switches from one state to another; it is just so wired-up that changes in temperature cause corrective reaction by the heating system. While you reason, the thermostat just switches.

The foregoing observations leave us with something of a puzzle. When you walk over to adjust the heating control – again, according to conventional wisdom – your movements are caused, insofar as they are caused at all, by physical processes in your brain. True, these physical processes of *inferring* and *deciding*, like the physical states of *believing* and *desiring* on which they depend, are incredibly complex affairs. But they are still just physical processes and states. True again, the 'wiring' connecting the nerve cells in your skin, via your brain, to the muscles

1

that you flex in the process of turning the knob is vastly more intricate than the wiring that connects the thermometer, via the thermostat, to the heaters. But it is still – in the broadest sense of the word – just wiring. So we are led to ask why there seems to be a qualitative difference here between you and the thermostat. What is it about the complicated processing that goes on in you, but not in the thermostat, that makes us inclined to say that you, but not the thermostat, make inferences on the basis of what you want and believe, and act or react at least sometimes as a result of those inferences?

Opinions vary. Part of the answer, it seems, lies in the enormous complexity of human behaviour compared to that of the thermostat, and in the variety of ways that complexity manifests itself. For example, if you find the temperature control has been set to what you regard as a ridiculously high level, you can try to work out who might have been responsible, and decide to have a word with him so that it does not happen again. Or, if you see that the temperature is at a level which you would normally regard as comfortable, you might wonder why you feel so hot, suspect an incipient illness, and decide not to turn the heating down after all. Thermostats do nothing like this: they display nowhere near this level of flexibility in their behaviour. Yet merely contrasting human complexity with thermostat simplicity can hardly be the *whole* explanation of the difference between thinking agents and unthinking devices. For we need to know precisely *which aspects* of the human's extra complexity are responsible for his counting as a thinking being. It is not just any old complexity that is required here, but complexity along certain specific dimensions. Question: what sorts of functional complexity are characteristic of thinking agents?

The practical importance of this question should not be underestimated. If human thought really is just a complex physical process, then it must be possible, at least in principle, to construct a mechanical device which thinks, or (for those who believe that machines cannot think) at least produces a simulation of thought indistinguishable from the real thing. And we would like to know *what* features, *what* sorts of complexity, to build into this device for us to be able to classify it as such. On the plausible assumption that such a device would, for practical reasons, have to be controlled by a digital computer, this question translates itself into the problem of programming a computer of which we can say that it has beliefs and desires, and that it infers and decides. The enterprise of solving this problem forms a large part of the discipline that has come to be called Artificial Intelligence. Thus, a large part of AI is the enterprise of programming computers to make inferences. It is this enterprise that forms the subject of this book.

Not all areas of AI can be so naturally regarded as the study of computer-based inference. Natural language processing, automated perception (especially computer vision), and motor control have been the subject of intensive research in recent decades, and yet are not obviously best regarded as merely inferential processes (this is especially true of work in motor control in robotics). Thus, in concentrating on the enterprise of programming computers to make inferences, there is much important work—particularly connected with how intelligent systems perceive and act in their environment—that will fall outside the scope of this book. Since most of these fields employ their own specialized techniques and knowledge, e.g. linguistics, digital signal processing, mechanical engineering, there is good reason to regard them as separate subjects, best treated elsewhere.

One caveat before we proceed. In declaring areas like natural language processing, automated perception and motor control as outside our remit, we must not regard them as being of secondary importance to AI – things which can always be bolted onto the outside of an inference system (once we have got one working) to make a useful device. On the contrary, work in the fields of perception and action must inform and stimulate the study of inference by helping to establish just *which* inferences an intelligent agent has to make. Thus, if we are designing an intelligent agent to respond to English commands, or inspect machine parts for defects, or sweep up litter on railway platforms, we may well want to think of that system as making inferences based on its knowledge of the environment and objectives. But what, exactly, this knowledge will be, what form it will be in, and what exactly the agent needs to decide in order for it actually to *do* something—these questions can be answered only by studying noninferential aspects of perception and action. Moral: bracketing inference as a self-contained subject may make expository sense for the purposes of this book; but it would make a poor research policy for the development of intelligent systems. With that caveat behind us, let us look in more detail at some inferential problems.

To help fix our ideas, we shall work through two simple inferential problems in this chapter. The purpose of the examples is to introduce some of the key concepts in AI which we shall encounter repeatedly in the course of this book: *knowledge representation, inference, heuristics* and *search*. Since our task in this chapter is to introduce important concepts, we shall avoid the technical details here as much as possible; there will be plenty of opportunity to return to them in due course.

1.2 A simple planning problem

Our first example concerns a robot – let us call him Bob – who inhabits the house shown in figure 1.1. The house contains just four rooms: hall, sitting-room, bedroom, and study; and all adjacent rooms have doors connecting them. Bob's function is to move various objects from one room to another. For simplicity, we will suppose that there are just two objects to be moved about: a table and a bookcase. Bob is programmed with a plan of the house, together with information as to where various things (including himself) happen to be at any time. Again, for simplicity, we always assume that Bob's information is correct and, in the relevant respects, complete. We take Bob's repertoire of actions to be limited to just two types of action: *carrying* an object from one room to another and *going* from one room to another. We further assume that nothing gets in Bob's way, that doors are always open and are never blocked, and that rooms never get full. Bob receives commands like: "Put the table in the bedroom, move the bookcase into the study

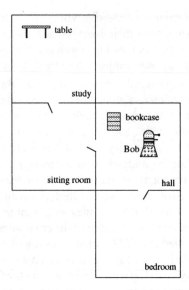

Figure 1.1   Bob's house and its contents

and leave yourself in the sitting-room"; he thereupon constructs a plan – that is, a sequence of actions he can perform – to achieve these goals. When he has devised such a plan, he executes it and awaits further instructions. Our task is to design a planning program controlling Bob.

1.2.1   Representing the problem

The first step is to decide how best to represent the problem in such a way that the computer program controlling Bob can make useful inferences with the information at its disposal. In particular, we need to represent (i) the possible *situations* Bob and his environment could be in, (ii) the *goals* that Bob has been set, (iii) the *actions* and sequences of actions that Bob will have to perform to achieve his goals and (iv) Bob's knowledge of the layout of the house.

(i) For our purposes, a *situation* is simply something which specifies the locations of all the movable objects in the house – i.e. the table, the bookcase and Bob himself. For example, if Bob is in the hall with the bookcase, and the table is in the study, that is a situation. We might represent that situation using the data-structure:

$$[in(bob,hall),in(bookcase,hall),in(table,study)]. \quad (1.1)$$

This data-structure can then be stored and accessed by the computer controlling Bob. (How such data-structures are *actually* realized in the computer depends on the details of the language in which Bob's programs are written; and implementations vary. But most practicable programming languages, and certainly AI-oriented languages such as LISP and Prolog, allow data-structures such as (1.1) to be easily created and accessed.)

(ii) Similarly, we can take Bob's set of *goals* to be simply something which specifies the desired locations of some, though not necessarily all, the movable objects in the house. For instance, if Bob wants the table in the sitting-room and himself in the hall, that is a set of goals. We might represent those goals using the data-structure:

```
[in(table,sitting-room),in(bob,hall)].                    (1.2)
```

(iii) We need to make a decision about how to represent the actions that Bob can perform. For example, carrying the bookcase from the study to the sitting room is an action. We might sensibly represent this action using the data-structure:

```
carry(bookcase,study,sitting-room).                       (1.3)
```

Likewise, going from the bedroom to the hall is an action, and we might represent this action using the data-structure:

```
go(bedroom,hall).
```

So far as Bob is concerned, a *plan* is just a sequence of actions to be performed in order to achieve his goals. For example, if Bob is initially in the situation (1.1) and has the goals (1.2), a suitable plan would involve *going* from the hall to the sitting-room, *going* from the sitting-room to the study, *carrying* the table from the study to the sitting-room, and finally *going* from the sitting-room to the hall. We might represent this plan using the data-structure:

```
[go(hall,sitting-room),go(sitting-room,study),
 carry(table,study,sitting-room),go(sitting-room,hall)].
```

(iv) Finally, we need to decide on a representation of the layout of the house. There are many possibilities here, but, for the simple planning task we are faced with, all that is really required is a list of facts specifying which rooms are adjacent to which. Thus, we can suppose that Bob's program has access to a list:

```
[adjacent(bedroom,hall),
 adjacent(hall,sitting-room),                             (1.4)
 adjacent(sitting-room,study)].
```

1.2.2 Representing knowledge about actions

So much for Bob's representations of situations, goals, actions, and the layout of the house. But if Bob is to devise plans to achieve his goals, the program controlling him needs to know about the various types of actions in his repertoire, including the conditions under which they can be performed and their effects when they are performed.

Consider the action-type of carrying an object from one room to another. Reasoning about this action depends upon knowing the following:

> For any object Object, and for any rooms Room1 and Room2:
> o Bob can perform the action carry(Object,Room1,Room2), provided that Room1 and Room2 are adjacent, that Object is in Room1 and that Bob is in Room1.
> o If Bob performs this action, some new facts will obtain: Object and Bob will be in Room2.
> o In addition, if Bob performs this action, some old facts will cease to obtain: Object and Bob will no longer be in Room1.

Again, this information can be represented easily as a computer data-structure, though this time a little more complexity is required. The data-structure shown below is one possibility. It has three parts: a *preconditions-list,* an *add-list* and a *delete-list.*

```
action-type(carry(Object,Room1,Room2),
    pre-conds([in(Object,Room1),
               in(bob,Room1),
               adjacent(Room1, Room2)]),              (1.5)
    add-list([in(bob,Room2),in(Object,Room2)]),
    del-list([in(bob,Room1),in(Object,Room1)])).
```

The preconditions are a list of facts which must hold in the current situation if the action is to be performable at all; the add-list specifies those new facts that will hold if the action is performed; the delete-list specifies those old facts which will cease to hold if the action is performed.

Corresponding information about the action of *going* from one room to an adjacent room (without carrying anything) can be represented similarly as follows:

```
action-type(go(Room1,Room2),
    pre-conds([in(bob,Room1),
               adjacent(Room1,Room2)]),              (1.6)
    add-list([in(bob,Room2)]),
    del-list([in(bob,Room1)])).
```

We will encounter data-structures of type (1.5) and (1.6) again in later chapters, and so we need a name for them. Since they are rules containing Preconditions, and Add-list and a Delete-list, we shall call them *PAD-rules.* Thus, we can use PAD-rules to represent the facts that Bob needs to know about the various kinds of actions he can perform.

Notice that we are interpreting Object, Room1 and Room2 in the PAD-rules (1.5) and (1.6) as *variables:* that is, they do not refer to *specific* objects or rooms such as do, e.g. `bookcase` or `sitting-room`. We will see how to make use of variables presently. To help us distinguish variables in data-structures, we shall always write variables with initial capital letters (e.g. `Room1`, and not `room1`); and we shall always write non-variables with initial small letters (e.g. `sitting-room`, and not `Sitting-room`). That is why, in our data-structures, we write `bob` with a small b.

It is no accident that we have begun our task by making decisions about how we are to *represent* the problem at hand. The design of most AI systems begins with such decisions, and the discipline of representing information for use by AI systems is sometimes referred to as *knowledge representation*. There are many different approaches to knowledge representation, and some central disputes in AI turn on the relative appropriateness of these approaches for various sorts of reasoning tasks. Issues in knowledge representation will never be far away in this book.

1.2.3 Making inferences

Representing facts about actions in the way suggested in section 1.2.2 enables Bob straightforwardly to compute the effect of a given action in a given situation. For example suppose Bob's representation of the current situation is the data-structure (1.1), and Bob needs to work out what will happen if he executes the action of carrying the bookcase from the hall to the sitting-room, i.e. the action

```
carry(bookcase,hall,sitting-room).
```

The procedure is as follows. First, Bob makes a copy of the PAD-rule (1.5), substituting `bookcase` for `Object`, `hall` for `Room1` and `sitting-room` for `Room2`, thus:

```
action-type(carry(bookcase,hall,sitting-room),
   pre-conds([in(bookcase,hall),
            in(bob,hall),
            adjacent(hall,sitting-room)]),          (1.7)
   add-list ([in(bob,sitting-room),
            in(bookcase,sitting-room)]),
   del-list ([in(bob, hall), in(bookcase, hall)]))).
```

Next, the preconditions of the rule-instance are checked against the current situation. In this case, the preconditions specify that Bob and the bookcase both be in the hall, and that the hall be adjacent to the sitting-room. These conditions can be seen to be fulfilled in the current situation as represented by list (1.1) and given the layout of the house as represented by list (1.4). Having verified that the preconditions in (1.7) are satisfied, Bob can then compute the effect of the action by taking the list (1.1), adding to it the facts in the add-list of (1.7), and deleting the facts in the delete-list of (1.7). The result is the data-structure:

```
[in(bob,sitting-room),in(bookcase,sitting-room),
 in(table,study)],
```

representing the resulting situation. Clearly, there is no special problem about programming a computer to carry out such manipulations. In fact, this is exactly the sort of thing that computers are very good at.

It is important to realize that we can think of the manipulation of data-structures just described – in which one situation is transformed into another by applying a PAD-rule – as an *inference*. In this case, the inference is of the form:

> The current situation is s
> Action a will be performed
> ———————————————————
> The new situation will be s'.

That is, the manipulation of data structures described above (test the preconditions; add the add-list; remove the delete-list) is a prescription to the program controlling Bob for how to revise its *beliefs* about its environment if an action is to be performed.

We have explained so far how the data-structures given in section 1.2.2 can be used to support inferences about the effects of individual actions. Clearly, these inferences can be chained together to reason about the effects of sequences of actions, i.e. plans. Suppose, for example, we take the initial situation

```
[in(bob,hall),in(bookcase,hall),in(table,study)]
```

and the proposed plan

```
[go(hall,sitting-room),go(sitting-room,study),
 carry(table,study,sitting-room),go(sitting-room,hall)].
```

It is clearly possible to write a program to step through this plan, checking, for each action, that its preconditions are satisfied and then computing the resulting situation using the appropriate add- and delete-lists. The sequence of situations obtained is:

1. `[ in(bob,hall),in(bookcase,hall),in(table,study)]`
2. `[in(bob,sitting-room),in(bookcase,hall),`
   `   in(table,study)]`
3. `[in(bob,study),in(bookcase,hall),in(table,study)]`
4. `[in(bob,sitting-room),in(bookcase,hall),`
   `   in(table,sitting-room)]`
5. `[in(bob,hall),in(bookcase,hall),`
   `   in(table,sitting-room)],`

so the above sequence of actions is a suitable plan for achieving the goals (1.2), since those goals are realized in the final situation. Again, the point to emphasize here is that these calculations can be regarded as *inferences* – transitions from one belief to another. Such inferences have the form:

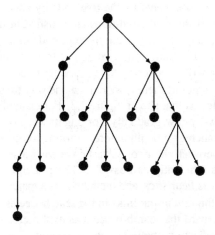

Figure 1.2   A search-tree

The current situation is *s*
Plan *p* will be executed
———————————————————
The new situation will be *s'*.

Such an inference will obviously be useful if *s'* is a situation in which Bob's goals are true.

Of course, merely checking that a given plan *p* achieves a given set of goals *G* is not what our original task demanded of us. What we have to do is *find* a plan that achieves *G*. For this, we must resort to another important idea in AI: search.

1.2.4   Searching for plans

We get a more global view of the planning task by looking at the collection of possible situations together with the actions that can be performed in them. Figure 1.2 shows how situations and actions can be usefully visualized. Each node in the tree represents a possible situation, and a link from one node to another below it represents an action which can be performed in the situation represented by the first node, and which results in the situation represented by the second node. The root node – the node at the very top of the tree – represents the initial situation. Thus, the tree is, in effect, a map of the possible sequences of action that Bob can take for a given initial situation. Remember: each node in the tree of figure 1.2 represents a complete situation (think of the node as being 'tagged' with a list such as (1.1)); likewise, each link in the tree represents an action (think of the arrow as being 'tagged' with the name of an action such as (1.3)). The problem of finding a plan to achieve a given set of goals can now be viewed in the following terms:

starting from the root node, generate the tree node by node, testing each node as it is generated to see if the goal conditions are satisfied in it. Once such a node is found, the route through the tree from the root node to this node will be a plan to achieve the goals. Programming a computer to perform this search is quite straightforward. (We will be covering the techniques to do so later in the book.)

Here is one crucial point: there is more than one way for a program to search a tree of inferences such as that shown figure 1.2. For example, the program could look at the nodes row-by-row, gradually working its way down the tree; or it could pursue individual branches in depth before returning to others; or it could opt for some compromise between the two. Clearly, we want a search procedure which finds a goal state as efficiently as possible. The principles which guide search processes are known as *heuristics*, and their study is a major research theme in AI.

So far, we have thought of the links in the search-tree as representing actions, and it is natural to regard the search process as exploration of a space of action-sequences. But, on reflection, the links can be thought of as standing not so much for *actions* which might be performed, as for *inferences* about what would happen if the actions in question were performed. And search through the search-tree can be regarded as exploration of a space of possible *inference*-sequences. That is, the heuristics which a program uses to find plans are really search procedures for finding an inference of the form: "If such-and-such a plan is executed, then my goals will be achieved".

This last observation is important, for it suggests that search plays a fundamental role not just in planning, but in inference generally. In Bob's planning program, the inferences in question are inferences about the effects of actions. But similar remarks apply to other sorts of inferences, as we shall see in the next section.

1.3   Inference outside planning

Consider a computer program whose job is to make inferences about family rela-tionships. We shall imagine that the program has access to a database of family trees, in the form of facts about parental and marital relationships involving the individuals in the database, as well as the usual definitions of common family relationships such as *father, brother, uncle* etc. The program's task is then to answer queries about such matters as, e.g. how many uncles someone has, whether two people are related, what the names of a person's brothers are, and so on.

As a simple example, consider just one specific sort of inference – inferring that one person is another person's ancestor. We shall suppose that the program's database contains the following specific facts:

> Sue is a parent of Noel
> Noel is a parent of Ann
> Ann is a parent of Dave.

A suitable definition of ancestor might be:

Any parent of someone is that person's ancestor
Any parent of someone's ancestor is that person's ancestor.

The program should, given this information, be able to make the inference:

Sue is an ancestor of Dave.

Let us see how this might be done.

As with the planning example considered above, our first task is to decide how to encode the program's knowledge. The set of facts about individuals might be represented using the data-structure:

$$[parent(sue,noel),parent(noel,ann), \atop parent(ann,dave)] \tag{1.8}$$

while the program's definition of the relation *ancestor* might be represented using the PAD-rules:

```
action-type(
    ancestor-rule-1(X,Y),
    pre-conds([parent(X,Y)]),
    add-list([ancestor(X,Y)]))
```
(1.9)

```
action-type(
    ancestor-rule-2(X,Y,Z),
    pre-conds([parent(X,Y), ancestor(Y,Z)]),
    add-list([ancestor(X,Z)])).
```
(1.10)

Notice that there are no delete-lists in the above PAD-rules. In terms of the kinds of inference considered here, where information simply accumulates, there is no use for delete-lists: once something has been inferred, it cannot be uninferred.

Making inferences is now a matter of applying these rules to generate new, larger, lists of facts. For example, consider the instance of rule (1.9) with ann substituted for X and dave substituted for Y, that is:

```
action-type(
    ancestor-rule-1(ann,dave),
    pre-conds([parent(ann,dave)]),
    add-list([ancestor(ann,dave)]))
```

Since the precondition of this rule-instance is satisfied by the list of known facts (1.8), an inference can be made by adding the add-list to that list, resulting in the data-structure:

```
[parent(sue,noel),parent(noel,ann),parent(ann,dave),
 ancestor(ann,dave)].
```

Having arrived at this enlarged list of facts, the program can now go on to apply further rule-instances, just as the planning program for Bob computed the effects of various action-instances in the example of section 1.2. For instance, the rule (1.10) can be applied, with noel substituted for X, ann substituted for Y and dave substituted for Z, to get the list of facts:

```
[parent(sue,noel),parent(noel,ann),parent(ann,dave),
  ancestor(ann,dave), ancestor(noel,dave)].
```

Finally rule (1.10) can be applied again, this time with sue substituted for X, noel substituted for Y and dave substituted for Z to get the list of facts:

```
[parent(sue,noel),parent(noel,ann),parent(ann,dave),
  ancestor(ann,dave), ancestor(noel,dave),
  ancestor(sue,dave)].
```

Thus, we have arrived at a list of facts containing the assertion that Sue is an ancestor of Dave. That is, we have made the inference we were seeking.

Again, as with the planning program of section 1.2, we can view the initial database and the PAD-rules as defining a tree as depicted in figure 1.2. Here, the nodes of the tree are lists of facts that have been derived – *knowledge-situations*, as it were – and the links are applications of the applicable instances of the PAD-rules transforming one knowledge-situation into another. In any given knowledge-situation, many inferences are possible, some leading towards the program's goal, others completely unhelpful. Finding an inference can be be viewed as a search through such a tree. The particular sequence of inferences just considered was of course chosen to lead directly to the sought-after conclusion. But a computer program trying to make these inferences for itself will in general need to perform extensive search in order to hit upon a suitable series of deductions. Again, in applications where the space of possible inferences is very large, the heuristics employed by the inference program – i.e. the order in which it explores the search-tree – will play a crucial role in determining its effectiveness.

Of course, the inferences that we have considered in this section – inferences which merely involve computing the ancestor-relation – are so simple that they can hardly be said to constitute examples of intelligent processing. (Do not worry about the simplicity of these examples: we will encounter plenty of complicated ones in chapters 4 and 5!) But what is at issue here is not the programming techniques used to tackle these examples, but the way of thinking about the processing of information that they suggest—in particular, the view of information processing as movement within a space of possible inferences implicitly defined by a knowledge-base. The consequences of this view will become clearer in the ensuing chapters; for the present, we must be content with the following general remarks.

1.4   Inference

1.4.1   *Beliefs versus heuristics*

One important aspect of inference we have repeatedly stressed in discussing the programs of sections 1.2 and 1.3 is that, in general, there are many sequences of *possible* inferences, but only a very few that will lead to the desired conclusion. And since the search-spaces in most non-trivial reasoning problems are usually large and often infinite, suitable heuristics for the problem at hand are a critical component of an effective inference mechanism. But this observation applies just as much to humans as to AI programs. What makes someone good at inference is not just a matter of the collection of things he believes and the rules of inference he accepts, but also, of the policies he uses to deploy those beliefs and rules of inference to good effect. The separation of a reasoner's competence into these two factors – *beliefs* and *heuristics* – is fundamental to inference.

Let us consider, for a moment, some of the differences between beliefs and heuristics. First of all, the things one believes are (at least in many cases) *true* or *false*. Thus, if you believe that the bookcase is in the sitting-room, there is a fact of the matter which makes that belief true or false; likewise, if you believe that the effects of a certain action are that such-and-such things become true and so-and-so things cease to be true, there is again a fact of the matter as to whether this is really so. But with heuristics, by contrast, it does not make sense to speak of truth or falsity. For a particular problem, it may be that focusing on one line of enquiry constitutes an effective way to find a solution whereas exploring others in depth tends to be inefficient. But that does not mean that the heuristics one deploys are *true* or *false*. There is nothing which could mean this.

Not only does it not make sense to talk about the truth or falsity of heuristics, but the evaluation of heuristics as effective or ineffective has a quite different impact on the final conclusion from the evaluation of beliefs as true or false. We can see the difference more clearly with an example. Suppose you have inferred a conclusion P on the basis of a belief Q that you previously held, but that you later discover that Q is false; it seems rational in that case to give up not only Q but P as well. Now suppose, by contrast, that you have inferred a conclusion P using a rather round-about proof, and that you later change the way you go about solving problems of that type – i.e. you give up your old heuristics. In this case, it does not seem rational to give up the conclusion P: the inference is still perfectly acceptable, however you hit upon it.

Here is a related case which also illustrates the difference between knowledge and heuristics. Suppose two people, A and B, are considering the same question, but working from different sets of assumptions. If A announces to B a conclusion P (together with his reasons), then that is not necessarily a reason for B to adopt that conclusion: after all, A and B do not agree on their basic premises. Now suppose, by contrast, that A and B begin from exactly the same set of assumptions, but using different heuristics. In this case, if as A tells B of a conclusion P

(together with his reasons), the fact that A and B are using different heuristics is no reason at all for B not to accept that conclusion.

In sum, a characteristic difference between beliefs and heuristics is that people normally exhibit a kind of *flexibility* – or openness to alternatives – with regard to their heuristics which they normally do not exhibit with regard to their beliefs. It is this special kind of flexibility that makes heuristics different from beliefs.

1.4.2   Heuristics, inference and search

We have explained, in broad outline, the difference between a person's *beliefs* and his *heuristics* in terms of the different ways these two components of his thought function. To characterize a reasoner as having beliefs and heuristics therefore presupposes a certain sort of complexity: in particular, the reasoner must display the characteristic flexibility regarding his heuristics that we took in section 1.4.1 to differentiate heuristics from beliefs. Few if any mechanical devices could sensibly be described as comprising a set of beliefs together with heuristics which combine to produce that device's overall input-output characteristics: there is just no sense in which they display the sort of flexibility that, as we argued, such a description presupposes. And that, we suggest, is one good reason (to be sure, there may be others!) why we should not think of such devices as making *inferences*: they lack the requisite structure to allow characterization in terms of interacting beliefs and heuristics.

Here is one way to think about that structure. When we say that a reasoner's inferences are the product of his beliefs and his heuristics acting together, we are suggesting that that his beliefs give him a sort of potential access to a collection of inferences which he cannot make unaided. Paradoxical as this may sound, it is true in the following sense: a reasoner can be shown chains of inference to which his heuristics would not have led him, and yet which he can accept given his beliefs and principles of inference. That is a consequence of the characteristic flexibility of heuristics, which we pointed out in section 1.4.1. Now, this division into interacting components – beliefs and heuristics – is modelled, albeit perhaps crudely, by a search-based architecture of the kind illustrated in the examples of sections 1.2 and 1.3, and which is prevalent in AI systems. In such systems, we typically distinguish the 'knowledge-base' (i.e. the system's 'beliefs') from the heuristics. Since, as we explained, the knowledge-base, together with the system's rules of inference, defines a search-tree, we can think of the inferences to which the system has 'access' as the inferences to be found within that search-tree. The separate heuristic component then directs the system's actual inferences, perhaps restricting the inferences that it will in practice make.

It is true that few if any AI programs exhibit quite the kind of flexibility or openness to suggestion that we expect of humans, and which we took in section 1.4.1 to be characteristic of the heuristic nature of inference. Nevertheless, in a system whose architecture is based on separation of knowledge-base and heuristics, and whose output can be seen as heuristically guided search through the search-tree, the potential for such flexibility is there. For it is possible to see how a heuristically guided inference program of the kind we have considered in this chapter might be given the additional feature of openness to suggestion that we took to be a necessary condition for inference. That, we argue, is why search is so important in AI: such architectures hold out the prospect of supporting one kind of complexity – heuristic flexibility – that is characteristic of the inferential behaviour of humans.

1.5 Conclusion

In this chapter, we have discussed some of the key concepts of AI – *knowledge representation, inference, search* and *heuristics* – with reference to two simple, but nevertheless illustrative, programming tasks. We explained the central role of inference in AI, how inference presupposes a structure in which the separate components of beliefs and heuristics interact, and how this structure is modelled in AI systems.

This is not to claim that we have found the fundamental difference between the inferential processes of thinking beings and the mechanical switching of a thermostat. No one can yet justifiably make that claim. But we have gone some way towards an answer by identifying one aspect of complexity – the separation of beliefs and heuristics – that seems to be characteristic of inference; and we have shown how computer programs could be based on an architecture tailor-made to support such a separation. But we must guard against too detailed a philosophical analysis at this early stage. The concepts just mentioned – *knowledge representation, inference, search* and *heuristics* – like concepts of proto-science generally, rest on whole rafts of associations both from other academic disciplines and from common usage, whose ultimate relevance to the discipline of AI is still unclear. Often, the best way to tackle high-level questions is first to acquire a better grasp of the low-level details: that way we benefit from a clearer idea of where the effort is needed. It is to the details, then, that we now turn.

Further reading

The philosophical foundations of AI are still in a state of flux, and it would not be fair to say that the view presented in this chapter is accepted by all, though it is fairly middle-of-the-road. A good collection of recent papers on this topic is to be found in Kirsh [2]. The central importance of search is elaborated by many writers, perhaps most monumentally by Newell [3]. It will be clear to readers, however, that Newell's reasons for taking search to be fundamental to AI are not those presented in this chapter. A good introduction to the philosophical issues surrounding AI is Haugeland [1].

The reader interested in gaining an impression of the different sorts of work currently being carried out in AI is referred to the major conference proceedings and journals in the field. Some important conferences are *The European Confer-*

ence on *Artificial Intelligence (ECAI)*, *The American Association for Artificial Intelligence (AAAI)*, *The International Joint Conference on Artificial Intelligence (IJCAI)* and *The Cognitive Science Society*. These proceedings contain mostly technical papers, but they are representative of mainstream work in the field. Some important journals are *Artificial Intelligence*, *Cognitive Science*, *Behavioural and Brain Sciences* and *Minds and Machines*, as well as many more journals dedicated to individual subfields. In addition, a useful and very general reference work is the two-volume *Encyclopedia of Artificial Intelligence* (Shapiro [4]).

Bibliography

[1] Haugeland, J. *Artificial Intelligence: the very idea*, Cambridge, MA: MIT Press, 1985.
[2] Kirsh, David (ed.) *Foundations of Artificial Intelligence*, Cambridge, MA: MIT Press, 1992.
[3] Newell, Allen *Unified Theories of Cognition*, Cambridge, MA: Harvard University Press, 1990.
[4] Shapiro, Stuart C. (ed.) *The Encyclopedia of Artificial Intelligence*, vols 1 and 2, New York: Wiley, 1987.

2 Search and Planning

Chapter 1 introduced some general ideas about the roles of knowledge representation and inference in AI, with particular emphasis on reasoning about plans of action. The aim of this chapter is to present the technical details required to turn these general ideas into computer programs. In doing so, we will encounter many of the central problems of search and planning, and some of the techniques that have been developed to tackle them. Mastery of these techniques will put us in a good position to appreciate the more theoretical issues raised in subsequent chapters.

2.1 The planning program for Bob

2.1.1 The problem and its representation

Recall the planning task of chapter 1. We discussed how to write a planning program for a robot, Bob, who inhabits the house shown in figure 2.1, and whose function is to move various objects from one room to another. We settled on the following knowledge representation scheme. Situations are represented as lists specifying the location of all movable objects, e.g.

$$[\text{in(bob,hall),in(bookcase,hall),in(table,study)]} \quad (2.1)$$

(this is actually the situation depicted in figure 2.1); goals are represented as a list specifying the desired locations of some of the movable objects, e.g.

$$[\text{in(bob,hall),in(table,sitting-room)]}; \quad (2.2)$$

actions are represented by combining action types with parameters, e.g.

$$\text{carry(bookcase,study,sitting-room)};$$

and the layout of the house is represented using a list of adjacency-facts

$$[\text{adjacent(bedroom,hall),adjacent(hall,sitting-room),}$$
$$\text{adjacent(sitting-room,study)]}.$$

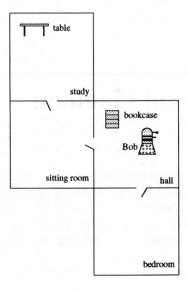

Figure 2.1   Bob's house and its contents

Finally, the properties of the two available action-types are represented using the PAD-rules:

```
action-type(
    carry(Object,Room1,Room2),
    pre-conds([in(Object,Room1),
               in(bob,Room1),
               adjacent(Room1,Room2)]),
    add-list([in(bob,Room2),in(Object,Room2)]),
    del-list([in(bob,Room1),in(Object,Room1)])).
```
(2.3)

```
action-type(
    go(Room1,Room2),
    pre-conds([in(bob,Room1),
               adjacent(Room1,Room2)]),
    add-list([in(bob,Room2)]),
    del-list([in(bob,Room1)])).
```
(2.4)

We saw in chapter 1 how the above decisions on knowledge representation allow the construction of a search-tree whose nodes are tagged with data-structures representing situations (with the root node representing the initial situation) and whose links are tagged with data-structures representing actions. Finding a plan is simply then a matter of constructing and searching the tree until a situation is found in which the goal conditions are satisfied. Our task in this section will be to establish precisely how best to do this.

2.1.2 The search-tree in detail

One point to be clear about is that we need not construct the entire search-tree (or some initial segment thereof) before we start searching. In practice, we generate the nodes one by one, starting with the node corresponding to the initial situation, and test the nodes as they are generated. Once a node has been found which satisfies the goals, or when the tree cannot be grown any further, the search stops. Testing a node to see whether it (or rather, the corresponding situation) satisfies the goals is a straightforward matter of determining whether the goals are all in the list tagging the node in question. Obtaining the children of a given node is a straightforward matter of looking at all the possible instances of the PAD-rules (2.3) and (2.4) and seeing which ones have their preconditions satisfied in the situation to which that node corresponds: the add- and delete-lists then allow the children of the node to be generated.

Before we describe the implementation of a planning program for Bob, there are two technical problems to be solved. The first concerns sequences of actions which lead us round in a circle back to some previously encountered situation. For example, in situation (2.1), Bob can perform the action go(hall,bedroom). In the resulting situation, he can perform the action go(bedroom,hall). Then, in the resulting situation, which is of course just the original situation (2.1), he can perform the action go(hall,bedroom). And so on, leading to an infinite branch of the search-tree in which Bob simply goes back and forth between the hall and the bedroom.

Since it can never be sensible to perform action sequences which take Bob round in circles, we want some method of preventing them from arising in the search-tree. The solution is to record, at each node, not just the situation that node stands for, but also, the *list of all previous situations encountered*. For example, a node in the third row of the tree could be tagged with a data-structure such as

$$
\begin{aligned}
&\texttt{sit-list([[in(bob,hall),in(bookcase,hall),}\\
&\qquad\texttt{in(table,study)],}\\
&\qquad\texttt{[in(bob,sitting-room),in(bookcase,hall),}\\
&\qquad\texttt{in(table,study)],}\\
&\qquad\texttt{[in(bob,study),in(bookcase,hall),}\\
&\qquad\texttt{in(table,study)]])}
\end{aligned}
\qquad (2.5)
$$

This tag represents the situation in which Bob and the table are in the study, and the bookcase is in the hall (i.e. the last situation in the list); but it also includes information about the preceding situations. Tagging nodes in this way lets us be more selective when generating the children of a node. Specifically, we can ignore those children corresponding to already-encountered situations, thus avoiding sequences of actions that would take Bob round in circles. Of course, it will often be the case that, when expanding a node, all the actions that are possible in the corresponding situation lead to situations which have been encountered. In that case, the node in question has no children at all. In fact, in the present planning problem, the practice of ignoring children corresponding to already-encountered situations guarantees that the search-tree will be finite.

Now for the second of our two technical problems. Suppose we find a node in which all Bob's goals are satisfied. What we want to do now is to return the *list of actions* that will lead from the initial situation to the goal-situation we have just encountered; that is, after all, the purpose of the planner. So we have the problem of recovering this list of actions. The solution is to record, at each node, not just the sequence of situations that node stands for, but also, the list of actions used to produce them. For example, instead of tagging a node in the third row of the tree with the data-structure (2.5), as suggested above, we will instead tag it with the more complicated data-structure:

```
[sit-list([[in(bob,hall),in(bookcase,hall),
            in(table,study)],
           [in(bob,sitting-room),in(bookcase,hall),
            in(table,study)],
           [in(bob,study),in(bookcase,hall),                    (2.6)
            in(table,study)]]),
   act-list([go(hall,sitting-room),
             go(sitting-room,study)])]
```

This tag represents the situation in which Bob and the table are in the study, and the bookcase is in the hall; but it also includes information about the preceding situations and the actions that were performed to reach them. Tagging nodes in this way ensures that the information we need is to hand whenever we find a situation in which Bob's goals are achieved.

Thus, the general form of the data-structure corresponding to a node is:

$$[\texttt{sit-list}([\textit{situation}_1, \dots \textit{situation}_n],$$
$$\texttt{act-list}([\textit{action}_1, \dots, \textit{action}_{n-1}])],$$

where $action_i$ leads from $situation_i$ to $situation_{i+1}$. Clearly, the nodes in the tree now have a complicated structure; but that of course is no problem for a computer. It is still relatively straightforward (if somewhat fiddly) to write programs to test whether the goals are satisfied at a node, and to generate the children of a node. (See exercise 1.)

Figure 2.2 shows some typical data-structures with which the nodes in the search-tree are tagged.

2.1.3 Search procedures

We are now ready to look at the various ways of searching the tree of figure 2.2. One possibility is to search the tree branch by branch, as shown in figure 2.3(a),

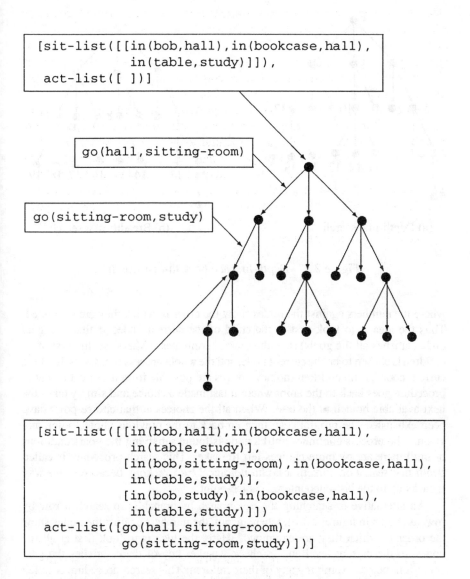

```
[sit-list([[in(bob,hall),in(bookcase,hall),
            in(table,study)]]),
 act-list([ ])]
```

```
go(hall,sitting-room)
```

```
go(sitting-room,study)
```

```
[sit-list([[in(bob,hall),in(bookcase,hall),
            in(table,study)],
           [in(bob,sitting-room),in(bookcase,hall),
            in(table,study)],
           [in(bob,study),in(bookcase,hall),
            in(table,study)]])
 act-list([go(hall,sitting-room),
           go(sitting-room,study)])]
```

Figure 2.2   A search-tree and the labels on some of its nodes and links

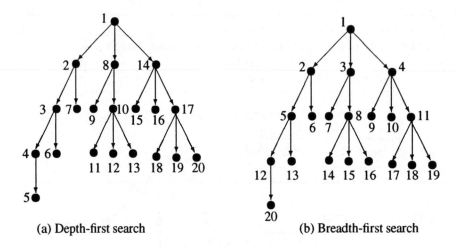

(a) Depth-first search   (b) Breadth-first search

Figure 2.3   Depth-first and breadth-first search

where the numbers against the nodes show the order in which they are examined.
Thus the idea is to look first at the child of the current node: if that is a goal
node (satisfies all the goals) then the search terminates. Otherwise, the first of its
children is chosen to be the current node, and the whole process repeats itself. If the
current node has no children (no new moves are possible from it), then the search
procedure goes back to the point where it last made a choice and simply takes the
next available branch in the tree. When all the choices at that choice-point have
been exhausted, the program can then go back to the previous choice-point, and
so on. The process continues until a node is found satisfying the goal conditions
or until there are no more choices left to make. This search procedure is called
depth-first search or, sometimes, *chronological backtracking*, because of the way
it backs up to the last-encountered choice-point.

An alternative to searching the tree branch by branch is to search it row by
row, as shown in figure 2.3(b), where, again, the numbers against the nodes show
the order in which they are examined. Here, the idea is to look first at all the
nodes on the current level and to check whether any of them satisfies the goal
conditions before examining any of their children. This search procedure is called
breadth-first search.

How might we implement the depth-first search procedure? The easiest way
is to maintain a queue of nodes, represented by a list-structure. The queue is
initialized to the list containing just the root node. The procedure for generating
the tree is then as follows. The first node in the queue is tested to determine if it
satisfies the goals. If it does, then the search is over. If not, its children, if there are
any, are generated and are added to the front of the queue. Then the first node in the
queue is examined again, and the process is repeated, until either a node is found

satisfying the goals, or the queue is empty (this happens when all possibilities have been exhausted). Since the children of each node are added to the front of the queue, the effect is to search each branch to its maximum depth before returning to other branches.

More formally, the algorithm is as follows:

> **begin** depth-first
>> **let** queue be the 1-element list containing the initial node
>> **until** queue is empty **do**
>>> **let** first-node be the first element of queue
>>> **if** first-node satisfies the goals, **then**
>>>> **halt** and **return** first-node
>>> **else**
>>>> delete first-node from start of queue
>>>> generate list of children of first-node
>>>> add those children to the *front* of queue
>>> **end if**
>> **end until**
>> **return** failure
> **end** depth-first

To implement breadth-first search, a similar algorithm can be employed as for depth-first search, except that the children of first-node are put at the *end* of the queue, instead of at the beginning. That way, the nodes already in the queue always get examined before these new children.

> **begin** breadth-first
>> **let** queue be the 1-element list containing the initial node
>> **until** queue is empty **then**
>>> **let** first-node be the first element of queue
>>> **if** first-node satisfies the goals **then**
>>>> **halt** and **return** first-node
>>> **else**
>>>> delete first-node from start of queue
>>>> generate list of children of first-node
>>>> add those children to the *end* of queue
>>> **end if**
>> **end until**
>> **return** failure
> **end** breadth-first

All that is needed to turn these search algorithms into planning programs for Bob are a procedure to generate the children of a given node in the search-tree, and a procedure to test whether a given node in the search-tree represents a situation in which the goals are satisfied. We discussed how to do this in section 2.1.2. The node returned by the search procedure will then be a data-structure containing a list of actions which will achieve the goals. (See exercise 2.) So, we have here all the elements needed for a planning program for Bob. The program is given knowledge of the current situation in the form of a list such as (2.1), and of the pre-conditions and effects of its actions in the form of data-structures such as (2.3) and (2.4). Its task is to plan a sequence of actions to achieve a set of goals such as (2.2). It is not too difficult to see that both the depth-first and breadth-first search procedures just described will always find a plan to achieve Bob's goals, if those goals are achievable at all. (See exercise 3.)

2.1.4   *Guiding the search process*

Although depth-first and breadth-first search can always be relied upon to find a plan for Bob's furniture-moving goals if a plan exists, these search-procedures are in general very inefficient. For example, if Bob is standing in the hall with the bookcase, and has the single goal of getting the bookcase into the sitting room, it is quite possible that the first action considered is that of carrying the bookcase into the bedroom – i.e. away from where it is supposed to be! Moreover, the depth-first search procedure will then go on to seek a plan which starts with this action before considering any others. Evidently, these planning procedures do not understand *towards* or *away from*: they have no notion of which moves are likely to lead to the goal state, and which will just make things worse.

The obvious response is to endow each situation with a measure of its distance from the goal conditions. Then, to make the search more efficient, we might concentrate on those moves which most reduce this distance. One search procedure embodying this idea is *best-first* search. In best-first search, we assume that, for a given node, a measure of *badness* or *distance from the goals* can be computed. Then, the search is directed by concentrating on the node which has the lowest badness of all the nodes examined so far.

What might such a badness-measure look like for Bob's planning program? The following is one possibility. Consider a node tagged with the data-structure (2.6), corresponding to the situation

[in(bob,study),in(bookcase,hall),in(table,study)].

Suppose Bob's goals are to get the table in the sitting-room and himself in the hall. Then, for each object mentioned in the goals – in this case, the table and Bob – we can count how far the current situation is from its desired position. Thus, the table is in the study and should be in the sitting-room, which is 1 room away; Bob is also in the study and should be in the hall, which is 2 rooms away. In that case we add up these distances, and say that the badness of node (2.6) is $1 + 2 = 3$. The badness of other nodes is calculated in the same way.

The badness-measure just defined can be easily computed by Bob's planning program, and used to save the search from consideration of some of the more perverse possibilities. Best-first search can them be implemented by simply ordering the nodes of queue in the above algorithms after the Children of first-node have been added. Here is the general algorithm:

begin best-first
    let queue be the 1-element list containing the initial node
    until queue is non-empty **then**
        let first-node be the first element of queue
        if first-node satisfies the goals **then**
            halt and **return** first-node
        else
            delete first-node from start of queue
            generate list of children of first-node
            add those children to queue
            re-order nodes in queue according to badness (least bad first)
        end if
    end until
    return failure
end best-first

(See exercise 4.)

Search procedures such as best-first search are sometimes called *heuristic search procedures*, because a serious attempt is made to concentrate on those inferences (remember, the search-tree is really a tree of possible inferences) which will be most likely to come up with a conclusion of the desired form. We stressed the importance of good heuristics in chapter 1: good heuristics – good choices about the sensible inferences to perform among the myriad available inferences – are in general an essential part of AI programs. True, in the present example the size of the search-tree is such that exhaustive search may be a viable option. (See exercise 5.) However, it is easy to increase the size of the problem to the point where this is no longer the case. Note in addition that the badness-measure just defined is specific to the present problem. It is common for heuristics to rely on features specific to the problem at hand in this way.

2.1.5 Finding optimal plans

We have introduced best-first search as a procedure for *efficiently* finding *some* plan to achieve Bob's goals. Note that this is not the same as a search-procedure for *somehow* finding an *efficient* plan to achieve Bob's goals. For example, if Bob is standing in the hall with the bookcase, and has the single goal of getting himself into the sitting room, it is quite possible that best-first search may find the plan of carrying the bookcase into the sitting room! After all, this plan will achieve Bob's goal of getting himself in the sitting room, and Bob has no goals as to where the bookcase should be. Evidently, the planning program we have designed so far does not understand *cost*: it has no notion of which moves are likely to lead cheaply to the goal state, and which moves are likely to involve unnecessary effort.

To tackle this issue, we need some way of representing the costs of various actions. One possibility would be by means of the data-structures:

```
cost(go(Room1,Room2),1)
cost(carry(table,Room1,Room2),2)                    (2.7)
cost(carry(bookcase,Room1,Room2),3)
```

with the obvious interpretation (note that Room1 and Room2 are variables here, which can take any values). The cost of a sequence of actions – i.e. of a plan – can then be defined as the sum of the costs of all the individual actions that go to make it up. Thus, what we seek is a planning program that produces plans with a low cost.

In this section, we present a search method known as A*, which finds *optimal* plans: that is, plans whose cost, for a given initial situation and given goal conditions, is guaranteed to be the lowest possible. The basic idea is as follows. First of all, we suppose that, for any given situation s, and any set of goals G, we can compute a *lower bound* for the cost of a sequence of actions to satisfy the goals G starting from the situation s (we will give an example of such a lower bound presently). That is, we know how much effort *at the very minimum* will be required to get from s to G. Given any node in a search-tree, then, we can calculate the *most optimistic estimate* (or MOE) of the eventual cost of any plan found in the search-tree below that node: it is simply the cost of the actions carried out so far plus the lower bound on the remaining cost of achieving the goals G. More precisely,

MOE(node) = Total cost of actions leading up to node + lower bound on remaining cost of satisfying the goals given the situation represented by node.

(We assume that this lower bound is a non-negative number.)

Now consider the best-first search algorithm of section 2.1.4. What if, instead of ordering the nodes in queue according to their *badness* (i.e. the distance of the represented situation from the goal conditions), we ordered them according to their MOE as defined above? If we do this, the first node found satisfying the goals must have been reached by an optimal plan. To see why, suppose that the first node, node, in the queue does indeed satisfy the goal conditions. In that case, the cost of achieving the goals is zero, and the lower bound on that cost must therefore also be zero, and the quantity MOE(node) equal to the cost of the actions leading up to node. Since the queue has been ordered according to the MOE-values, even on the most optimistic estimate, the total cost of any plan found by expanding any other nodes in the queue will be at least as great as the cost of the actions leading up to node, and so those actions form an optimal plan.

This idea can be put into practice using the following algorithm:

```
begin a-star
    let queue be the 1-element list containing the initial node
    until queue is non-empty then
        let first-node be the first element of queue
        if first-node satisfies the goals then
            halt and return first-node
        else
            delete first-node from start of queue
            generate list of children of first-node
            add those children to queue
            re-order the nodes in queue according MOE (least first)
        end if
    end until
    return failure
end a-star.
```

Finally, in order to apply the A* procedure to the planning program for Bob, we need a suitable lower bound on remaining cost of achieving the goals in a given situation. By coincidence, the badness measure defined in section 2.1.4 will do nicely, as the reader may like to verify for himself. The implementation of A* in a computer program is then routine. (See exercise 6.)

We have described the A* procedure at this point because of its obvious affinities, in programming terms, with the heuristic search procedures presented above. However, it is important to distinguish two quite different objectives which we might want our search procedures to achieve. One objective is that of efficiently finding *a* plan to achieve the goals in question. This is the true job of a heuristic as we explained the notion in chapter 1. Here, the inferential task is simply to find *any* plan which can be seen to achieve the planner's goals, and the heuristics serve to guide the inference so that that inferential task is accomplished as painlessly as possible. A second, and quite different objective, however, is that of finding *an efficient* plan to achieve the goals in question. Here, the inferential task is the more demanding one of finding an *efficient* – sometimes an *optimal* – plan; that is, the efficiency sought is not efficiency of inference, but efficiency in the final plan. And inferring that a plan is optimal involves the use of knowledge encoded somewhere in the knowledge-base and inference procedures which must be distinguished from true heuristics. (Consider the distinctive feature of heuristics alluded to in chapter 1: a reasoner should not reject the results of someone else's reasoning just because he does not accept the heuristics that were employed in constructing it. Clearly, if a planning program seeks not any old plan, but an optimal one, it will not be interested in the results of a search procedure which does not guarantee optimality.) It is to inferences about optimal plans that A* aspires, and so it cannot properly be regarded as a pure heuristic.

2.2   Working on goals separately

In our treatment of the planning program for Bob, we took those nodes in the search-tree satisfying *all* of the goal conditions to be success nodes, and all others to be failure nodes. Suppose, for example, that Bob has three goals, say

```
[in(bob,hall),in(table,sitting-room),
 in(bookcase,bedroom)].
```

Then, if a node is generated representing a situation in which the first two goals are achieved, but the third is not, that node is simply deemed to be a failure, and replaced by its children, just as would have happened for a node in which *none* of these goals were satisfied. The planning algorithms outlined in the previous sections are tough markers: they give no credit for partial success.

In many planning domains, this policy of – in effect – *throwing away* plans which achieve some but not all of the goals wastes valuable effort. What we would like is some way of tackling the individual goals separately (usually a much more tractable problem), and then combining the resulting plans into a big plan that will achieve all of the goals together. The snag, however, is that planning for goals separately and then simply executing the plans in sequence usually does not work. Consider again the initial situation

```
[in(bob,bedroom),in(bookcase,hall),in(table,hall)]
```

and the goals

```
[in(bob,hall),in(table,sitting-room)].
```

And let us see what happens when we try to plan for the two goals separately. A plan to achieve the first goal is not hard to devise: it is simply the 1-action plan

```
[go(bedroom,hall)].
```

Likewise, a plan to achieve the second goal (given the situation that results from achieving the first goal) might be

```
[carry(table,hall,sitting-room)].
```

But the two plans appended together in that order, i.e.

```
[go(bedroom,hall), carry(table,hall,sitting-room)].
```

do not achieve the original goals.

The problem is, of course, that the plan to achieve the second goal, in(table,sitting-room), undid the first goal, in(bob,hall). In the planning programs of the previous sections, we dodged this problem by treating the goal conditions as one indivisible block, which a given situation either did or did not satisfy. However, as we shall see in section 2.4.1, this policy can have its drawbacks. Indeed, for most practical planning purposes, treating the goals as an indivisible block would lead to unmanageably large search spaces, and the alternative of working on separate goals independently is unavoidable. The difficulty associated with combining interacting plans is largely what makes planning an interesting and non-trivial topic in AI. Before we investigate this matter in more detail, however, we need to understand one further issue concerning search procedures.

2.3 Forward and backward chaining

We have developed a number of programs, based on different search procedures, to solve a simple planning problem. However, all of these programs have one thing in common: they all *begin* with a description of the initial situation and terminate when a situation is found satisfying the goals. The effect of such a procedure is that, when a plan is found, the actions in that plan are always added in the order in which they are to be executed in the plan. Or, if we think of matters in terms of inference, the steps in the inference are thought up in logical order – that is, starting with the initial knowledge-base and working forwards towards the program's inferential goals. This general inference strategy is known as *forward chaining*.

Forward chaining:
  Start with a node corresponding to the initial set of beliefs.
  For each node, corresponding to a set of beliefs, expand that node by examining all the possible inferences that can be made on the basis of those beliefs. For each such possible inference, add the conclusion of that inference to the set of beliefs, and let the resulting collection of beliefs be a child of the node. Search terminates when a node is generated which satisfies the reasoner's inferential goals.

However, there are alternative strategies. In particular, instead of starting with the initial knowledge-base and working towards the goals, we could just as well start with the goals and work backwards towards the initial knowledge-base. Let us see how this works in detail.

2.3.1 The family-tree inference program

Recall the second example in chapter 1, where we described how a program might make inferences about family relationships using forward-chaining search. In this section, we consider an alternative approach.

We settled on the following knowledge representation scheme. The set of known facts about individuals is represented using a data-structure such as

[parent(sue,noel),parent(noel,ann),parent(ann,dave)] (2.8)

(we can think of such a list as specifying a *knowledge-situation*); and the program's definition of the relation *ancestor* is represented using the PAD-rules:

```
action-type(
    ancestor-rule-1(X,Y),
    pre-conds([parent(X,Y)]),                    (2.9)
    add-list([ancestor(X,Y)]))
```

```
action-type(
  ancestor-rule-2(X,Y,Z),
  pre-conds([parent(X,Y),ancestor(Y,Z)]),        (2.10)
  add-list([ancestor(X,Z)])).
```

The job of the program is to try to infer some conclusion in which we are interested, e.g.

$$ancestor(sue,dave).   \qquad (2.11)$$

Instead of adopting the Bob-like approach of starting from the initial knowledge-situation and generating a search-tree of all possible inferences until a node is found containing the sentence ancestor(sue,dave), we shall adopt the reverse strategy of working back from the goal, by seeing what could have led up to it.

Consider, for example, which instances of the rules (2.9) and (2.10) could have led up to the goal (2.11). One possibility is rule (2.10) with X = sue, Z = dave and Y set to some other value – say, Y = noel:

```
action-type(
  ancestor-rule-2(sue,noel,dave),
  pre-conds([parent(sue,noel), ancestor(noel,dave)]),
  add-list([ancestor(sue,dave)])).
```

This rule-instance would indeed add the sought-after conclusion (2.11) to the known facts. But in order to apply it, it is first necessary to establish its preconditions, namely

```
[parent(sue,noel),ancestor(noel,dave)].
```

These two preconditions can now be regarded as the program's new inferential goals; and we can again see what rules could have led to inferring them. Notice, first of all, that the first of our two new goals, parent(sue,noel), is in the original knowledge-base – it is one of the things the program already believes. So it is only necessary to establish the second goal, ancestor(noel,dave). Again, there are a number of instances of rules (2.9) and (2.10) which would yield this conclusion. One of these is rule (2.10) with X = noel, Y = ann and Z = dave. That would indeed establish ancestor(noel,dave), and would leave two new goals to establish, namely

```
parent(noel,ann),ancestor(ann,dave).
```

Once again, the first of these goals is already in the program's knowledge-base; only the second goal remains to be inferred. Again, there are various possibilities, and one of these is rule (2.9) with X = ann, and Y = dave. This time, there is just one precondition to be established, namely

```
[parent(ann,dave)],
```
which is already in the knowledge-base, and we are done.

Let us consider what has been going on here. We started with one goal – one inferential objective – and found an instance of one of the PAD-rules which would allow us to reach our objective on condition that we could establish its preconditions. These preconditions then became our new goals, which again we sought to establish by the application of a PAD-rule instance. This in turn yielded new goals to establish, until eventually, we found that all our inferential goals were satisfied by the program's initial knowledge-base.

Since this strategy is more or less the opposite of forward chaining, as described above, we call it *backward chaining*:

Backward chaining:

Start with a node corresponding to the initial set of goals.

For each node, corresponding to a set of goals, expand that node by examining all the possible inferences that would establish one or more of those goals. For each such possible inference, add the preconditions of that inference to the unachieved goals, and let the new set of goals be a child of the node.

Search terminates when a node is generated in which all of the inferential goals are satisfied by the reasoner's current set of beliefs.

It is important to be clear about the direction of inference in backward chaining reasoning. Logically speaking, inference is *from* the original knowledge-base – e.g. the facts (2.8) and the rules (2.9) and (2.10) – *to* the conclusion – e.g. the conclusion (2.11). The fact that the chain of inference-steps connecting the two was found by starting at the putative conclusion does nothing to change this. Thus, we might say that, while in forward chaining the steps in the inference are thought up in logical order, in backward chaining, they are thought up in reverse-logical order. But to repeat, the inference is still *from* the initial knowledge-base *to* the conclusion, irrespective of how it is thought up.

2.3.2 *Variables*

The discussion of section 2.3.1 omitted one important element found in most practical inference systems. Consider again the inferential goal (2.11). As was pointed out, rule (2.10) could be used to reduce this goal using the substitution X = sue, Z = dave and Y set to *some other value*. The value *we* chose was Y = noel (simply because this was the one that was going to lead to success); but for a computer program, all possible values of Y might have to be tried out in the search process. The result will be search-trees with a large branching factor, especially if there are many individuals that could be substituted for Y.

What we would like our backward chaining to do when applying rule (2.10) is to leave the value of Y *open*. That is, given the goal (2.2) we would like to apply rule (2.10) using the substitution X = sue and Z = dave to get the goals

```
parent(sue,Y),ancestor(Y, dave).
```

The new goals contain a variable – a slot for a value – which is left open until we have some better idea as to how best to fill it in. Now, since the first of these goals is is parent (sue, Y), and since the fact parent (sue, noel) is already in the knowledge-base, choosing Y = noel will result in a goal that is already achieved (which of course is a good thing). Making this substitution, the current goals become

> parent(sue,noel),ancestor(noel,dave)

and the backward chaining proceeds as before. But notice that the selection of the values for X, Y and Z is no longer a matter of blind search. The value of Y was left open until it was known which value would result in a goal that is easily solved. The assignment of values to variables so as to make rules match to goals can bring about a huge saving in the search space compared with considering all rule-instances as links in the search-tree, so much so, that no serious backward-chaining system would fail to incorporate this feature. (See further reading.)

2.4   Interacting plans and means-ends analysis

In section 2.2, we described how interactions between plans can lead to problems for a planner which works on goals one at a time and then attempts to combine the resulting plans to achieve all of the goals. In this section, we examine just such a planning strategy, and explain how these problems are addressed.

2.4.1   Backward chaining with Bob

By way of introduction, let us consider how we might approach the planning problem for Bob using backward chaining. It is certainly possible to do this. Suppose, for example, that Bob's initial situation is

[in(bob,sitting-room),in(table,study),in(bookcase,hall)]

and his goals are

> [in(bob,hall),in(table,sitting-room)].   (2.12)

Then we can look for an action, e.g. go(sitting-room,hall), which will achieve one of these goals, and add the preconditions of this action to the remaining goals, thus

> [in(bob,sitting-room),in(table,sitting-room)].

We then look for an action whose add-list contains one of these new goals. In fact the add-list of carry(table,study,sitting-room) achieves both of them. Its preconditions then become the new goals, namely

> [in(bob,study),in(table,study)].

Finally, by considering the action go(sitting-room,study), these goals can be reduced to

[in(bob,sitting-room),in(table,study)]

which are true in the initial situation, and we are done.

However, things do not always work out so neatly with backward-chaining planning, and a certain amount of care is required. Let us look at some of the pitfalls we must avoid. The first pitfall is straightforward enough. Suppose the planner selects an action *a* to achieve one of its goals. What the planner must also check, is that action *a* does not delete any of the other goals. Consider again the goals (2.12). The action carry(table,hall,sitting-room) would achieve the second of these goals, *but it would also undo the first*. In fact it is easy to see that no plan to achieve these goals can have, as its final action, moving the table into the sitting-room.

The second pitfall is related, but more subtle. When tracing through the backward chaining of the family-tree program, we occasionally noted that certain goals could be ignored on the grounds that they were true in the initial knowledge-situation. However, when reasoning about actions, we need to be careful about ignoring goals that are already achieved. Suppose, for example, the planner has the goals (2.12), but this time is starting from the situation

[in(bob,hall),in(bookcase,hall),in(table,hall)].

Then the first goal – that Bob be in the hall – is already achieved in the initial situation. That is: it can be achieved by the 'null plan' of doing nothing at all. Suppose, then, we ignore this goal, and simply use backward chaining to devise a plan to achieve the second goal of getting the table in the sitting room. One plan we might come up with is:

[carry(table,hall,sitting-room)].

Executing this plan, followed by the null plan of doing nothing, will put Bob in the sitting-room, when he wanted to end up in the hall. The problem is that the plan of doing nothing *would* have achieved the goal of getting Bob in the hall, *if* it had been executed in the initial situation; but of course, that is not the situation in which it gets executed if it is preceded by plans to achieve the other goals.

The third pitfall is more subtle still. We pointed out above that the action carry(table,hall,sitting-room) would achieve the second of Bob's goals (getting the table into the sitting-room), but that it would also undo the first (getting Bob into the hall). This is because the relevant PAD-rule instance has in(bob,hall) in its delete-list. But what if, in choosing an action to achieve the second goal, Bob considered not carry(table,hall,sitting-room), but instead, carry(table,study,sitting-room)? This action would also achieve the second goal (getting the table into the sitting-room), since this fact is in its add-list. Moreover, it would not delete the first goal (getting Bob into the hall), since the delete-list of this action is [in(bob,study),in(table,study)].

Good. So, suppose now that Bob takes the remaining unachieved goal and adds the preconditions of this action to get a new set of goals. The result will be

```
[in(bob,hall),in(table,study),in(bob,study)]
```

thus requiring Bob, impossibly, to be in two places at once. Exploring ways of achieving *these* goals is obviously a waste of time: they are unachievable. So we will at least need some method for pruning inconsistent goal sets from the search-tree.

The fundamental problem here is this. What a planner's PAD-rules provide is, in effect, sensible sets of preconditions which would enable a planner to achieve a given goal. What they do not provide – at least, not without some further effort – are sensible sets of preconditions for achieving a given *set* of goals. That is, they do not immediately provide inference-steps of the form

I can achieve goals $G_1, \ldots G_n$ by performing the action by action α
   if I can first achieve $G'_1, \ldots G'_{n'}$

with which a planner can chain backward from the original set of goals. And that is why a backward-chaining version of the planner for Bob is more difficult to implement than the forward-chaining version considered above.

It is, of course, all the fault of the delete-lists. That is why these problems cannot arise with the family-tree program considered above. The delete-lists tell us how one action – or one plan – can interfere with the work of another. And it is this that makes simple backward-chaining awkward in many cases. It is important to realize that the pitfalls mentioned here do not show that backward chaining is in any way faulty as an inference strategy. No: *provided* that inference-steps of the above form can be generated, chaining backwards produces valid inferences. The problem is that – and this is what the example just considered shows – such inference steps can be tricky to generate. (But see exercise 7.)

The conclusion of this section is that it is sometimes more convenient to work on goals one at a time, and then to combine the resulting plans together. In practice, most serious planning programs operate in this way. It is to just such a planning strategy that we now turn.

2.4.2 Means-ends analysis

Consider the following strategy for a planning program. The program starts by selecting an action α which, if performed, would achieve *one* of its goals. In general, α's preconditions will be unsatisfied in the initial situation. So the program sets these preconditions as new goals, and devises a plan to achieve them. Once a plan π has been found to achieve the preconditions of α, the program works out what the situation will be after π and α have been carried out; then it devises a plan to achieve the remaining goals given this new situation. Hopefully, the task of planning for α's preconditions and the task of planning for the remaining goals after α has been performed should be easier than the original planning task.

This strategy is sometimes called *means-ends analysis*. More generally, means-ends analysis is the following procedure:

o Take the initial situation S, and the set of goals **G**.
o Find an action α which, if it could be performed, would achieve some goal G in **G**.
o Find (using means-ends analysis) a plan π, which will achieve the preconditions of α.
o Compute the situation I produced by executing π and then α and find (using means-ends analysis) a plan π' which will achieve the remaining goals in **G** (minus G) in situation I. Let the final plan be $[\pi, \alpha, \pi']$ (i.e. π followed by α followed by π').

Means-ends analysis was employed in an early and influential robot planning program called STRIPS. STRIPS uses PAD-rules to represent knowledge about actions, and lists of formulae to represent situations and goals, much as described here. (See further reading.)

Notice that the first action to be thought of, α, occurs, in general, neither at the beginning of the final plan (as with forward chaining), nor at the end (as with backward chaining), but somewhere in the middle. Logically speaking, if we view the planner as inferring that the plan $[\pi; \alpha; \pi']$ will achieve its goals, then the inference-step concerning the effects of α will also occur in the middle of the chain of inference from the facts in its knowledge-base to its new conclusion.

Notice also that, having found a plan (i.e. the plan $[\pi, \alpha]$) to achieve the first goal G, means-ends analysis computes the situation I that would result from executing it, and then uses I as a new initial situation when devising a plan to achieve the remaining goals in **G**. In this way, side effects of $[\pi, \alpha]$ are taken into account when deciding which actions are required to achieve subsequent goals. Means-ends analysis therefore requires slightly more complicated book-keeping than the forward-chaining planning programs of section 2.1, since it has to reason both about the unsolved goals still on its books and the situations resulting from the partial plan that it has so far devised.

The standard implementation of this sort of planning strategy keeps, as data-structures: (i) `current-situation`, which records the effect of the actions so far thought-up, and (ii) `goal-stack`, which records the goals yet to be achieved. These data-structures are initially set to the planner's description of the initial situation and to its list of goals, respectively. The procedure then examines the top goal on `goal-stack`. If this goal is already satisfied in `current-situation`, it is simply removed. Otherwise, an action is found which would achieve that goal. Before this action is carried out however, *its* preconditions are added to the top of the goal stack, and the whole cycle is repeated, with the preconditions of α at the top of `goal-stack`. Only when all the goals that are subsequently added to achieve the preconditions of α have been satisfied is the effect of α on `current-situation` actually computed.

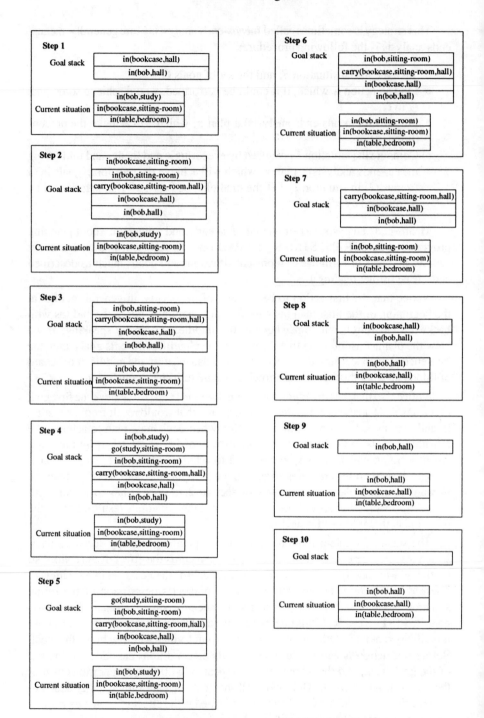

Figure 2.4   Trace of a planning program based on means-ends analysis

The best way to understand this procedure is to see it in action. Consider again the planning problem for Bob. Let us take the initial situation to be

```
[in(bob,study),in(bookcase,sitting-room),
 in(table,bedroom)]
```

and set Bob the task of getting the bookcase and himself into the hall. Figure 2.4 shows how means-ends analysis can be used to find a suitable plan.

Step 1 shows the initial situation and the initial goal stack. Since the uppermost goal in the goal stack is not satisfied in the current situation, the planner finds an action to achieve it. The action `carry(bookcase,sitting-room,hall)` is suitable, since its add-list contains `in(bookcase,hall)`. This action is added to the goal stack (the point of doing so will become clear presently), with its preconditions `in(bookcase,sitting-room)` and `in(bob,sitting-room)` piled on top. The result is shown in step 2. In step 2, the planner finds that the top goal, `in(bookcase,sitting-room)` is satisfied in the current situation, and so it is removed from the goal stack. In step 3, the top goal is not satisfied in the current situation, so the planner again finds an action whose add-list contains that goal. The action `go(study,sitting-room)` is suitable, so it is added to the goal stack, together with its precondition, `in(bob,study)`. In step 4, we again find that the top goal is satisfied in the current situation, and so it is removed. In step 5 we get to process our first action, `go(study,sitting-room)`. The add- and delete-lists are used to compute the new situation, and the action is removed from the goal stack. The result, with the updated `current-situation` and the action `go(study,sitting-room)` removed from `goal-stack`, is shown in step 6. The remaining steps basically repeat the pattern of steps 4 and 5, with satisfied goals being removed from the goal stack and the final action `carry(bookcase, sitting-room, hall)` being processed, until the goal stack is empty. Thus the plan found is

```
[go(study,sitting-room),carry(bookcase,sitting-room,hall)]
```

which is easily recoverable from the above process.

More formally, the following algorithm describes the means-ends analysis procedure given a collection of goals $\mathbf{G} = \{G_1, \ldots, G_n\}$ and an initial situation S (the symbol $\star$ indicates a so-called choice point, and will be explained below):

begin means-ends-planner
      put the goals $G_1, \ldots, G_n$ onto the stack goal-stack in some order $(\star)$
      let current-situation be S
      until goal-stack is empty **do**
          if the top item on goal-stack is a goal G
          and G is satisfied in current-situation **then**
             remove G from goal-stack
          else if the top item on goal-stack is a goal G, **then**
             find a PAD-rule instance A that contains G in its add-list $(\star)$

          put *A* onto `goal-stack`
          put preconditions of *A* onto `goal-stack` in some order (⋆)
       else if the top item on `goal-stack` is an action *A* **then**
          remove *A* from `goal-stack`
          update the `current-situation` using the add- and
             delete-lists for *A*
       end if
     end until
end `means-ends-planner`

In our example, choices had to be made for actions which would achieve the top goal, for example, the action `carry(bookcase,sitting-room,hall)` in step 1. This was a good choice, as it happened. But of course there is nothing in general to stop the planner choosing, for example, the action `carry(bookcase, bedroom, hall)`, since that would also have the desired effect of getting the bookcase into the hall. Unfortunately, it would also have the undesired effect of sending the planner on an extensive and unnecessary tour of the premises, since achieving the preconditions of this action (which, remember, would be added to `goal-stack`) means devising a plan to get the bookcase into the bedroom! The algorithm described above has no idea of how to choose an action which will achieve the top goal in `goal-stack` *and whose preconditions have the best chance of being achieved.* In practice, a real planning program would use the trick mentioned in section 2.3.2 here, leaving an uninstantiated variable for `Room1` in the PAD-rule instance, binding it only when necessary for matching. However, we shall not describe the implementation details of this process here.

There is another problem. Suppose that, at some point in the planning processes, the top goal in `goal-stack`, G_1, is found to be true in `current-situation`, and so is removed, leaving a second goal, G_2, uppermost. An action *A* is chosen to achieve G_2, and *A* together with its preconditions are added to `goal-stack`. As the planning process proceeds, these preconditions are achieved, and *A* and G_2 are eventually removed from the goal stack. However, in the process of achieving G_2, an action may have been performed which makes G_1 false (i.e. an action with G_1 in its delete-list). That is, the achievement of G_2 may undo the previously achieved goal G_1. And of course, if G_1 and G_2 are preconditions for some action further down the goal stack, the planner may find itself in the position of having an action on top of the goal stack which cannot be carried out in the current situation because its preconditions are not all satisfied.

How might the algorithm be modified to deal with this problem? Here is one possibility. We stipulate that, whenever an action is on top of `goal-stack`, its preconditions are checked against `current-situation` to see if they hold. If they do, then the action is removed from the goal stack and `current-situation` is updated as before. If they do not, a failure is reported and the program *backtracks to the last choice point.* This is where the points marked ⋆ in the algorithm are important. At these points, a choice is available: for instance, there may be a choice of action to achieve a certain goal, or a choice as to which order to put a collection of preconditions onto the goal stack. If, then, the program encounters a problem (unsatisfied preconditions) when trying to remove an action from a goal, it goes back to the point where it last made a choice and simply makes the next available choice at that point. When all the choices at that choice-point have been exhausted, the program can then go back to the previous choice-point, and so on. This kind of backtracking is of course familiar from our discussion of depth-first search. And indeed, we can think of this process of making and revising choices as a search through a search-tree. (See exercise 8.)

2.5 Search in Game-Playing

2.5.1 The minimax procedure

We conclude this chapter with a brief introduction to the use of search-techniques in programming computers to play adversarial games such as chess. Finding a sequence of moves to win a board game poses similar problems to finding a sequence of actions to achieve a goal. We can think of the former problem as a matter of searching a tree whose nodes correspond to possible board positions, and whose links correspond to possible moves transforming one board position into another. The difference with game playing is that one has an opponent trying to thwart one's plans.

In game trees, we distinguish two sorts of nodes – 'white' nodes and 'black' nodes – to indicate whose move it is in the corresponding situation. Figure 2.5 shows a game tree. The node at the top of the tree is the current board position, and the three links hanging from it, the possible moves for the white player. The links in the next tier correspond to possible moves for black, those in the tier after that, possible moves for white, and so on.

For interesting games, the search-trees consisting of all possible moves from the start to the finish (containing all possible ways in which the game may develop) are *huge*; and it is quite impractical to try to generate the whole tree until a goal state (win for the computer) is encountered. So, rather than marking some situations as goal situations, as in the planning problems considered above, we will imagine that *each* situation has a numerical *goodness value* or *utility* from the white player's point of view. (Thus, a win-situation for white will be assigned the highest possible utility, and win-situation for black, the smallest possible utility.) The point about assigning utilities in this way is that the computer can decide on a move by generating just *part* of the search-tree – say, corresponding to the next 4 moves by each player. Even though this tree may contain no win-states, it is sensible for the computer to try to reach the state which gives it the best position available from its point of view.

Suppose, for definiteness, that the computer is playing white. At each point in the game, its choice of move (at the white nodes) must take account of the fact

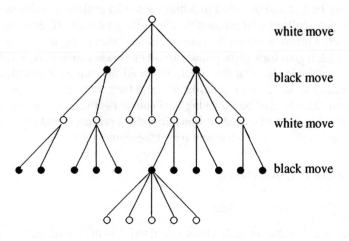

white move

black move

white move

black move

Figure 2.5   A game-playing tree

that its opponent (at the black nodes) will be trying to thwart its aims. Assuming optimal play by the opponent, it seems sensible for the computer to suppose that, whichever move it makes, its opponent will reply in such a way as to lead to the situation with minimum utility. So the computer should choose that move which maximizes the minimum utility among its possible moves. But what is the minimum utility for a given move? Well assuming optimal play by the computer, it seems sensible for the opponent to suppose that, whichever move it makes, the computer will reply in such a way as to lead to the situation with maximum utility. So the opponent should choose that move which minimizes the maximum utility among its possible moves. And so on.

Thus we arrive at the simplest and most common procedure for searching a game tree: the *minimax* procedure. This procedure finds a path (i.e. a sequence of moves) to a board position which is the best that can be hoped for (assuming optimal play by the opponent). The first move in this sequence is then the chosen move to be executed by the game-playing program. Once this move is made, the program awaits its opponent's response, at which point the process begins over again from the new board position.

More formally, the procedure can be described recursively as follows:

begin minimax(node)
   if node is at limit of search-tree **then**
      let utility be the utility of node
      return [node, utility]
   else if node is a white node, **then**
      apply minimax to children of node
      return result which has maximum utility
   else if node is a black node, **then**
      apply minimax to children of node
      return result which has minimum utility
   end if
end minimax

One final technicality. As described, the above procedure returns a node in the search-tree, describing the best board position it can achieve, assuming optimal play by its opponent. But what the computer needs is not so much a description of that board position as the first element in the sequence of moves that would lead to it; for it is this move that the computer must make. Thus, we must resort to the programming trick explained in section 2.1.2, of tagging nodes in the search-tree with the list of the moves that lead up to them. This modification is completely routine, and will be ignored here.

2.5.2 Alpha-beta pruning

The minimax procedure, as just described, invokes unnecessary search. The best way to see this is to work through the algorithm on the fragment of a game tree shown in figure 2.6. Here, the labels n_i on the non-terminal nodes are for reference only; the numbers below the terminal nodes represent the utilities of the board positions at the limit of search.

To execute minimax on node n_1, we must first execute minimax on n_2 and n_3, and select the result that has minimum utility (since n_1 is a black node). To execute minimax on n_2, we must execute minimax on n_4, n_5 and n_6, and select the result that has maximum utility (since n_2 is a white node). The result of applying minimax to the black node n_4 is the terminal node below it with utility 1, and the result of applying minimax to the black node n_5 is the terminal node below that with utility 6 (since n_4 and n_5 are black nodes). So far, so good. But now look what happens when minimax is applied to n_6. One of the children of n_6 is a terminal node with utility 3. Since n_6 represents a situation where black moves, it follows that, if the white player makes the move from n_2 to n_6, he will be faced with a board position of utility no more than 3. By contrast, if in the situation represented by n_2 white had moved to node n_5, he could have guaranteed himself a terminal node of utility 6. So there is clearly no point in white choosing the move from n_2 to n_6, *whatever utilities the other children of n_6 may have*. Thus, searching any additional children of n_6 is a waste of time, since the system will never want to move to this node.

Looking at the same game tree one level up, similar observations show that, once node n_8 has been processed, there is no point in looking at any other children of n_3. For suppose that black moves from n_1 to n_3. Then, since it is white's move at n_3, white can guarantee a terminal node of utility 8 by moving to n_8. But if black had moved to n_2 instead of n_3 (remember: it is black's move at n_1) the best white could have done would have been a terminal node with utility 6. Clearly, then, black would never move to n_3 in preference to n_2. And so we need look at no more of n_3's children after n_8.

α-β pruning is a method for reducing the number of paths searched using the minimax procedure, based on a generalization of the above reasoning. Two types of parameters are kept at the nodes: an α-parameter at maximizing (white) nodes, and a β-parameter at minimizing (black) nodes. These parameters function as follows. Suppose a maximizing (white) node, node, is being examined. Clearly, the parent of node will be a minimizing node. In general, node will have several siblings in the tree, some of which will have been examined already. The parameter β, stored at the parent of node, contains the minimum of the results of minimax on all of these already-examined siblings – i.e. the worst result for white. Now, let us consider what happens as the children of node are processed by the minimax algorithm. That algorithm will return a utility for each of the children examined. This is where the parameter α comes in: as the children of node are examined, α is set to the maximum of the results of minimax on all the children examined so far.

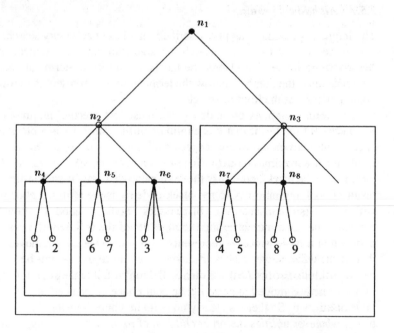

Figure 2.6   Fragment of a game tree invoking unnecessary search.

Since the parent of node is a minimizing node – i.e. a node in which black chooses the move – it is clear that, if ever an outcome that white can achieve by choosing its move at node is greater than β, the search can stop, since black will never choose the move that leads to node in preference to one of the already-examined alternatives. Thus, since the parameter α stored at node represents a utility which white could achieve if ever the node node were reached, the process of examining the children of node can stop whenever its value becomes greater than the value of β associated with the parent of node.

Exactly corresponding remarks apply where node is a minimizing node. In that case, the value of α (stored at the parent of node) represents the maximum outcome of the minimax-procedure applied to those siblings of node which have been examined so far. As the children of node are examined, the parameter β (stored at node) is set to the minimum value of the minimax procedure applied to those children examined so far. If α exceeds β, we can abandon the search of node and its children, because we know that white will inevitably choose one of the already-examined siblings of node in preference to node, since that way white can force a greater utility.

Thus we arrive at the procedure ab-minimax. It takes two arguments: node, the node being currently processed, and parent, its parent in the game tree. It returns with a pair consisting of a node and a utility: this node represents the best board position that can be hoped for, assuming optimal play by both players. A special case must be made if node is the root node of the tree, so that it does not have a parent. In this case, we imagine a 'dummy' parent to be supplied, and we set $\alpha(\text{parent})$ to $-\infty$ and $\beta(\text{parent})$ to ∞.

begin ab-minimax(node,parent)
    if node is at limit of search-tree **then**
      let U be the utility of node
      return [node,U]
    else if node is a white node **then**
      let $\alpha(\text{node})$ be $-\infty$
      for each child in children of node **do**
          let U be utility of ab-minimax(child,node)
          let $\alpha(\text{node})$ be max(U, $\alpha(\text{node})$)
          if $\alpha(\text{node}) > \beta(\text{parent})$ **then**
             prune node and all its descendants from tree
          end if
      end for each
      return the result of whichever call to ab-minimax
      above yielded greatest utility
    else
      let $\beta(\text{node})$ be ∞
      for each child in children of node **do**
          Let U be utility of ab-minimax(child,node)

         let $\beta(\texttt{node})$ be min(U, $\beta(\texttt{node})$)
         if $\alpha(\texttt{parent}) > \beta(\texttt{node})$ **then**
            prune node and all its descendants from tree
         end if
      end for each
      return the result of whichever call to `ab-minimax`
         above yielded smallest utility
     end if
end `ab-minimax`

Minimax with α-β pruning can be rather difficult to understand. The best way to get a feel for what is going on is to work through the example given above to see how redundant search is indeed avoided. But it is important to understand that alpha-beta pruning is just a technique for speeding up minimax search: the moves it chooses are the same as those minimax would have chosen; it simply chooses them faster.

Figure 2.7(a) shows a game played on a square board with opposing pieces (black and white) lined up along the end ranks. The players take turns to move, and skipping a move is not allowed. The pieces can move only straight forward, one square at a time (onto unoccupied squares), and can capture an opposing piece only one square diagonally forward (just like regular pawn capture in chess). Figure 2.7(b) shows what the board can look like after a number of moves. The object is to get a pawn to the other side of the board; the game is drawn if the player whose turn it is cannot move. The board shown in figure 2.7 is 8 by 8 squares; but the game works quite well for any size greater than 3 by 3.

The minimax search procedure with α-β pruning gives good results on this game (even with a quite trivial evaluation function), and can be programmed, using the above algorithm, to search to 8 ply (i.e. 4 moves by each player) using a 5-by-5 board without intolerable delays. The resulting performance should be adequate (with that sort of look-ahead) against a casual human opponent. (See also exercise 10.)

2.5.3 *More advanced considerations in game playing*

The approach to game-playing just outlined suffers from a number of limitations. For example, one problem is that it has no notion of a board situation which is interesting and worth investigating in detail. Thus, in the situation of figure 2.7(a) – i.e. the initial board situation – nothing much is happening: moves by each player will lead to small changes in the utility of the current board state. The position in figure 2.7(b), by contrast, is much less stable. With successive moves, each side can loose a piece, resulting in much more rapid changes in the utility of the board states. A state in which the utility function does not change by large amounts from one side to another is called a *quiescent state*. A human player would spend less time analysing the development of the quiescent state in figure 2.7(a)

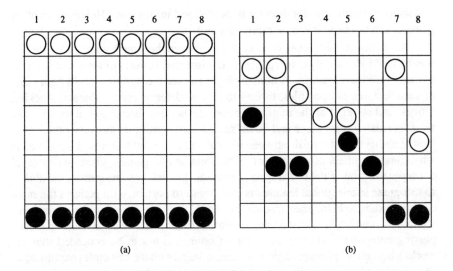

Figure 2.7   A simple game which a computer can easily play

than the nonquiescent state in figure 2.7(b); for it is in the second case that deep analysis is likely to be important. Likewise, a more sophisticated approach to game-playing would be able to look for quiescent states, and to vary the amount of search accordingly.

One problem that arises from using a fixed search depth is the so-called horizon effect. The problem is that, for a player using minimax, serious problems can be made to 'go away' as a result of frivolous and irrelevant moves. Consider figure 2.7(b), with black to move. If black moves his piece on file 3, white can move the piece on file 4 forward, at which point victory for white is certain: he simply needs to push the piece on file 4 three more squares forward. However, if black is played by a computer using minimax search to 8 ply, it will not be able to see that white's victory is inevitable here. For imagine that black does move the piece on file 3. The problem is that, while white is progressing along file 4 to victory, black could move forward the piece on file 1. White must respond to this move (say, by taking), otherwise black would win. The effect of this exchange would merely be to delay white's victory. But if black is only looking ahead 8 ply, that delayed victory lies beyond the limit of the look-ahead, and will not be noticed. So black will not see that moving the piece on file 3 is (necessarily) a losing move. The inevitable defeat has been pushed beyond the horizon of the look-ahead by a move which has no real effect on the outcome of the game. The horizon effect is a particularly difficult problem to deal with, because the minimax algorithm has no conception of the long-term significance of its moves. (In fact, for the game of figure 2.7, the horizon effect is not a significant problem, because there are not that many opportunities for disaster to be delayed in this way. However, in other games, such as chess, it can be more serious.)

The ability to play games such as chess, or even the simple game of figure 2.7, is enhanced by an ability to reorganize and reinterpret features of the board in terms of their significant features. A human player can see the significance, in figure 2.7, of such features as open files, threats to pieces, defence against threats, blocking moves, and so on. For the minimax game player described above, none of these features exists: every piece and board square is as significant as every other. This lack of ability to distinguish between pivotal and irrelevant features of a position is why computer chess programs tend to be weak at end-games, where higher-level conceptualization of the board is so important. Indeed, in some games, the ability to recognize subtle global features is even more important, with perhaps the most extreme example being the game of go. Thus, the mere use of search (even with alpha-beta pruning) is at best a partial solution to the problem of developing game-playing computers. Having said that, of course, it has to be conceded that the world's best chess-playing computers, based largely on the principles explained in this chapter, play extremely well. The program *Deep Thought*, for example, plays at grand master level, with a rating of about 2,600. (See further reading.) And in the simple game of figure 2.7, alpha-beta minimax does, as I can confirm from personal experience, play convincingly!

2.6   Conclusion

In this chapter, we have seen how the general ideas introduced in chapter 1 can be put into practice. In particular, we have seen how programs can be made to search the spaces of inferences generated by knowledge-bases to solve simple inferential problems, including problems in planning and game-playing. Since we have been mainly concerned with the practical problems that need to be solved in writing such programs, we have have paid relatively little attention to the theoretical basis of our approach to knowledge representation and inference. That is the subject of the next chapter.

Exercises

1. (Programming) Write a program to take a search-tree node in the form of (2.6) and generate the list of its children given the PAD-rules (2.3) and (2.4). Beware of the way we have represented adjacency facts. If the program knows adjacent(hall,bedroom), does it also know adjacent(bedroom,hall)?

2. (Programming) Implement the algorithms for depth-first and breadth-first search in section 2.1.3. Using the program written for exercise 1, construct a planning program for Bob.

3. (To think about) Breadth-first search will, for the planning program for Bob, tend to produce better plans than depth-first search. Why is this? What are the computational disadvantages of breadth-first search in this case?

4. (Programming) Implement the best-first search algorithm, and use it as the basis of a planning program for Bob.

5. (To think about) How many nodes are there in the search-tree for Bob's planning program?

6. (Programming) Implement the A* search algorithm, and use it as the basis of a planning program for Bob.

7. (Programming) In spite of the reservations of section 2.4.1, it is possible to construct a backward-chaining planning program for Bob. Remember, the nodes of the tree represent collections of goals, not situations. Write a program which, when given a set of goals $G_1, \ldots G_n$ for Bob, finds all actions α and sets of goals $G'_1, \ldots G'_{n'}$ such that, if $G'_1, \ldots G'_{n'}$ can be achieved, performing α will achieve $G_1, \ldots G_n$. Then use breadth-first search (this works much better than depth-first) to construct a backward-chaining planner. Bear in mind the three pitfalls pointed out in section 2.4.1, and do not forget the programming tricks described in section 2.1.3. Good luck!

8. (To think about) Given that the means-ends planning algorithm of section 2.4.2 requires search, can we apply all of the search-methods described in section 2.1? In particular, how would heuristics be used to guide the making of suitable choices? Is the algorithm of section 2.4.2 guaranteed to find a plan for Bob?

9. (To think about) Why does the problem of interacting plans not arise with the forward-chaining planning algorithms of section 2.1?

10. (Programming) Program a computer to play the game of figure 2.7, using minimax search with alpha-beta pruning.

    You will need to devise a board evaluation function to calculate utilities. One possibility (no doubt not the best) is simply to give both players one point for every square they have moved towards the opposite end of the board (summed over all pieces) and then to subtract black's score from white's. In addition, of course, board positions in which one player has won will have to be assigned huge (positive or negative) utilities. Once you have decided how to represent a board state and compute its utility, you will need to write a program to generate, for any given board state, all the states that can be reached from it in one move. Then the algorithm of section 2.5.2 can be applied directly. It makes the program more fun to play if you can write a graphical interface.

    Once you have got the program working, you can investigate the effect of alpha-beta pruning. By counting the number of times that the condition $\alpha > \beta$ is or is not satisfied as the algorithm runs, you can determine the frequency of pruning. By playing the same game with alpha-beta pruning disabled, you can count the number of nodes that were pruned off.

11. (To think about) If you have done exercise 10 (or even if you have not), in what respects does the way you play this game differ from the way the computer plays it?

Further reading

Planning in general – and the key issue of managing goal interactions in particular – is a vast topic, of which this chapter has barely scratched the surface. The interested reader is referred to the collection of articles on all aspects of planning to be found in Allen, Hendler and Tate [1].

For those readers not familiar with the Prolog programming language, this is recommended as an excellent way of gaining a practical grasp of the issues concerning search and planning discussed in this chapter, especially the use of variables to as described in section 2.3.2. There are many adequate guides to Prolog programming available. Perhaps the best is still Clocksin and Mellish [2].

The mathematical study of heuristics is well-developed, to which Pearl [4] amply testifies; quite how significant this work is for practical AI systems, however, is less clear.

Game-playing is also a major topic in AI, and in this chapter, we have presented only the rudiments. Readers interested in computer chess are referred to the article by Feng-hsiung Hsu, T. Anantharaman M. Campbell and A. Nowatzyk [3] on a famous chess-playing computer called *Deep thought*.

Bibliography

[1] Allen, J, J. Hendler, and A. Tate (eds.) *Readings in Planning*, San Mateo: Morgan Kaufmann, 1990.
[2] Clocksin, W.F. and C.S. Mellish *Programming in Prolog*, 2nd ed., Berlin: Springer Verlag, 1984.
[3] Hsu, Feng-hsiung, T. Anantharaman, M. Campbell and A. Nowatzyk "A Grandmaster Chess Machine", *Scientific American*, vol. 263, no. 4 (1990) pp. 18–24.
[4] Pearl, J. *Heuristics. Intelligent Search Strategies for Computer Problem Solving*, Reading, Mass: Addison-Wesley, 1984.

3 Logic and Inference

In the first half of this century, great strides were taken in the development of formal logic. Although largely motivated by puzzles in the philosophy of mathematics, the development of systems of formal logic in general, and of one such system in particular – the predicate calculus – revolutionized the study of inference. With its combination of expressive power and mathematical simplicity, the predicate calculus was unquestionably superior to the (basically) Aristotelian Logic which had gone before, and deduction in the predicate calculus came to be seen as a paradigm of rational inference. Moreover, where deduction seemed not to suffice as a model for inference – most notably, in the confirmation of scientific theories by empirical testing – the search began for an 'inductive logic' which was to be the equal of its deductive sibling in formality and rigour. (We shall have more to say about inductive logic in chapter 9.) Given the pre-eminence of the predicate calculus in providing a paradigm of rational inference, it was only to be expected that AI took the predicate calculus as its point of departure as a method for performing inference automatically. But, as we shall see, a surprise was lurking in the shadows.

Since many readers of this book will already be familiar with the predicate calculus, we will not interrupt the flow of the argument by explaining it here. For the benefit of readers with no background in logic, and for those who would like some quick revision, the appendix contains a tutorial introduction to the predicate calculus.

3.1 Logic and inference

The logical approach to inference views a system's knowledge-base as an unstructured collection T of formulae in a formal language. The role of logic is to provide a proof theory – usually a system of axioms and rules of inference – which effectively defines the permissible inference-sequences that the system can make from T. Of course, the system's actual inferential behaviour will depend in part on its heuristics – the policies it uses for deciding which inferences to try – and these lie outside the concern of logic proper. What the axioms and rules of inference in the logic do is simply to define the tree of possible inferences to which the system has 'access' (in the sense explained in chapter 1).

In addition to a proof theory, logics typically provide a formal semantics, which delimits the permissible interpretations of the formulae of the language concerned, and specifies the conditions under which any given formula is true. Of particular interest from the point of view of inference is the relation of *semantic entailment* between T and a formula ψ. T is said to semantically entail ψ when ψ is true in all interpretations of the formulae which make T true, that is:

for any interpretation M, if $M \models T$ then $M \models \psi$,

or, as we shall write:

$$T \models \psi$$

A system which infers only those sentences that are semantically entailed by its knowledge-base will never pass from truth to falsity. Now, in the ideal case, the proof theory for a logic is *correct* and *complete* in the sense that it provides a definitive test of semantic entailment, i.e.:

$$T \vdash \psi \quad \text{iff} \quad T \models \psi.$$

Thus, the attraction of using a correct and complete proof theory to define the tree of inferences the system can make from its knowledge-base is that it guarantees the system has access to just those chains of inference which will never lead it from truth to falsity. One might say: the system has access to those chains of inference to which ought to have access, given the interpretations of the representations with which it is reasoning.

To be sure, there is much more to be said about inference than what logic has to tell us. Firstly, as we have just observed, heuristics are required to guide the system through the space of possible inferences to get to its inferential objective, and heuristics lie outside logic proper. Secondly, there must exist some mechanism for selecting inferential goals in the first place; truly intelligent agents do not, after all, spend their whole time taking inferential orders from others. Again, this is not something which logic provides. Thirdly, though there are many different kinds of logic, it is doubtful whether logic, in any recognizable sense of the word, is the best way of reasoning with certain sorts of beliefs, for example, vague or uncertain beliefs. (We will examine inference under uncertainty in chapter 8.) Fourthly, a real inference system will need some policy for what to do if it ever *revises* some of its beliefs. Suppose, to take an extreme example, the system notices that its beliefs are contradictory. Now, from a contradiction, in standard logics (and in many non-standard logics too), anything follows. But the system should not under those circumstances infer anything: it should give up some of its beliefs so that the contradiction no longer arises. More generally, the problem of managing revisions to the system's beliefs – including giving up beliefs as well as adopting them – is one for which logic writes surprisingly few prescriptions.

Logic, then, is not a theory of inference; it is at best a part of such a theory. Nevertheless, many AI researchers believe that logics of various types at least play an important part in the study of inference, for the reasons given above. We will have much to say in this book on the role of logic in a theory of inference.

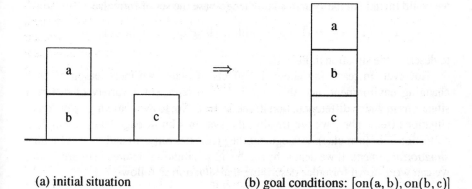

(a) initial situation   (b) goal conditions: $[\mathrm{on}(a, b), \mathrm{on}(b, c)]$

Figure 3.1   Blocks world – initial situation and goal conditions

3.2   A simple AI problem

To fix our ideas about how logic might be used to guide inference, we again turn to a simple but illustrative AI problem. In this section, we will investigate how logic can be used to solve this problem, and in later sections, we shall explore some of the difficulties that emerge from this investigation.

Our example concerns a robot whose job is to manipulate named blocks which are stacked in vertical piles on a table. The robot can pick up only one block at a time from the top of any pile, and can place it either on the table top (which never becomes cluttered) or directly on top of an existing pile. Perhaps the initial situation contains just three blocks stacked in two piles as in figure 3.1(a), and perhaps the robot must stack the blocks vertically in order as shown in figure 3.1(b).

The robot must plan a sequence of actions – in this case, the picking up and putting down of various blocks – which will achieve the stated goal, given the situation in which it initially finds itself. It is understood that certain simplifying assumptions hold: for example, there are no objects in the environment other than those explicitly stated, the robot never errs in performing its actions, the piles of blocks never totter and collapse, there are no influences on the environment apart from the robot's actions, and so on. Everything is predictable, and everything relevant is known. Our task is to write a planning program for the robot.

3.2.1   Representing the problem

The obvious way to represent a situation in the predicate calculus is to employ a predicate $\mathrm{on}(x, y)$ denoting that one block is on top of something else, and, perhaps a predicate $\mathrm{clear}(x)$, denoting that the top of x is not cluttered by blocks. For then we could include in the system's knowledge-base the set of formulae:

$$\{on(a, b), \ clear(a), \ on(b, table), \ clear(c), \ on(c, table)\}$$

to describe the situation in fig 3.1(a).

However, in reasoning about the effects of plans, we must reason about a changing environment, and this requires us to represent a variety of different situations in which different propositions are true. So, to avoid mixing up different situations (remember, we are treating the system's knowledge-base as simply a collection T of formulae), we augment the predicates $on(x, y)$ and $clear(x)$ with a *situation argument*. If we denote by s_0, the initial situation pictured in figure 3.1(a), we can write down formulae describing that situation as follows.

$$\{on(a, b, s_0), \ clear(a, s_0), \ on(b, table, s_0), \ clear(c, s_0), \ on(c, table, s_0)\}. \ (3.1)$$

Here, $on(a, b, s_0)$ says that block a is on block b in situation s_0, $clear(a, s_0)$ says that block a is clear in situation s_0, and so on.

This notation allows us to represent the effects of actions using function symbols. Consider the action of moving block a from block b to the table. Performing this action will transform the initial situation s_0 into a new situation which we can represent as

$$do(move(a, b, table), s_0).$$

Then, to represent the fact that, for example, block b will be clear if block a is moved from block b to the table, the system need only generate the formula

$$clear(b, do(move(a, b, table), s_0)).$$

In words: block b is clear in the situation which results from performing the action $move(a, b, table)$ in situation s_0. Here, $move(x, y, z)$ and $do(a, s)$ are functions. For any block x, and for and y and z, $move(x, y, z)$ denotes the action of moving block x from y to z; and for any action a and situation s, $do(a, s)$ denotes the situation that results by performing a in s. The predicate calculus, when used with situation-arguments to represent facts about changing environments, is sometimes referred to as the *situation calculus* in AI. But it is really no more than plain old predicate calculus.

In the situation calculus, names for situations are just plans with the actions written in reverse order. For example, the term

$$do(move(a, table, b), do(move(b, table, c), do(move(a, b, table), s_0)))$$

names the situation that results from performing the sequence of actions:

$$[move(a, b, table), move(b, table, c), move(a, table, b)]. \qquad (3.2)$$

Given this method of representing situations, how might an AI system reason about the effects of plans? For example, how might such a system infer that the plan (3.2) achieves the goals of stacking block a on block b and block b on block c, in the problem of figure 3.1? Well, according to the logical approach, the system must *prove*, in the predicate calculus, the corresponding formula:

$$
\begin{aligned}
&\text{on}(a, b, \text{do}(\text{move}(a, \text{table}, b), \\
&\qquad \text{do}(\text{move}(b, \text{table}, c), \\
&\qquad\qquad \text{do}(\text{move}(a, b, \text{table}), s_0)))) \ \& \\
&\text{on}(b, c, \text{do}(\text{move}(a, \text{table}, b), \\
&\qquad \text{do}(\text{move}(b, \text{table}, c), \\
&\qquad\qquad \text{do}(\text{move}(a, b, \text{table}), s_0)))),
\end{aligned}
\tag{3.3}
$$

for this formula states that the relevant conditions obtain in the situation resulting when plan (3.2) is performed.

In order to prove proposition(3.3), the system needs to include, in its knowledge-base, a collection of premises encoding its knowledge about the preconditions and effects of the move-action. This can easily be done. For instance, we know that block x can be moved from a location y onto a new location z (where z is not equal to x) if (i) x is on y to start with, and (ii) x and z are clear; and we know that, in the resulting situation, x will be on z and y will be clear. So the axiom is:

$$
\begin{aligned}
&\forall x \forall y \forall z \forall s \\
&\quad ((\text{on}(x, y, s) \ \& \ \text{clear}(x, s) \ \& \ \text{clear}(z, s) \ \& \ x \neq z) \rightarrow \\
&\quad (\text{on}(x, z, \text{do}(\text{move}(x, y, z), s)) \ \& \ \text{clear}(y, \text{do}(\text{move}(x, y, z), s))))).
\end{aligned}
\tag{3.4}
$$

In addition, the system can be given other general knowledge about the blocks world. For example, we might express the relationship between $\text{clear}(x, s)$ and $\text{on}(x, y, s)$ using the following axiom:

$$
(\forall x)(\forall s)(\text{clear}(x, s) \leftrightarrow (\neg(\exists y)\text{on}(y, x, s) \lor x = \text{table}))
\tag{3.5}
$$

since the table is always clear. And we might represent the distinctness of the various blocks using an axiom such as:

$$
a \neq b \ \& \ b \neq c \ \& \ a \neq c \ \& \ a \neq \text{table} \ \& \ b \neq \text{table} \ \& \ c \neq \text{table}.
\tag{3.6}
$$

3.2.2 *Making inferences*

Let us suppose, then, that the system's knowledge-base T consists of: formulae (3.1) specifying the initial situation, formula (3.4) specifying the properties of the move-action, as well as other general pieces of knowledge-such as, e.g. formulae (3.5) and (3.6). We want the system to prove proposition (3.3) as a theorem. The question is, can it do it?

The answer is no. For although we seemed in the above discussion to have fully characterized the effects of the move-action on the blocks world, we in fact neglected a crucial detail: we omitted to specify what things the action did not change. Thus, it is impossible to prove, using the above axioms, that, for example, when block a is moved from b to the table, block b remains on the table. Of course, this is obvious to us: blocks which are not moved remain as they are. But it is not obvious to a computer programmed with the above axioms, for it does not follow from those axioms. The critical (and to us, obvious) facts which we have not declared are the following:

$$\forall x \forall y \forall z \forall u \forall v \forall s$$
$$((\text{on}(x, y, s) \,\&\, \text{clear}(x, s) \,\&\, \text{clear}(z, s) \,\&\, \text{on}(u, v, s) \,\&$$
$$x \neq z \,\&\, u \neq x) \rightarrow \text{on}(u, v, \text{do}(\text{move}(x, y, z), s)))$$

$$\forall x \forall y \forall z \forall w \forall s$$
$$(\text{on}(x, y, s) \,\&\, \text{clear}(x, s) \,\&\, \text{clear}(z, s) \,\&\, \text{clear}(w, s) \,\&$$
$$x \neq z \,\&\, w \neq z) \rightarrow \text{clear}(w, \text{do}(\text{move}(x, y, z), s))).$$

(3.7)

The first of these says that, if block u is on v in situation s, and if some block x (other than u) is moved from y to z, then u will still be on v in the resulting situation. The second says that if w is clear in situation s, and and if some block x is moved onto some location z (other than w), then w will still be clear in the resulting situation. When, and only when, these two propositions are added to our collection of axioms can we prove formula (3.3) and so verify that the plan (3.2) will work. (See exercise 1.)

Of course, proving that a suggested plan achieves a given set of goals is not what our original task demanded of us. What we have to do is *find* such a plan from scratch. How can we understand this latter task in terms of predicate calculus theorem-proving?

3.2.3 *Searching for plans*

In fact, the answer is remarkably simple. Suppose that the system is given the goals of getting block a on block b and block b on block c, as shown in figure 3.1(b). Then the system's inferential task is to prove *some* theorem of the form

$$\text{on}(a, b, \sigma) \,\&\, \text{on}(b, c, \sigma)$$

where σ is a term denoting a situation – i.e. a term from which a plan can be read off.

Notice first that proving the formula

$$(\exists s)(\text{on}(a, b, s) \,\&\, \text{on}(b, c, s) \,\&\, \text{on}(c, \text{table}, s))$$

would establish that a plan *exists* to achieve the goals in question, since the only situations the system knows about are those whose names correspond directly to sequences of actions. Now, it turns out that certain automatic theorem-provers, known as resolution theorem-provers, can prove existentially quantified propositions by finding values of the existentially quantified variables which make the proposition true. In the present case, the value of the variable s making the above proposition true can only be a plan to achieve the corresponding set of goals. Thus, even *finding* a plan can, in practice, be viewed as a matter of theorem-proving.

The reader may be wondering at this point what part the notions of heuristics and search play in this process. The answer is that they are still there, because, when trying to prove a theorem, there are always many inferences that can be made at any stage, only a few of which will lead to the desired conclusion. In general, many possibilities must be tried, and this trying of possibilities is the search. Good heuristics – good policies for searching the space of possible inferences – are what make the difference between an effective and an ineffective theorem-prover.

Before we go on to look at the difficulties of the logic-based approach to inference presented here, it is worth pointing out one of its attractive features. The point about getting a system to make inferences by proving theorems is that, in some sense, we *know* that its inferential policies are right, given the interpretation of the formulae with which it is reasoning. For the predicate calculus has a correct and complete proof theory: by making that proof theory define the system's search-tree, we are giving the system access to just those chains of inference which will never lead it from truth to falsity. The prospect of being able to validate a system's inferential policies in this way remains an important motivation among those who advocate logic as a basis for AI.

3.3 The frame problem

So far, so good. We can indeed state axioms governing the move-action in a way which is sufficient for reasoning about the effects of any given sequence of actions in the blocks world. However, all is not well. Consider again our observation that, in order to reason about the effects of actions using the predicate calculus, axioms are needed to specify the things those actions do not change, as well as the things they do change. In the blocks world, this requirement was easily discharged with the formulae (3.7); but it is clear that, in more complicated domains, it is impossibly onerous. Suppose, for example, that I knock over the cup of tea on my desk. As a result of that that action, various changes occur: the contents of the cup drain out and wet the desk, the nearby books and papers are stained brown, and the cup assumes a new position and orientation. Other things, however, are unaffected. The colour of my next-door neighbour's wallpaper remains what it was before, Bill Clinton is still president of the USA, the orbit of Pluto is not (measurably) affected, and so on. Now it is impossible that a computer system reasoning by means of the predicate calculus about such matters should have an axiom for each of these myriad non-changes; there would just be too many such axioms to store. Yet if these axioms were not present, the system would have most of its beliefs wiped out by a single, trivial action. For, from $\text{president}(\text{usa}, \text{bill\_clinton}, s_0)$, it does not follow that $\text{president}(\text{usa}, \text{bill\_clinton}, \text{do}(\text{spill\_tea}, s_0))$ unless there is also an axiom stating that spilling tea does not affect who is president of what:

$$(\forall x)(\forall y)(\forall s)(\text{president}(x, y, s) \rightarrow \text{president}(x, y, \text{do}(\text{spill\_tea}, s)))$$

For historical reasons, axioms expressing the non-effects of actions are known as *frame axioms*. And the problem raised by the plethora of such axioms required to reason about almost any non-trivial domain has consequently come to be called the *frame problem*. The frame problem is one of the most important insights thrown up by artificial intelligence, because it tells us something unexpected about the inadequacy of theorem-proving in the predicate calculus as a paradigm of rational inference. The qualifier 'rational' in the last sentence is important. To be sure, it is easy to believe (and in fact true) that human beings seldom reason by theorem-proving. But it was only with the advent of AI research that it became apparent that even a computer reasoning system expressly constructed to be as rational as possible could not rely on the predicate calculus for many everyday reasoning tasks.

It is important to distinguish the frame problem from different, though related, problems in reasoning about actions. Matters are not helped in this regard by the various uses for which writers in the field have appropriated the term 'frame problem'. As we have represented it, the frame problem is a problem about the *space* requirements of a predicate-calculus-based reasoning system – about how big, if you like, such a system's *disk* would have to be. That is different from, though related to, the problem of the excessive *time* taken to prove a given goal when the system has a galaxy of axioms to choose from. And it is different from, though related to, the problem of deciding what to bother proving in the first place. This last point deserves some explanation. Consider again the action of spilling my tea. And suppose that I did use the predicate calculus to represent the world. Then it is a consequence of my (frame- and other) axioms that, in this new, post-tea-spilling world, Bill Clinton is still the US president. OK, so I deduce that. Of course, it is also a consequence of my axioms that next-door's wallpaper has not changed colour, so I deduce that; and the orbit of Pluto is still the same, so I deduce that; and so on. The point should be clear: all this is going to take a long time (so long you can be sure Bill Clinton will have been succeeded as president by the time I get around to him). Thought will become paralysed, effective decision-making impossible. Of course, it may not be necessary to run through all of these frame inferences explicitly: after all, no one can explicitly deduce all the consequences of his beliefs, for they are endless. But then the problem arises as to how these frame inferences might be scheduled so as not to make simple questions impossibly difficult to answer. After all, I sometimes do need to know who the president of the USA is, and it would be a shame if I had to run through the thousands of trivial events that had occurred since I last thought of the matter, in order to check that it was still who I last thought it was. And that is why there is a problem of deciding what to bother proving: I cannot deduce every non-effect of spilling my tea; but if I deduce none, then it looks as if simple yes-or-no questions like "Is Bill Clinton (still) the president of the United States?" will take years to answer.

There is another sort of problem which it is important to distinguish from the frame problem, as we have characterized it. The blocks world we considered above is particularly inference-friendly in the following respect: the preconditions of the move-action can be briefly stated, and its effects are assumed to be deterministic. The robot arm always functions perfectly. Children never wander onto the scene and knock down all the towers. Other robots, with different ideas about what to do with the blocks, do not exist. There are no power cuts, hurricanes, tidal waves, or earthquakes. And so on. But in more realistic domains, these possibilities cannot always be ignored, so that the conditions under which an action will have its normal range of effects become massively complicated. For example, executing the action move(x, y, z) will result in x's being on z, but only if the robot arm is in good working order, and the tower does not become too wobbly, and no other agents disturb the tower and no earthquake topples it, and so on. And the axioms required to take these possibilities into account would need antecedents of horrendous complexity. This problem is sometimes called the *qualification problem*.

3.4 An alternative to logic

In section 3.2, we saw that it is possible, theoretically, to encode knowledge of the blocks world in the situation calculus so that reasoning about actions can be viewed as theorem-proving. In section 3.3, however, we also saw what crippling practical difficulties such an approach entails. However, there are other ways to represent our knowledge about the blocks world; indeed, we have already met one of them in chapters 1 and 2. The purpose of this section is to examine this alternative, and compare it with the logic-based approach. The comparison will prove instructive.

Recall how, in chapter 1, the planning program for Bob represented information about situations as lists of facts that are true in them, e.g.:

[in(bob,hall),in(bookcase,hall),in(table,study)]. (3.8)

Suppose, then, we adopt the same approach to the blocks world. For example, we might represent the initial situation in figure 3.1(a) as the list:

[on(a,b),on(b,table),on(c,table),clear(a),clear(c)]. (3.9)

(If it is necessary to distinguish several situations, there is no problem about tagging such a list with an appropriate label, e.g. a label consisting of the sequence of actions that led from the initial situation to the situation being represented; however, this feature is inessential to the discussion here and can be ignored without affecting the argument.) If we represent situations in this way, then we can represent the facts about the action move(x, y, z), which we previously captured by the axioms (3.4) and (3.5), using a PAD-rule as follows:

```
action-type(move(X,Y,Z),
    pre-conds([on(X,Y),clear(X),clear(Z),
               X≠Z,Y≠Z]),                        (3.10)
    add-list([on(X,Z), clear(Y)]),
    del-list([on(X,Y),clear(Z)])).
```

That is, the action of moving X from Y to Z makes it true that X is on Z and that Y is clear, and makes it false that X is on Y and that Z is clear. Note that, in order to check the preconditions of these rules, it will be necessary to give the program access to facts about identity, perhaps in the form of a list

$$[a≠b,a≠c,b≠c,a≠table,b≠table,c≠table,...]$$

or, perhaps, in some more compact way. But we can take it that this is unproblematic. (However, see exercises 2, 3 and 4.)

Using this representation scheme, it is possible to infer what the effects of an action will be in a given situation. The process simply involves taking the list representing the current situation and then adding all the (appropriately instantiated) formulae in the add-list and deleting all the (appropriately instantiated) formulae in the delete-list. To determine whether a given plan – i.e. a sequence of actions – will achieve a given set of goals, it is only necessary to step through each action in the plan, applying the appropriate instance of the above rule at each step. The result, assuming that the preconditions of each action are satisfied, will be a list of atomic formulae representing the final situation after executing the plan. If and only if the goal conditions are in this list is the plan verified. And the problem of *finding* a plan to achieve a given set of goals can also be solved using search as explained in chapter 2.

We can bring out the difference between these two approaches if we consider the frame axioms (3.7), which specify the non-effects of the move-action. For it turns out that these axioms need no counterpart in the PAD-rules. There is no need to mention that, after moving block a from block b to block c, block b remains on the table, because, *if no mention of this proposition is made in the add- or delete-lists, it will simply remain where it is in the representation of a situation when the PAD-rule is applied to it.* Herein lies the appeal of this representation scheme: if non-effects of actions are simply not mentioned in the PAD-rules, then they exhibit the appropriate behaviour for non-effects, i.e. they are not affected. No need to bother with clauses explicitly stating that this or that fact does not change as the result of applying an action: only the actual changes need be mentioned. The relevance of PAD-rules to the frame problem is now immediate. For the frame problem just is the problem of needing to store a titanic listing of axioms specifying the non-effects of actions. And, on the PAD-rules approach, no such listing is required. (Notice, however, that the PAD-rule scheme does not obviously do anything to alleviate the qualification problem. PAD-rules do not allow for probabilistic connections between actions and their effects, so that, in realistic domains, their precondition-lists will have to be hopelessly complicated.)

This, then, is the basic difference between the situation calculus and the PAD-rule scheme: the latter, but not the former, allows the representation of facts by omission. While the axioms (3.7) in the situation calculus are required to state that the locations of unmoved blocks are not affected by the move-action, the PAD-rule representation merely fails to mention any other blocks in its add- and delete-lists: and, because of the way PAD-rules are applied, that suffices to represent the relevant facts about what is not affected by the action in question.

In representing positive information by omission, the PAD-rule scheme has certain features in common with maps. For example, if a map shows a railway line with stations indicated along its course using certain symbol, e.g. a small red circle, then the absence of a red circle at specific point X represents that fact that there is *no* station at the location corresponding to X – not merely that the map is *not saying whether* there is a station there. And, of course, there is no need for the legend to include a special symbol meaning "place where there is no station" – the mere absence of a red circle will do. Thus, maps constitute another good example of why it is sometimes advantageous to represent information by omission.

An alternative way of thinking about the PAD-rule representation scheme is as a *simulation-based* approach, in which the PAD-rule instances simulate, albeit crudely, the causal powers of the actions they represent. When I knock my tea over, the reason next-door's wallpaper remains whatever colour it is or that Bill Clinton remains US president is that the effects of the former event peter out before they reach the latter states of affairs. A PAD-rule encoding knowledge about knocking over a cup of tea would aspire to have exactly this property: its add- and delete-lists would induce changes in some of the facts I believe, and these changes might conceivably induce further updating of my beliefs via some other rules; but the effects of the PAD-rule would peter out before they reached the vast majority of my beliefs.

Thus the PAD-rule approach addresses not only the frame problem, but also some of the related problems identified above. It addresses the problem of the time taken to make the large number of frame inferences, because these inferences, on the PAD-rule scheme, come free: one does not even need to think about the president of the USA when one spills one's tea, yet one's belief that it is still Bill Clinton will survive the action. And, by making all these inferences free, the PAD-rule approach addresses – or rather dissolves – the problem of deciding when to make them. Drew McDermott [6] has called this approach to the frame problem the *sleeping dog strategy*. On this approach, the non-effects of actions are the sleeping dogs of reason; and we should let them lie. This insight is important, and transcends questions of the appropriateness of PAD-rules, or whatever we might put in their place. For the lesson of the frame problem is surely that the vast bulk of our beliefs are simply not accessed when we reason about the effects of an action. It is not that we infer that these beliefs should be unaffected; it is rather that we do not think of them at all. The secret of effective reasoning is just this ability not to think about the multitude of things that do not change whenever something trivial happens. It seems that this ability rests on the encoding of information by omission.

In fact, if we are in the business of representing facts by omission, we can make our representation of the blocks-world more compact. Consider the data-structure (3.9) representing the situation figure 3.1(a). The term `clear(a)` is simply equivalent to the fact that there is no block on block a. But if we decide to interpret a list such as (3.9) as encoding *all* the relevant facts about what is on what, we can dispense with `clear(a)`: the mere absence of any term of the form `on(_,a)` can then be taken to imply that there is nothing on top of block a in that situation. In that case, we can reduce (3.9) to

$$[on(a,b),on(b,table),on(c,table)]. \tag{3.11}$$

Of course, we would have to modify the PAD-rule as well. The terms `clear(Y)` and `clear(Z)` would no longer have to appear in the add- and delete-list, and the inference program would have to check the preconditions `clear(X)` and `clear(Z)` by scanning the situation for corresponding terms of the form `on(_X)` and `on(_Z)`. But again, this is easy to program.

3.5   Closed world assumptions and their problems

3.5.1   The closed world assumption

Let us see if we can get clearer as to what is going on, logically, when we represent information by omission, in the way just suggested. We proposed representing a situation by means of a data-structure listing the facts which hold in that situation, for example:

$$[on(a,b),on(b,table),on(c,table)].$$

Now this data-structure corresponds to the following set of predicate calculus formulae:

$$\{on(a,b),on(b,table),on(c,table)\}.$$

But, in taking the data-structure to represent the negative facts which have been omitted, we are, in effect, taking it to encode, *in addition*, the formulae:

$$\neg on(c,a),\ \neg on(b,a),\ \neg on(a,table),\quad \text{etc.}$$

(Note: we ignore the predicate $clear(x)$ for this purpose, and we assume that the only individuals are the table and blocks a, b and c.)

Let us generalize this idea. First, some terminology. A formula is *atomic* if it consists of one predicate letter and its arguments; a formula is *ground* if it contains no variables. Thus, for example, on(c, a), on(b, a) and on(a, table) are all ground atomic. Now, if T is a set of formulae, we define the *naive closure* of T to be the set of formulae

$$CW_T = \{\neg\psi \mid \psi \text{ is ground atomic and } T \nvdash \psi\}$$

(See exercise 5.)

We can think of CW_T as the set of basic facts encoded in T by omission. Thus, the naive closure of a knowledge-base (or set of facts) is really just a precise way of saying what we are assuming when we say that we are encoding information by omission: we take the knowledge contained in an explicit knowledge-base T to include all those facts in $T \cup CW_T$. In interpreting a knowledge-base in this way, one is sometimes said to be making a *closed world assumption*.

At the start of this chapter, we suggested that the predicate calculus might contribute towards a theory of inference in the following way: if a reasoning system believes a set of facts T, and if it can be determined that

$$T \vdash \psi$$

for some formula ψ, then ψ might be a suitable thing for the system to infer. Making the closed world assumption with respect to a knowledge-base T can be seen as giving the system a commitment to infer ψ when

$$T \cup CW_T \vdash \psi$$

which, obviously, will allow the system to infer more things from a knowledge-base of a given size.

This way of looking at things suggests a version of the logical approach to inference which might address the frame problem (at least in the narrow sense given above). The tree of inferences to which a system with knowledge-base T has access is still defined by the proof rules of the predicate calculus, *but in conjunction with the formulae of the closed world assumption*. This approach allows the system's knowledge-base to encode information by omission, whilst at the same time putting its inferential practices on a sound footing. We shall have much to say about closed world assumptions in chapter 4.

3.5.2 Encoding ignorance

Representation by omission can be used to tackle some of the problems discussed in section 3.3, but there is a price to pay, as we shall see.

One problem with naive closure is that it makes it difficult to encode ignorance or lack of information. Suppose the system knows where block b and block c are, but has no idea where block a is. Then it cannot encode its knowledge using the set of formulae

$$T = \{\text{on}(b, \text{table}), \text{on}(c, \text{table})\},$$

since this will be interpreted as saying that block a is *not* on block b, *not* on block c, and *not* on the table, which is of course not what we want.

Here is a similar case, this time involving disjunction. Suppose the system is not sure whether block a is on block b or on block c. Then it cannot encode its knowledge using the set of formulae

$$T = \{on(a, b) \lor on(a, c), on(b, table), on(c, table)\},$$

since $\neg on(a, b)$ and $\neg on(a, c)$ are in CW_T, whence $T \cup CW_T$ contains the inconsistent trio $\{\neg on(a, b), \neg on(a, c), on(a, b) \lor on(a, c)\}$. True, it is possible to restrict the formulae in T so that this kind of inconsistency does not arise. (For example, one possibility is to restrict T to containing only horn clause formulae – i.e. disjunctions of literals at most one of which is unnegated.) But these restrictions are a heavy price to pay. Certainly, we would like a reasoning system to be able to think that block a is either on block b or on block c without knowing which.

3.5.3 Deciding on the language

Another problem with naive closure (in fact, with closed-world assumptions in general) is that it makes the set of derivable facts critically dependent on the *language* chosen. Consider the predicate *fridgeon*, defined in Fodor[3] as follows:

x is a *fridgeon* (at time t) if and only if x is an elementary particle and my fridge is on (at time t).

Suppose we have $fridgeon(x)$ as one of our predicates. It is a strange predicate, to be sure, but nothing has been said so far to discriminate against strange predicates. The trouble is that, if this is a predicate in my language, my PAD-rule for switching the fridge on (or off) had better contain a clause specifying that all the elementary particles in the universe change from being non-fridgeons to being fridgeons (or the other way around). If this clause is omitted, the PAD-rule is wrong. And there are rather many elementary particles. So $fridgeon(x)$ had better not be in my language. But the problem is now that we have so far not been given any criterion for distinguishing between sensible predicates such as $clear(x)$ or $on(x, y)$ that are not going to cause this sort of problem, and silly, gerrymandered properties such as $fridgeon(x)$, that are. If this problem of choosing the predicates of the representation language seems bizarre and recherché, be warned that it will not go away: we will meet it again in later chapters and in other guises.

3.6 Conclusion

In this chapter, we have examined the relationship between logic and inference. We began by explaining why logic might be seen to have a role in inference – namely in defining the space of inferences to which a reasoning system should have access. We then went on to see that a simplistic application of this idea leads to the frame-problem (and its relatives). The conclusion we drew was that effective inference relies on the ability *not to think of* the vast majority of states that are not affected by various actions, and we saw that this ability rests on the encoding of information by omission. We explained how PAD-rules incorporate such a feature, and how they avoid the frame-problem in the blocks world (at least in the narrow sense defined above). We concluded by pointing out some of the difficulties of trying to represent information by omission, difficulties which we take up in the next chapter.

Exercises

1. Suppose that, in the situation s_0, the blocks a, b and c are stacked as shown in figure 3.1; this would be represented in the predicate calculus by the axiom:

    $$on(a, b, s_0) \ \& \ clear(a, s_0) \ \& \ on(b, table, s_0) \ \& $$
    $$clear(c, s_0) \ \& \ on(c, table, s_0).$$

    Using the predicate calculus formalization of the blocks-world suggested in formulae (3.4), (3.5) and (3.7) (and any other reasonable axioms you think you might need), prove using resolution theorem-proving (or some other theorem-proving technique) the proposition

    $$on(b, c, do(move(b, table, c), do(move(a, b, table), s_0))).$$

2. The PAD-rule (3.10) is not quite correct if Z is instantiated with `table`. Identify the problem, and write a PAD-rule (or -rules) to avoid it.

3. Suppose that the blocks a, b and c are stacked as figure 3.1; this would be represented in the PAD-rule scheme of section 3.4 by the list:

    `[on(a,b),on(b,table),on(c,table),clear(a),clear(c)]`.

    Show, using the correct specification of the action `move(X,Y,Z)` (see previous exercise), that the goal `on(b,c)` is achieved by the plan

    `move(a,b,table);move(b,table,c)`.

4. (Programming) Write a program which takes as input a list-representation of a situation, e.g.

    `[on(a,b),on(b,table),on(c,table),clear(a),clear(c)]`.

    together with a plan in the form of a sequence of actions, e.g.

    `[move(a,b,table);move(b,table,c);move(a,table,b)]`

    and computes the effects of the plan, outputting the list-representation of the resulting situation.

5. Suppose a system's knowledge-base is

    $$T = \{on(a, b), on(b, c), on(c, table)\}.$$

where a, b and c and table are the only individual constants in the language, and on(x, y) the only predicate. What is CW_T? Why, when forming the naive closure of a set, do we need to take into account the language used?

Suppose that, in order to allow reasoning about multiple situations, we give the predicate a situation argument, thus: on(x, y, s). And suppose we include in the language the individual constant s_0 naming the initial situation, as well as the familiar functions move(x, y, z) and do(a, s). What is the naive closure of T now? How many formulae does it contain?

Further reading

The debate on the role of logic in AI continues unabated. See, for example, the paper "Logic and Artificial Intelligence", by Nils Nilsson in Kirsh [4] for a defence of the 'logicist' position. A lively discussion of the frame problem is to be found in the collection of papers edited by Zenon Pylyshyn (Pylyshyn [8]). A more in-depth and mathematical treatment of the frame problem (and its relatives) is to be found in Shoham [9]. See also Morgenstern and Stein [7].

Some readers may be particularly interested in pursuing the topic of automated theorem-proving. There are several theorem-proving programs available: one recent such program (in the public domain) is the OTTER 2.0 theorem-proving system (McCune [5]). For another approach to automated theorem-proving, see Boyer and Moore [2].

Bibliography

[1] Allen, J, J. Hendler, and A. Tate (eds.) *Readings in Planning*, San Mateo: Morgan Kaufmann, 1990.

[2] Boyer, Robert S. and J. Strother Moore *A Computational Logic Handbook*, Boston: Academic Press, 1988.

[3] Fodor, J. "Modules, Frames, Fridgeons, Sleeping Dogs, and the Music of the Spheres", in Pylyshyn [8], pp. 139–149.

[4] Kirsh, David (ed.) *Foundations of Artificial Intelligence*, Cambridge, MA: MIT Press, 1992.

[5] McCune, William "Otter 2.0 Users' Guide", Argonne National Laboratory report ANL-90/9, Argonne, Illinois.

[6] McDermott, Drew "We've been framed: or, why AI is innocent of the frame problem", in Pylyshyn [8], pp. 113–122.

[7] Morgenstern, L. and L.A. Stein: "Why things go wrong: a formal theory of causal reasoning", in Allen, Hendler and Tate [1], pp. 641–646.

[8] Pylyshyn, Z. (ed.) *The Robot's Dilemma: the frame problem in artificial intelligence*, Norwood, N.J: Ablex, 1987.

[9] Shoham, Yoav *Reasoning about Change*, Cambridge, MA: MIT Press, 1986.

4 Closed World Assumptions

The lesson of chapter 3 is that theorem-proving in the predicate calculus constitutes a poor mechanism for reasoning about a complex, dynamic environment such as the one we inhabit. In particular, we drew attention to the problem of representing *negative* information – information about the non-existence of objects or events or processes or influences. Negative information, we argued, must sometimes be encoded by the mere absence of positive information to the contrary: propositions which are not given, or which are not deducible from those which are given, should be assumed to be false. This type of assumption is sometimes referred to as a *closed world assumption*, and the logical properties of closed world assumptions occupy centre stage in one important strand in AI research. They also form the topic of this chapter.

4.1 A closed world assumption

Let us briefly recapitulate the example of chapter 3, in which we saw how to formalize knowledge about the action move(x, y, z) in the situation calculus. The relevant axioms are:

$\forall x \forall y \forall z \forall s$
$\quad$ ((on(x, y, s) & clear(x, s) & clear(z, s) & $x \neq z$) $\rightarrow$ $\qquad$ (4.1)
$\quad$ (on(x, z, do(move(x, y, z), s)) & clear(y, do(move(x, y, z), s)))))

which specifies the 'positive' effects of the action move(x, y, z), and

$\quad \forall x \forall y \forall z \forall u \forall v \forall s$
$\qquad$ ((on(x, y, s) & clear(x, s) & clear(z, s) & on(u, v, s) &
$\qquad$ $x \neq z$ & $u \neq x$) $\rightarrow$ on(u, v, do(move(x, y, z), s)))

$\qquad\qquad\qquad\qquad\qquad\qquad\qquad\qquad\qquad\qquad\qquad$ (4.2)
$\quad \forall x \forall y \forall z \forall w \forall s$
$\qquad$ (on(x, y, s) & clear(x, s) & clear(z, s) & clear(w, s) &
$\qquad$ $x \neq z$ & $w \neq z$) $\rightarrow$ clear(w, do(move(x, y, z), s)))

which specify its non-effects. As we argued, in more realistic domains than the blocks-world, it will not in general be possible to axiomatize an action's non-effects anything like as succinctly as we can with formulae (4.2); that is the whole nub of

65

the frame problem. So we would like to be able to dispense with formulae (4.2) and rely instead on the assumption that things in general do not change unless there is a positive reason for their doing so.

In order to formalize this idea, it will help to change the notation slightly. Instead of writing

$$\text{on}(a, b, s_0), \quad \text{on}(b, \text{table}, s_0), \quad \text{clear}(c, s_0), \quad \text{etc.}$$

we shall use instead:

$$\text{holds}(\text{on}(a, b), s_0), \quad \text{holds}(\text{on}(b, \text{table}), s_0), \quad \text{holds}(\text{clear}(c), s_0), \quad \text{etc.}$$

Notice that, here, expressions such as $\text{on}(a, b)$, $\text{clear}(c)$ etc. are not formulae, but terms – they name states of affairs which may or may not hold in various situations. Such states of affairs are sometimes known as *fluents*.

Then we can introduce a predicate $\text{affected}(p, a)$ with the intuitive interpretation: "the fluent p is affected by action a". Our new notation might then be used to write down the axiom:

$$\forall p \forall a \forall s((\text{holds}(p, s) \& \neg\text{affected}(p, a)) \rightarrow \text{holds}(p, \text{do}(a, s))). \qquad (4.3)$$

saying that fluents which are not affected by an action a remain true after that action has been performed. Now, given axiom (4.1) and (4.3), together with other suitable axioms (stating such things as that only one block can rest on top of another block, and that each block can only be in one place in a given situation), it can be proved that any instance of the action-type $\text{move}(x, y, z)$ affects the facts $\text{on}(x, y)$ and $\text{clear}(z)$. That is, it can be proved that:

$$\forall x \forall y \forall z \, \text{affected}(\text{on}(x, y), \text{move}(x, y, z)),$$
$$\forall x \forall y \forall z \, \text{affected}(\text{clear}(z), \text{move}(x, y, z)).$$

The idea that we wish to explore here is the following. We would like to assume that *any fluent that we have no reason to believe is affected by an action will not be affected by that action*. That is, we would like to stipulate that the only statements of the form

$$\text{affected}(p, a)$$

that are true are those which we can prove to be true from our axioms; all others are false. Clearly, this is a kind of closed world assumption. The advantage of such an assumption is that it holds out the prospect of avoiding having to list axioms stating all the non-effects of actions. The problem, as we saw in chapter 3, is that it is difficult to make a closed world assumption in an unrestricted logic, without generating an inconsistency. In this chapter, we see how, with a certain amount of effort, this problem can be overcome.

In section 4.2, we begin by considering two preliminary approaches to this problem: one *semantic* or *model-theoretic*, the other *syntactic* or *proof-theoretic*.

In section 4.3, we put right some defects in these preliminary approaches. In section 4.4, we are finally in a position to see how a computer might represent facts about the noneffects of the move-action in the blocks world using a closed world assumption. Our approach in this chapter will take us across some difficult terrain. But be patient: our goal is an ambitious one; and we will get there in the end.

4.2 p-minimal models and predicate circumscription

The above axiomatization of the blocks world, although highly idealized in comparison to real-life situations, is nevertheless quite complex, so to clarify our ideas, we shall concentrate on a simpler example which has often been discussed in the literature. Consider the theory T_{flies} consisting of the formulae:

$$\{\forall x((\text{bird}(x)\&\neg\text{ab}(x)) \rightarrow \text{flies}(x)), \text{bird}(\text{tweety}),$$
$$\text{bird}(\text{oscar}), \text{oscar} \neq \text{tweety}, \text{ab}(\text{oscar})\}$$

with the intended interpretation that all birds which are not abnormal fly, that Tweety and Oscar are (distinct) birds, and that Oscar is abnormal. Of course, these formulae do not license the conclusion that Tweety flies, because they have models in which Tweety is in the extension of the predicate $\text{ab}(x)$. Yet in the absence of any reason to the contrary, it would be nice to be able to assume that Tweety is not an abnormal bird, and so can fly.

4.2.1 p-Minimal models

Let us step back a little. Suppose that, given a theory T (i.e. a knowledge-base of premises $\phi_1, \ldots, \phi_n$) in the predicate calculus, we establish, by means of theorem-proving, the conclusion ψ:

$$T \vdash \psi. \tag{4.4}$$

The point of proving such a theorem is that it shows us that the argument from the premises in T to the conclusion ψ is *valid*: if the theory T is true, so is the conclusion ψ. Put more technically, it shows that every interpretation M that makes the formulae $\phi_1, \ldots, \phi_n$ in T true also makes the conclusion ψ true:

$$\text{for any interpretation } M, \text{if } M \models T \text{ then } M \models \psi, \tag{4.5}$$

or, as it is usually written:

$$T \models \psi.$$

But suppose now we confine our attention to those models in which the extension of some predicate is *minimized*. We might consider, for example, what is true in all models of T_{flies} in which the predicate $\text{ab}(x)$ has the smallest possible extension. If a formula ψ is true in all such models, we might say that ψ follows from T *under the minimization of* $\mathrm{ab}(x)$. If we could make this notion precise, then perhaps it will yield a solution to the problem of encoding the assumption that things are normal unless we have reason to believe otherwise. In the case of the theory T_{flies}, we would want to say that, if M is a model of T in which the extension of the predicate $\mathrm{ab}(x)$ is made as small as possible, then Tweety must be in the extension of flies in M, that is:

> for any interpretation M, if $M \models T$ and the extension of $\mathrm{ab}(x)$ in M is minimal, then $M \models \mathrm{flies}(\mathrm{tweety})$.

The task before us, then, is to make precise what we mean by "the extension of $\mathrm{ab}(x)$ in M is minimal".

One possibility is as follows. We begin with a definition:

Definition *Let M and M' be models of a theory T and $p(x)$ a predicate. We say that M' is a p-submodel of M if*

1. *M and M' have the same domain;*
2. *the denotations of all terms and function letters are the same in M and M';*
3. *the extension of $p(x)$ in M' is a proper subset of the extension of $p(x)$ in M;*
4. *the extensions of all other predicates are the same in both M and M'.*

We then say that a p-minimal model of a theory T is a model M of T which has no p-submodels.

We shall need to return to the notion of p-minimal model in the sequel, but at least we now have the germ of an idea which we can apply to the blocks world problem above. Given a theory T, and a predicate $p(x)$, we have the following way of putting into effect the assumption that the only things which have the property $p(x)$ are those things which T says have the property $p(x)$: we draw, as our conclusions, formulae ψ with the property that:

> for any interpretation M, if $M \models T$ and M is p-minimal, then $M \models \psi$,

or, as we shall write:

$$T \models_p \psi,$$

a condition which should be compared with (4.5) above.

4.2.2 Database completion

Section 4.2.1 outlined an approach to minimality-assumptions based on model-theoretic considerations. In this section we examine an alternative approach with a more proof-theoretic flavour.

Suppose we have a theory T_{ab} consisting of axioms specifying certain birds to be abnormal:

$$\{\ \forall x(\mathrm{penguin}(x) \rightarrow \mathrm{ab}(x)),\ \forall x(\mathrm{emu}(x) \rightarrow \mathrm{ab}(x)),\ \mathrm{ab}(\mathrm{oscar})\ \}$$

These axioms constitute a set of sufficient conditions for abnormality: penguins, emus and Oscar have got to number among the abnormals. We can gather together the axioms of theory T_{ab} into the single, equivalent axiom:

$$\forall x((\text{penguin}(x) \vee \text{emu}(x) \vee x = \text{oscar}) \rightarrow \text{ab}(x)). \tag{4.6}$$

Now, another way of capturing the assumption that the only abnormal things are those which T_{ab} says are abnormal is to make the *sufficient* condition (4.6) for abnormality a *necessary* condition, by reversing the implication:

$$\forall x(\text{ab}(x) \rightarrow (\text{penguin}(x) \vee \text{emu}(x) \vee x = \text{oscar})). \tag{4.7}$$

Formula (4.6) says that *all* things which are penguins or emus or Oscar are abnormal; formula (4.7) says that *only* things which are penguins or emus or Oscar are abnormal. Thus, formula (4.7) expresses the assumption that the only abnormal things are those which T_{ab} says are abnormal.

Formula (4.7) is called the *database completion* of $\text{ab}(x)$ in the theory T_{ab}. More generally, suppose T is a theory in which the predicate $p(x)$ occurs only in the formulae:

$$\forall x(\text{cond}_1(x) \rightarrow p(x))$$
$$\forall x(\text{cond}_2(x) \rightarrow p(x))$$
$$\cdots$$
$$\forall x(\text{cond}_n(x) \rightarrow p(x)).$$

Together, these formulae are equivalent to the formula

$$\forall x((\text{cond}_1(x) \vee \text{cond}_2(x) \vee \ldots \vee \text{cond}_n(x)) \rightarrow p(x)).$$

We define $\text{comp}(p, T)$, the *database completion* of $p(x)$ in T, to be the formula obtained by reversing the implication, thus:

$$\forall x(p(x) \rightarrow (\text{cond}_1(x) \vee \text{cond}_2(x) \vee \ldots \vee \text{cond}_n(x))).$$

(Note: for these purposes, we convert a formula of the form $p(a)$, where a is a name, to the equivalent form $\forall x(x = a \rightarrow p(x))$ and we take the completion of a predicate $p(x)$ which has no defining clauses to be the formula $\forall x \neg p(x)$.)

Here again, then, we have the germ of an idea which we will eventually be able to apply to the blocks world problem. Given a theory T, and a predicate $p(x)$, we have the following way of putting into effect the assumption that the only things which have the property $p(x)$ are those things which T says have the property $p(x)$: we draw, as our conclusions, formulae ψ which we can prove from T together with $\text{comp}(p, T)$, i.e. formulae with the property that:

$$T \cup \{\text{comp}(p, T)\} \vdash \psi,$$

a condition which should be compared with (4.4) above.

4.2.3   *Predicate circumscription*

So far, we have considered a model-theoretic and a proof-theoretic approach to expressing a closed world assumption. Let us now try to make these two approaches converge. Suppose we have theory T involving a predicate $p(x)$ which we want to minimize: i.e. we want to assume that the only things in the extension of $p(x)$ are those things which the axioms in T force to be there. The proof-theoretic approach discussed in section 4.2.2 relies on the idea of taking a sufficient condition for $p(x)$ and assuming it to be a necessary condition. We will need to generalize this idea slightly to bring it into line with the p-minimal models approach of section 4.2.1. Let $\Phi(x)$ be any predicate calculus expression which expresses a sufficient condition for $p(x)$. That is:

$$\forall x(\Phi(x) \rightarrow p(x)).$$

And suppose that, when we substitute $\Phi(x)$ for every occurrence of $p(x)$ in T, we get a list of formulae which we can prove from the original theory T. (Intuitively, we are supposing that $\Phi(x)$ is a suitable substitute for $p(x)$ according to T.) We can write the result of substituting all occurrences of $p(x)$ in T by $\Phi(x)$ as

$$T(\Phi).$$

(Note: it will help if, in the sequel, we think of a theory T as being not a set of formulae, but a single, big, conjunctive formula.) Finally, we can assert the fact that $\Phi(x)$ is also a necessary condition for $p(x)$ using the formula:

$$\forall x(p(x) \rightarrow \Phi(x)).$$

Thus, to force $p(x)$ to have minimal extension, we can add to our theory T, as new axioms, all formulae of the form:

$$[T(\Phi) \;\&\; \forall x(\Phi(x) \rightarrow p(x))] \rightarrow \forall x(p(x) \rightarrow \Phi(x)) \qquad (4.8)$$

where $\Phi(x)$ is any predicate calculus expression having one free variable, and where $T(\Phi)$ is the result of replacing all occurrences of $p(x)$ in the theory T by $\Phi(x)$. The set of formulae (4.8), which we may denote $\mathrm{circ}(p, T)$, is called the *predicate circumscription* – for short, the *circumscription* – of the predicate $p(x)$ within the theory T.

To see the relationship between $\mathrm{circ}(p, T)$ and $\mathrm{comp}(p, T)$, consider again the theory T_{ab}:

$$\{ \forall x(\mathrm{penguin}(x) \rightarrow \mathrm{ab}(x)), \forall x(\mathrm{emu}(x) \rightarrow \mathrm{ab}(x)), \mathrm{ab}(\mathrm{oscar}) \}$$

and see what happens when we circumscribe the predicate $\mathrm{ab}(x)$ in this theory. Taking T to be the theory T_{ab} and $p(x)$ the predicate $\mathrm{ab}(x)$ in (4.8) yields:

$$[\forall x(\mathrm{penguin}(x) \rightarrow \Phi(x)) \;\&\; \forall x(\mathrm{emu}(x) \rightarrow \Phi(x)) \;\&\; \Phi(\mathrm{oscar}) \;\& \\ \forall x(\Phi(x) \rightarrow \mathrm{ab}(x))] \rightarrow \forall x(\mathrm{ab}(x) \rightarrow \Phi(x)). \qquad (4.9)$$

Remember, (4.9) is a *collection* of formulae, rather than a single formula. Let us just focus on one of these formulae, namely, that obtained by substituting the expression

$$(\text{emu}(x) \vee \text{penguin}(x) \vee x = \text{oscar})$$

for $\Phi(x)$. (We will see the motivation of this particular substitution presently.) The result is the slightly daunting:

$$
\begin{aligned}
&[\forall x(\text{penguin}(x) \rightarrow(\text{emu}(x) \vee \text{penguin}(x) \vee x = \text{oscar})) \;\&\\
&\forall x(\text{emu}(x) \rightarrow (\text{emu}(x) \vee \text{penguin}(x) \vee x = \text{oscar})) \;\&\\
&(\text{emu}(\text{oscar}) \vee \text{penguin}(\text{oscar}) \vee \text{oscar} = \text{oscar}) \;\& \qquad\qquad (4.10)\\
&\forall x((\text{emu}(x) \vee \text{penguin}(x) \vee x = \text{oscar}) \rightarrow \text{ab}(x))] \rightarrow\\
&\qquad\qquad \forall x(\text{ab}(x) \rightarrow (\text{emu}(x) \vee \text{penguin}(x) \vee x = \text{oscar})).
\end{aligned}
$$

We now see that, if T_{ab} is true, then the antecedents in formula (4.10) are all true as well. For

$$\forall x(\text{penguin}(x) \rightarrow (\text{emu}(x) \vee \text{penguin}(x) \vee x = \text{oscar}))$$
$$\forall x(\text{emu}(x) \rightarrow (\text{emu}(x) \vee \text{penguin}(x) \vee x = \text{oscar}))$$
$$(\text{emu}(\text{oscar}) \vee \text{penguin}(\text{oscar}) \vee \text{oscar} = \text{oscar})$$

are all logical truths, and

$$\forall x((\text{emu}(x) \vee \text{penguin}(x) \vee x = \text{oscar}) \rightarrow \text{ab}(x))$$

is just the original theory T_{ab}. But then the conclusion of formula (4.10) must also be true, namely:

$$\forall x(\text{ab}(x) \rightarrow (\text{emu}(x) \vee \text{penguin}(x) \vee x = \text{oscar}))$$

which is exactly the database completion of $\text{ab}(x)$ in T. Thus, circumscription is at least as strong as database completion.

In the previous section, we suggested minimizing the predicate $p(x)$ in a theory T by drawing, as conclusions, formulae ψ with the property that:

$$T \cup \{\text{comp}(p, T)\} \vdash \psi.$$

As a result of the discussion of this section, we might equally well consider instead drawing conclusions ψ with the property that

$$T \cup \text{circ}(p, T) \vdash \psi,$$

or, as we shall write:

$$T \vdash_p \psi.$$

We can now answer our question about the relationship between the model-theoretic and proof-theoretic approaches to minimization. The connection between $T \vdash_p \psi$ and $T \models_p \psi$ can be stated in the following theorem (which will not be proved here):

$$\text{If } \; T \vdash_p \psi, \; \text{ then } \; T \models_p \psi. \qquad\qquad (4.11)$$

If a conclusion ψ can be proved by p-circumscription from T, then ψ is true in all p-minimal models of T. That is, if we intend a knowledge-base to be taken with the assumption that $p(x)$ is to be minimized, theorem-proving with p-circumscription will always produce correct results. The converse of the result (4.11) does not in general obtain. However, there is a restricted completeness theorem according to which, in certain special cases, if a conclusion ψ is true in all p-minimal models of a theory T, then ψ is provable from T together with the circumscription of $p(x)$ in T. The technical details involved in stating this restricted completeness theorem would take us too far afield, and we shall not develop them here. (See further reading.)

If, then, we intend that a system's knowledge-base be taken with the assumption that p is to be minimized, the above results show us the attraction of getting the system to reason by theorem-proving under p-circumscription. For, if we use theorem-proving under p-circumscription to define the tree of inferences the system can make, we know that the system has access only to those inferences which will never lead it from truth to falsity, given the interpretation of the representations it is using.

4.3 (p, p)-minimal models and formula circumscription

4.3.1 (p, p)-*minimal models*

Plausible as they may seem, the notions of predicate circumscription and p-minimal models do not furnish us with a solution to the problem of chapter 3. The best way to see this is to consider again the theory T_{flies}

$$\{\forall x((\text{bird}(x) \& \neg \text{ab}(x)) \rightarrow \text{flies}(x)), \text{bird}(\text{tweety}),$$
$$\text{bird}(\text{oscar}), \text{ab}(\text{oscar}), \text{oscar} \neq \text{tweety}\},$$

and to circumscribe the predicate $\text{ab}(x)$ in it. Ignoring those conjuncts in $T_{\text{flies}}(\Phi)$ which do not involve Φ and which are therefore simply formulae in T_{flies}, $\text{circ}(\text{ab}(x), T_{\text{flies}})$ is the collection of formulae:

$$[\forall x((\text{bird}(x) \& \neg \Phi(x)) \rightarrow \text{flies}(x)) \& \Phi(\text{oscar}) \& \forall x(\Phi(x) \rightarrow \text{ab}(x))] \rightarrow$$
$$\forall x(\text{ab}(x) \rightarrow \Phi(x)).$$

$$(4.12)$$

Common sense suggests the substitution of $x = \text{oscar}$ for $\Phi(x)$ in order to prove a theorem of the form

$$\forall x(\text{ab}(x) \rightarrow x = \text{oscar}),$$

from which flies(tweety) would immediately follow.

Unfortunately, there is a problem. All we can prove with the substitution of $x = \text{oscar}$ for $\Phi(x)$ is:

$$[\forall x((\text{bird}(x) \& x \neq \text{oscar}) \rightarrow \text{flies}(x))] \rightarrow \forall x(\text{ab}(x) \rightarrow x = \text{oscar})$$

which says that, if we can show that all birds other than Oscar fly, then the only abnormal bird is Oscar. But that is of course useless. The only reason we want to show that all birds other than Oscar are not abnormal was *so that* we could show that all birds other than Oscar can fly!

Is there perhaps a cleverer substitution for $\Phi(x)$ which enables us to prove the desired result? A little model-theoretic reflection shows us that the answer is no. Consider the model M_{bad} with domain {tweety, oscar}, in which the extension of flies(x) is empty and the extension of ab(x) is the whole domain, {tweety, oscar}. Strangely, enough, even though nothing in the axioms forces Tweety to be abnormal, and even though M_{bad} does indeed put Tweety in the extension of ab(x), it transpires that M_{bad} is nevertheless ab(x)-minimal. Remember that M is ab(x)-minimal just in case it has no ab(x)-submodels. But, according to clause 4 of definition of *minimal model*, for M' to be an ab(x)-submodel of M, it is required that the extensions of all predicates other than ab(x) be the same in both M and M'. And it is this clause that causes the trouble. For it is clear that any model of T_{flies} in which the extension of flies(x) is the same as in M_{bad} (i.e. is the empty set) must have both Tweety and Oscar in the domain of ab(x) (otherwise the first formula in T_{flies} would not come out true). So M_{bad} is ab(x)-minimal, according to our definition. (Intuitively, of course, this is an unwelcome result.) It follows that the formulae $\forall x(\mathrm{ab}(x) \rightarrow x = \mathrm{oscar})$ and flies(tweety) are not true in all ab(x)-minimal models (M_{bad} is a counterexample!), so that, by the result (4.11), these formulae are not derivable from T_{flies} together with circ(ab, T_{flies}). Predicate circumscription – and indeed concentration on p-minimal models – does not yield the desired results. (But see exercise 1.)

With a little perseverance, however, it turns out that these difficulties can be overcome. In terms of minimal models, the solution is that, in minimizing the predicate ab(x), we must allow the extensions of other predicates to vary. Thus, we define:

Definition *Let M and M' be models of a theory T, $p(x)$ a predicate, and $\mathbf{p} = \{p_1(x), \ldots, p_n(x)\}$ a set of predicates. We say that M' is a $(p, \mathbf{p})$-submodel of M if*

1. *M and M' have the same domain;*
2. *the denotations of all terms and function letters are the same in M and M';*
3. *the extension of $p(x)$ in M' is a proper subset of the extension of of $p(x)$ in M;*
4. *the extensions of all predicates other than $p(x), p_1(x), \ldots, p_n(x)$ are the same in both M and M'.*

We then say that a $(p, \mathbf{p})$-minimal model of the theory T is a model M of T which has no $(p, \mathbf{p})$-submodels.

The idea here is that the old definition in section 4.2.1 was too restrictive, because it refused to compare models M and M' in which not all predicates other than $p(x)$ have the same extension. The new definition seeks to remedy this problem by allowing us to specify a set of predicates which are allowed to vary freely in our attempts to minimize $p(x)$. If, in the theory T_{flies}, we let $p(x)$ be the predicate $\text{ab}(x)$ and $\mathbf{p}$ be the set of predicates $\{\text{flies}(x)\}$, then it is easy to see that any $(p, \mathbf{p})$-minimal model M of T_{flies} must make Tweety normal and so able to fly. For if Tweety is abnormal and unable to fly in M, then by transferring Tweety from the extension of $\text{ab}(x)$ to the extension of $\text{flies}(x)$ and leaving everything else unchanged, we obtain a $(p, \mathbf{p})$-submodel of M. Thus, in every $(p, \mathbf{p})$-minimal model of T_{flies}, Tweety flies. Or, as we shall write:

$$T_{\text{flies}} \models_{(p, \mathbf{p})} \text{flies}(\text{tweety})$$

which is the desired conclusion.

4.3.2   Formula circumscription

This new notion of minimality has a syntactic counterpart known as *formula circumscription*. Recall that the predicate circumscription $\text{circ}(p, T)$ of a predicate $p(x)$ in a theory T is simply the collection of formulae:

$$[T(\Phi)\&\forall x(\Phi(x) \to p(x))] \to \forall x(p(x) \to \Phi(x)). \qquad (4.13)$$

Corresponding to our new notion of $(p, \mathbf{p})$-minimal models, we now define the *formula circumscription* $\text{circ}(p, \mathbf{p}, T)$ of a predicate $p(x)$ in a theory T with respect to a set $\mathbf{p} = \{p_1(x), \ldots, p_n(x)\}$ of predicates to be the set of formulae:

$$[T(\Phi, \Phi_1, \ldots, \Phi_n)\&\forall x(\Phi(x) \to p(x))] \to \forall x(p(x) \to \Phi(x)) \qquad (4.14)$$

where $\Phi(x), \Phi_1(x), \ldots, \Phi_n(x)$ are any predicate calculus expressions having one free variable and where $T'(\Phi, \Phi_1, \ldots, \Phi_n)$ is the result of replacing all occurrences of $p(x)$ in T by $\Phi(x)$ and all occurrences of $p_i(x)$ $(1 \leq i \leq n)$ in T by $\Phi_i(x)$. (Again, we should think of T as being not a set of formulae, but a single, big, conjunctive formula.) Note that in $T'(\Phi, \Phi_1, \ldots, \Phi_n)$, we have, not a single formula, but a collection of formulae, and that we are allowed to make any substitution we like for the $\Phi, \Phi_1, \ldots, \Phi_n$.

Remember, the point of $\text{circ}(p, \mathbf{p}, T)$ is to put into effect the assumption that the only things which have the property $p(x)$ are those things which our theory T says have the property $p(x)$. The idea is that we draw, as our conclusions, formulae ψ with the property that:

$$T \cup \text{circ}(p, \mathbf{p}, T) \vdash \psi,$$

or, as we shall write:

$$T \vdash_{(p, \mathbf{p})} \psi.$$

As an example, consider the formula circumscription of $\text{ab}(x)$ in T_{flies} with respect to the set of predicates $\mathbf{p} = \{\text{flies}(x)\}$. Here, the set $\mathbf{p}$ of predicates contains just one member, and schema (4.14) becomes:

$$[T(\Phi, \Phi_1)\&\forall x(\Phi(x) \to p(x))] \to \forall x(p(x) \to \Phi(x)). \qquad (4.15)$$

Ignoring those conjuncts in $T_{\text{flies}}(\Phi, \Phi_1)$ which do not involve $\Phi(x)$ or $\Phi_1(x)$

and which are therefore simply formulae in T, $\text{circ}(\text{ab}(x), \{\text{flies}(x)\}, T_{\text{flies}})$ is the collection of formulae:

$$[\forall x((\text{bird}(x) \ \& \ \neg\Phi(x)) \rightarrow \Phi_1(x)) \ \& \ \Phi(\text{oscar}) \ \& \\ \forall x(\Phi(x) \rightarrow \text{ab}(x))] \rightarrow \forall x(\text{ab}(x) \rightarrow \Phi(x)). \tag{4.16}$$

Since we are allowed to make any substitution we like for Φ and Φ_1, let us substitute $x = \text{oscar}$ for $\Phi(x)$ and $\text{bird}(x)$ for $\Phi_1(x)$. We obtain the formula:

$$[\forall x((\text{bird}(x) \ \& \ x \neq \text{oscar})) \rightarrow \text{bird}(x)) \ \& \ \text{oscar} = \text{oscar} \ \& \\ \forall x(x = \text{oscar} \rightarrow \text{ab}(x))] \rightarrow \forall x(\text{ab}(x) \rightarrow x = \text{oscar}).$$

Since the antecedents of this conditional are all clearly theorems of T_{flies}, we can see that:

$$T \cup \text{circ}(\text{ab}(x), \{\text{flies}(x)\}, T_{\text{flies}}) \vdash \forall x(\text{ab}(x) \rightarrow x = \text{oscar})$$

and hence

$$T \cup \text{circ}(\text{ab}(x), \{\text{flies}(x)\}, T_{\text{flies}}) \vdash \text{flies}(\text{tweety}).$$

or, to use the notation introduced above:

$$T \vdash_{(\text{ab}, \{\text{flies}(x)\})} \text{flies}(\text{tweety}),$$

which is the desired conclusion.

The connection between $T \vdash_{(p,\mathbf{p})} \psi$ and $T \models_{(p,\mathbf{p})} \psi$ can be stated in the following theorem (which will not be proved here):

$$\text{If} \ \ T \vdash_{(p,\mathbf{p})} \psi, \ \ \text{then} \ \ T \models_{(p,\mathbf{p})} \psi. \tag{4.17}$$

If a conclusion ψ can be proved by $(p, \mathbf{p})$-circumscription from T, then ψ is true in all $(p,\mathbf{p})$-minimal models of T. That is, if we intend a knowledge-base to be taken with the assumption that p is to be minimized, allowing the predicates in $\mathbf{p}$ to vary, theorem-proving with $(p,\mathbf{p})$-circumscription will always produce correct results.

The converse of the result (4.17) does not in general obtain. However, there is a restricted completeness theorem according to which, in certain special cases, if a conclusion ψ is true in all $(p,\mathbf{p})$-minimal models of a theory T, then ψ is provable from T together with the formula circumscription of $p(x)$ in T with respect to the predicates in $\mathbf{p}$. The technical details involved in stating this restricted completeness theorem would take us too far afield, and we shall not develop them here. (See further reading.)

If, then, we intend that a system's knowledge-base be taken with the assumption that p is to be minimized, allowing the extensions of the predicates in $\mathbf{p}$ to vary, the above results show us the attraction of getting the system to reason by theorem-proving under $(p, \mathbf{p})$-circumscription. For, if we use theorem-proving under $(p, \mathbf{p})$-circumscription to define the tree of inferences the system can make, we know that the system has access only to those inferences which will never lead it from truth to falsity, given the interpretation of the representations it is using.

4.4   Back to the blocks world

We are now, at long last, ready to answer the question with which we began this chapter: can we avoid axioms detailing the non-effects of an action such as move(x, y, z) by writing our knowledge of its positive effects in the form of axiom (4.1) (or some notational variant thereof), defining the predicate affected (p, a) as in axiom (4.3) and assuming that the extension of affected (p, a) is as small as possible? In this section, we will see that the answer is yes – with some difficulty.

4.4.1   Representing the problem

We begin by setting out a theory T_{blocks} of the blocks world. In fact, T_{blocks} is somewhat different from the formalization of chapter 3. The approach taken here starts by defining an *allowable* situation as one which can be achieved from the initial situation by repeated application of the move-action. Specifically: the initial situation, s_0 is allowable, and, for any situation s, if s is allowable, and if the preconditions of move(x, y, z) hold in s, then the situation do(move(x, y, z), s) is also allowable. In symbols:

allowable(s_0)

$\forall x \forall y \forall z \forall s$
   ((allowable(s) & block(x) & ($y = $ table $\lor$ block(y)) & $x \neq y$ &   (4.18)
   ($z = $ table $\lor$ block(z)) & $x \neq z$ & $y \neq z$ & holds(on(x,y), s) &
   holds(clear(x), s) & holds(clear(z), s)) $\rightarrow$
   allowable(do(move(x, y, z), s))).

Clearly, the only situations we are interested in are the allowable ones. We can then write the axiom specifying the positive effects of move(x, y, z) quite simply as

$$\forall x \forall y \forall z \forall s \text{ (allowable(do(move}(x, y, z), s)) \rightarrow}$$
$$\text{holds(on}(x, z), \text{do(move}(x, y, z), s)))$$

(4.19)

$$\forall x \forall y \forall z \forall s \text{(allowable(do(move}(x, y, z), s)) \rightarrow}$$
$$\text{holds(clear}(y), \text{do(move}(x, y, z), s))),$$

and the axiom stating that unaffected propositions persist as

$$\forall p \forall a \forall s \text{ ((allowable}(a, s) \text{ & holds}(p, s) \text{ &}}$$
$$\neg \text{affected}(p, a)) \rightarrow \text{holds}(p, \text{do}(a, s))).$$

(4.20)

A natural next step would be to add axioms expressing general constraints applying to the blocks world, such as that no block can be resting in two places at once, that every block must be somewhere, and so on, from which it would be possible to prove results such as

$$\forall x \forall y \forall z \text{affected}(\text{on}(x, y), \text{move}(x, y, z)),$$
$$\forall x \forall y \forall z (\text{block}(z) \rightarrow \text{affected}(\text{clear}(z), \text{move}(x, y, z))). \tag{4.21}$$

However, things are considerably simplified if we simply add these two formulae (4.21) as *axioms*. After all, they are certainly true. Finally, of course, we have axioms specifying the initial conditions (we assume three blocks for brevity):

$$\begin{aligned}
&\text{block}(a) \,\&\, \text{block}(b) \,\&\, \text{block}(c), \\
&a \neq b \,\&\, a \neq c \,\&\, b \neq c, \\
&a \neq \text{table} \,\&\, b \neq \text{table} \,\&\, c \neq \text{table}, \\
&\text{holds}(\text{clear}(a), s_0) \,\&\, \text{holds}(\text{clear}(\text{table}), s_0), \\
&\text{holds}(\text{on}(a, b), s_0) \,\&\, \text{holds}(\text{on}(b, c), s_0) \,\&\, \text{holds}(\text{on}(c, \text{table}), s_0).
\end{aligned} \tag{4.22}$$

So, our theory T_{blocks} consists of the formulae (4.18)–(4.22).

4.4.2 Making inferences

Next we consider the formula circumscription of the predicate $\text{affected}(p, a)$ in T_{blocks}, allowing the predicates $\{\text{allowable}(s), \text{holds}(p, s)\}$ to vary:

$$[T_{\text{blocks}}(\Phi, \Phi_1, \Phi_2) \,\&\, \forall p \forall a (\Phi(p, a) \rightarrow \text{affected}(p, a))] \rightarrow$$
$$\forall p \forall a (\text{affected}(p, a) \rightarrow \Phi(p, a)) \tag{4.23}$$

where $T_{\text{blocks}}(\Phi, \Phi_1, \Phi_2)$ is the result of substituting $\Phi(p, a)$ for $\text{affected}(p, a)$, $\Phi_1(s)$ for $\text{allowable}(s)$, and $\Phi_2(p, s)$ for $\text{holds}(p, s)$. Remember that (4.23) is a *set of* formulae – namely, those obtained by substituting any predicate calculus expressions for $\Phi(p, a)$, $\Phi_1(s)$ and $\Phi_2(p, s)$.

We let Φ be the predicate:

$$\Phi(p, a) \equiv \exists x \exists y \exists z ((p = \text{on}(x, y) \lor p = \text{clear}(z)) \,\&\, a = \text{move}(x, y, z))$$

and we let Φ_1 and Φ_2 be (trivial) predicates which are always true of their arguments. Under these substitutions, (4.23) reduces to

$$\forall p \forall a (\text{affected}(p, a) \rightarrow$$
$$\exists x \exists y \exists z ((p = \text{on}(x, y) \lor p = \text{clear}(z)) \,\&\, a = \text{move}(x, y, z)))$$

which suffices – with a little technical help – to show that nothing changes except that which is stated by T_{blocks} to change. The technical help required is just a collection of axioms to ensure the uniqueness of state- and action-descriptions:

$$\forall x \forall y \forall z \forall x' \forall y' \forall z' (\text{move}(x, y, z) = \text{move}(x', y', z') \rightarrow$$
$$(x = x' \,\&\, y = y' \,\&\, z = z')),$$
$$\forall x \forall y \forall x' \forall y' (\text{on}(x, y) = \text{on}(x', y') \rightarrow (x = x' \,\&\, y = y')),$$
$$\forall x \forall x' (\text{clear}(x) = \text{clear}(x') \rightarrow x = x').$$

Now it is possible to prove simple results such as

$$\text{holds(on}(b, a), \text{do(move}(b, c, a),$$
$$\text{do(move}(a, b, \text{table}), s_0))),$$
$$\text{holds(on}(c, b), \text{do(move}(c, \text{table}, b), \qquad\qquad (4.24)$$
$$\text{do(move}(b, c, a),$$
$$\text{do(move}(a, b, \text{table}), s_0)))),$$

which require inferences about the non-effects of the actions in question. (See exercise 2.)

Thus, formula circumscription can be used to reason under the assumption that the only effects which actions have are those the knowledge-base implies that they have. Moreover, the minimal model semantics of formula circumscription means that we have at least some independent characterization of what we are doing when we circumscribe predicates in theories. And even if the development of formula circumscription and its semantics set out in this chapter is rather complex and confusing at first sight, the solution we have arrived at does possess a certain mathematical elegance and simplicity, and it does – at least in the above case – do the job.

4.4.3   Problems with circumscription

Unfortunately however, the blocks-world example we have just examined in fact paints a flattering picture of circumscription. For circumscription is, in general, *murderously* difficult to work with. The problem is that, when one writes down a theory T, and decides to use $(p, \mathbf{p})$-circumscription, it is often very hard to determine what the minimal models are and hence very difficult to know whether one has captured one's intentions correctly. True, the problem of knowing whether one has captured one's intentions correctly occurs with any formalization scheme – even ordinary predicate calculus. But there is a qualitative difference in the kinds of difficulties one encounters: usually, it takes an enormous amount of effort to decide whether a theory has any $(p, \mathbf{p})$-minimal models at all, let alone whether those models are the ones that one intends the knowledge-base to represent. Human beings, it seems, just do not think naturally in terms of minimal models. (See exercise 4.)

Not only is circumscription difficult to work with from the point of view of the knowledge engineer, who must construct the system's knowledge-base: it is also difficult for a computer to prove theorems with. In the above examples, we used our own understanding of the situation to select sensible substituends for the Φ's, bearing in mind the sorts of things we knew we were going to have to prove. (Even then it was not easy!) But, of course, automatic theorem provers are inevitably less directed in the possibilities they try; and the circumscription schemas are clearly in general difficult things to work with. In some cases, it may be possible to use advanced techniques in logic automatically to reduce circumscription schemas to single first-order formulae in those cases where it is possible; however, such approaches are, at the time of writing, still under investigation.

Recall from chapter 3 that we were careful to distinguish the frame problem proper – which we took to be a problem about the storage requirements of a logic-based reasoner – from related problems, such as the *time* taken to make inferences, or deciding *which* inferences to make. These distinctions are important here. For while circumscription does – in some cases at least – enable a small knowledge-base to encode large amounts of information by omission (thus solving the problem of the system's storage requirements), it does not obviously alleviate the problem of the time taken to make inferences, or the problem of deciding which things to infer. The trouble is that, in *proving* that a formula ψ follows by circumscription from the knowledge-base T, the system is tackling an intrinsically difficult problem – that of showing that ψ is true in all the minimal (in the relevant sense) models of T. Recall the example we gave in chapter 3 of what happens when I spill the cup of tea on my desk: we asked how it was that I managed still retain most of my beliefs after this action was performed. And we argued that it is important that I simply *do not think of* the myriad things that are not affected by this event. Somehow, establishing that they hold in all the minimal models of a set of axioms does not seem to be what is called for. The moral: despite the intuitive appeal of circumscription as a means of encoding information by omission, we should not think that it necessarily solves all the problems concerning the use of logic to perform inference.

4.5   Nonmonotonic logics

4.5.1   The idea of nonmonotonicity

The previous sections of this chapter have been concerned with the development of a notion of proof-under-circumscription. That is, we have defined a relation of implication

$$T \vdash_{(p,\mathbf{P})} \psi$$

holding between a knowledge-base and formulae implied by that knowledge-base under the convention that the predicate $p(x)$ is to be minimized. As this nota-tion suggests, this relation is supposed to contrast with the ordinary relation of implication in the predicate calculus:

$$T \vdash \psi.$$

One striking difference between these two implication-relations deserves men-tion here. Let T be any theory from which a formula ψ can be deduced, via some proof in the predicate calculus. Then, clearly, if T' is a theory which contains all the formulae of T and others besides, ψ must still be derivable from T': in fact, the very same proof would do. Thus: the more premises you put in, the more conclusions you can get out. In symbols:

$$\text{If } T \vdash \psi \text{ and } T \subset T' \text{ then } T' \vdash \psi. \tag{4.25}$$

A proof relation $\vdash$ is said to be *monotonic* just in case property (4.25) holds for all T, T' and ψ. If, now, we consider the relation of provability-under-circumscription – i.e. $\vdash_{(p,\mathbf{P})}$ – then it is clear that the monotonicity property fails. That is, it is possible to have two theories, T and T' with

$$T \vdash_{(p,\mathbf{P})} \psi, \quad T \subset T', \quad \text{and} \quad T' \nvdash_{(p,\mathbf{P})}\psi.$$

When making deductions under circumscription, adding facts to the knowledge-base can cause previously derivable formulae to cease to be derivable. This is to be expected: for example, if we add information which allows us to deduce that a fact p is affected by an action a, then the previously derivable conclusion that p is not affected by a will cease to be derivable. Accordingly, we say that circumscription is *nonmonotonic*.

There are, however, other nonmonotonic logics, and the study of such logics forms a major sub-discipline within artificial intelligence. For example, McDermott and Doyle [5] and McDermott [4] investigate a logic which includes an operator M that allows us to frame such default rules such as

$$(\text{bird}(\text{tweety}) \& M(\neg\text{ab}(\text{tweety}))) \rightarrow \text{flies}(\text{tweety})$$

with the intuitive interpretation that, if Tweety is a bird and if *it is consistent to assume that* Tweety is not abnormal, then tweety can fly. Together with the single axiom bird(tweety), then the conclusion flies(tweety) follows on McDermott and Doyle's system because the proposition $\neg$ab(tweety) cannot be disproved. On the other hand, taken together with the three axioms,

$$\{\text{bird}(\text{tweety}), \text{penguin}(\text{tweety}), \forall x(\text{penguin}(x) \rightarrow \text{ab}(x))\},$$

the formula $\neg$ab(tweety) can be disproved and so the conclusion that Tweety flies cannot be drawn. We will not investigate all the technical details of this family of logics here. The reader is referred to the citations just given. One further, extensively investigated, system of nonmonotonic logic is Reiter's *default logic* [7]. We shall describe this logic in some detail in chapter 5.

4.5.2   Two uses of nonmonotonic logic

Let us consider again the theories T_{blocks} and T_{flies}. The former theory was constructed as a knowledge-base which encodes – when taken with the circumscription of the predicate affected(p, a) – facts about a blocks world. We said from the outset in chapter 3 that we were making certain idealizing assumptions about this world, for example, that the robot arm always functions perfectly, that other robots do not interfere, that there are no power cuts, hurricanes, or earthquakes, and so on. In short, the effects of all the actions performed are known with certainty. The point of using circumscription here is as a means of *encoding information by omission*, because we wanted to avoid having to write down frame axioms (which we argued would be very numerous in more realistic domains). In particular, the function of circumscription is not to encode any sort of *uncertainty*, for uncertainty has been idealized away in this example.

The theory T_{flies}, by contrast, suggests a very different interpretation of circumscription. For we took the critical axiom of that theory, namely

$$\forall x(\text{bird}(x) \,\&\, \neg\text{ab}(x) \rightarrow \text{flies}(x)),$$

to have the intuitive interpretation (under the circumscription of the predicate $\text{ab}(x)$) that birds *normally* fly. Here we *are* dealing with uncertainty. When we say that birds normally fly, we commit ourselves to the inference that the next bird we come across will fly, unless of course, we have information to the effect that it is abnormal. And that inference, though perhaps extremely robust, is not entirely certain: it may be, as we say, *defeated* by additional information. Moreover, it seems distinctly odd to say that, in believing that birds normally fly, we are *representing information by omission*. True, we may infer that Tweety will fly if we have no information from which to infer that he is abnormal. But that does not mean that our knowledge-base represents by omission the fact that Tweety is not abnormal (or that he flies). If it did, then there would be no uncertainty in the inference.

It should be clear that representing facts by omission and being uncertain are two quite different things (that has not stopped some writers on nonmonotonic logic from mixing them up, of course), yet circumscription seems to have something to say about both. Let us try to understand what is going on here.

Consider a computer system which must reason with statements like "Birds normally fly", "Elephants are normally grey", and so on. We would like such a reasoner to infer that the next bird it sees will fly, or that the next elephant it stumbles across will be grey, unless it has reason to believe that this particular bird or elephant is abnormal in the relevant respect. And one way to model this kind of inferential tendency is to get the computer to *concentrate on models of its knowledge-base in which abnormality is minimized*. Hence the use of circumscription in a theory like T_{flies}. Now consider a computer system which must reason about a certain environment such as we assumed the blocks-world to be. We would like such a reasoner to encode information about the noneffects of actions by omission, since this will save disk space. And one way to implement this kind of representation scheme is to get the computer to *concentrate on models of its knowledge-base in which effects are minimized*. Hence the use of circumscription in a theory like T_{blocks}. But what is intended by "concentrating on minimal models" is different in the two cases.

Suppose we design a computer reasoning system using circumscription to encode information by omission, as in T_{blocks}. What we, as designers of the system are in effect doing is to interpret the system's knowledge-base as encoding the belief that the world is a minimal model of a certain theory T_{blocks}. In this case, then, we concentrate on minimal models in precisely the following sense: the minimal models of T_{blocks} are the *intended interpretation* of T_{blocks} as it is being used by the system. Here, then, predicate circumscription is evidently an appropriate reasoning process, for, as the result (4.17) tells us, the space of possible inferences which it generates is (within) the space of inferences that are correct according to the intended interpretation of the symbols being used.

Suppose, by contrast, we design a reasoning system using circumscription to license uncertain inferences, as in T_{flies}. Here, we do not interpret the system's knowledge-base as encoding the belief that the world is a minimal model of T_{flies}, for the simple reason that we want to admit the possibility that there are abnormal birds which the system (like ourselves) does not know about. In this case, then, we concentrate on minimal models in precisely the following sense: the minimal models of T_{flies} specify how we want the system to assume things to be *unless and until additional information arrives which contradicts this assumption*. Here, the emphasis is on getting the knowledge-base T_{flies} to license a probable inference in the face of uncertainty, while retaining consistency if additional information (specifically, something implying that Tweety is abnormal) arrives to defeat that inference.

But notice that, when we want a reasoning system to represent beliefs about what is normally the case, as in T_{flies}, it is no longer so obvious that circumscription – or, more generally, the policy of drawing inferences that hold in all the minimal models – is at all sensible. For it is not obvious that the belief expressed by the English sentence "Birds normally fly" really is captured by a commitment to infer sentences true in all $ab(x)$-minimal models of one's current knowledge. Now, of course, it might be *argued* that circumscription does indeed model what speakers of English mean by normally-sentences. But it is important to see that an argument is needed here. And it is furthermore important to see that the result (4.17) does not help in this regard. It just shows that, if the system's knowledge-base is given a minimal-model interpretation, proving theorems under circumscription will never lead us astray. But it does not show that, when we say that birds normally fly, we commit ourselves, unless and until shown otherwise, to the assumption that the world is a minimal model of a particular collection of formulae.

This distinction in the use of nonmonotonic logics is important, because such logics are so often used to model (defeasible) reasoning under uncertainty. And it is precisely when nonmonotonic logics are used in this way that we must take care that the technical characteristics of the logic in question really capture the uncertainty that we are out to model. In the rush for non-standard logics, it is all to easy to forget that, just because a logic has a formal semantics with respect to which it is correct, that does not mean to say that the semantics in question capture the intended interpretation of the symbols. We will examine this problem in more detail in chapter 5.

4.6 Conclusion

In this chapter, we have outlined one approach to reasoning under closed world assumptions. We have also examined some of its drawbacks. Whether this approach will ultimately emerge as the best way to formalize the representation of knowledge by omission, only time will tell.

Notice though, how we have remained within the overall conception of intelligent processing set out in chapter 1: that of movement within a space of possible inferences implicitly defined by a knowledge-base. All that has changed is that the way in which the knowledge-base defines the space of possible inferences has become more complicated. In particular, the relationship between these two is seen to be nonmonotonic, in that adding information to the knowledge-base can cause previously sanctioned inferences to cease to be so.

Exercises

1. Let the theory T_{flies}^- be the theory T_{flies} *except for* the first axiom: i.e.

$$\text{bird(tweety)}$$
$$\text{bird(oscar)}$$
$$\text{ab(oscar)}$$
$$\text{oscar} \neq \text{tweety}$$

   Write down the predicate circumscription of $\text{ab}(x)$ in T_{flies}^-.
   We saw in section 4.3 flies(tweety) cannot be proved from T_{flies} plus the circumscription of $\text{ab}(x)$ in T_{flies}. Show that flies(tweety) *does* follow from T_{flies} plus the circumscription of $\text{ab}(x)$ in T_{flies}^-!

2. Prove the result

$$\text{holds(on(b, a), do(move(b, c, a), do(move(a, b, table), s_0)))}$$

   from T_{blocks} using formula circumscription. (Hint: use the substitutions for $\psi(x)$, $\psi_1(x)$ and $\psi(x)$ suggested in section 4.3.)

3. Formula circumscription really is stronger than predicate circumscription. Write down the predicate circumscription of $\text{affected}(p, a)$ in T_{blocks}. What exactly prevents the derivation of useful results?

4. In the theory T_{blocks}, we did not give the predicate $\text{affected}(p, a)$ a situation-argument, since the effects of actions (in the blocks world) are situation-independent (except insofar as the situation determines whether the action can be carried out at all). But of course there is no reason why we could not give $\text{affected}(p, a)$ an extra argument, thus: $\text{affected}(p, a, s)$ (read: fact p would be affected by action a if it were performed in situation s). And we could easily modify T_{blocks} by universally quantifying over this extra argument in the sensible way. Write down the new versions of T_{blocks}.

Explain informally what happens when we minimize the predicate, affected(p, a, s) (while allowing holds(p, s) and allowable(s) to vary)? Why does circumscription no longer given the intended results? (Hint: imagine a model in which the action move(x, y, z) has some strange additional effects which *limit* the number of different situations that can be reached.)

5. (Programming in Prolog) The theory T_{blocks} in section 4.4, consisting of the formulae (4.18)–(4.22), can be transcribed directly into the programming language Prolog and run. If you have access to a Prolog interpreter, try it. What does this tell you about the relationship between circumscription and the 'negation-as-failure' feature of Prolog? N.B. the axioms

$$a \neq b \,\&\, a \neq c \,\&\, b \neq c$$
$$a \neq \text{table} \,\&\, b \neq \text{table} \,\&\, c \neq \text{table}$$

can be ignored, so far as Prolog is concerned.

Further reading

Nonmonotonic logic forms a major research sub-discipline, and has its own vast and still mushrooming literature. An excellent, though technically rather challenging overview of this area is provided by Brewka [1]. Brewka's book also contains an (at the time of writing) up-to-date bibliography. The reader interested in pursuing this topic can still benefit from reading the original articles in the issue of the journal *Artificial Intelligence* 13 (1980) which contains the seminal articles by McCarthy, McDermott and Doyle and Reiter. The restricted completeness results for circumscription with respect to minimal model semantics are proved in Perlis and Minker [6].

Bibliography

[1] Brewka, G. *Nonmonotonic Reasoning: Logical Foundations of Commonsense*, Cambridge: CUP, 1991.

[2] Etherington, D. "A semantics for default logic", *Proceedings, IJCAI-87*, Milan (1987) pp. 495–498.

[3] McCarthy, J. "Circumscription: a form of nonmonotonic reasoning", *Artificial Intelligence*, 13 (1980).

[4] McDermott, D. "Non-Monotonic Logic II: Non- monotonic modal theories", *Journal of the ACM* 29 (1982) pp. 33–57.

[5] McDermott, D. and J. Doyle "Non-Monotonic Logic I", *Artificial Intelligence*, 13 (1980) pp. 41-72.

[6] Perlis, D. and J. Minker "Completeness results for circumscription", *Artificial Intelligence*, 28 (1986) pp. 29–42.

[7] Reiter, R. "A logic for default reasoning", *Artificial Intelligence*, 13 (1980) pp. 81–132.

5 Defeasible Inference

In this chapter, we examine some recent attempts to formalize inferences with generalizations that hold not *always*, but only *normally* or *for the most part*. For instance, from the fact that elephants are normally grey, normally live in the wild and normally have four legs, we can conclude that Clyde, an elephant with which we are unacquainted, probably has these characteristics himself. We have already met one approach to this kind of inference: circumscription. However, we argued in chapter 4 that the applicability of circumscription to this kind of inference is at best unclear. So it is time to examine some of its competitors.

5.1 Property Inheritance

Interesting cases of this type of inference arise when we have a chain of generalizations. If Clyde is an elephant, and if elephants are normally grey, and if grey things are normally hard to see at dusk, we might conclude that Clyde is probably hard to see at dusk. Pictorially (figure 5.1), we can think of Clyde 'inheriting' the property of being hard to see at dusk through the properties of being grey and being an elephant, as one might inherit an ancestral title through one's grandfather and father. Here, an arrow from one property X to another property Y has the interpretation: "Normally, X are Y", and an arrow from an individual, x to a property X has the interpretation: "x is an X". Terminology: the links from properties to properties are sometimes called *a-kind-of* links; the links from individuals to properties are sometimes called *is-a* links.

It is easy to see the advantages, in terms of storing information efficiently, of associating properties with types of entities by arranging those entities within a hierarchy, and storing the properties at the highest (most general) node possible. Thus, if I ask you *Do elephants wear pyjamas?* you can answer that question, not because you have explicitly stored the fact in memory (the odds are you had never considered the proposition before), but rather, because you know that elephants are animals, and you know that pyjamas are clothes, and you have stored explicitly the fact that animals normally do not wear clothes. Well, that story involves a psychological claim which we cannot justify here, but the plausibility of encoding real-world knowledge in this way should be clear. Rather than storing the propositions: *aardvarks don't wear pyjamas, baboons don't wear pyjamas, crocodiles don't wear pyjamas*, etc. people just store the information once at the

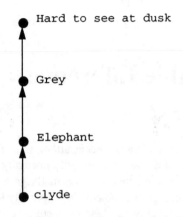

Figure 5.1   Property-inheritance

superordinate level *animal*, declaring exceptions as necessary. Because of the efficiency and simplicity of storing information in this format, property inheritance forms a part of many knowledge-based systems in practical use.

An *inheritance network* is a collection of nodes, representing individuals or categories of objects, arranged in a hierarchy, through which they inherit properties. Figure 5.2 illustrates the basic idea. In that network, the nodes jumbo, clyde and tweety inherit Breathes through various intermediate nodes. Notice the crossed-out arrow from Penguin to Fly. This has the interpretation: "Penguins normally do not fly". Thus Tweety, being a penguin, should inherit the property of not flying. Much of the work that has gone into devising algorithms for property inheritance has focused on what to do in tricky cases involving exceptions and exceptions-to-exceptions. In this chapter, we shall be examining the logic of property inheritance, raising, in the process, some fundamental questions as to how this useful technique should be understood.

5.1.1   The basic intuitions

The basic pattern of inference underlying all types property-inheritance is the so-called schema of *direct inference:*

$$\frac{\text{Normally, } A \text{ are } B}{\text{Normally, } A \text{ are } C.}$$

$$(5.1)$$

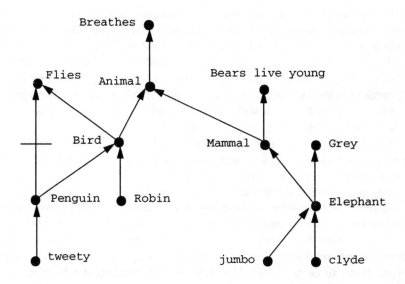

Figure 5.2   An inheritance network

Thus: normally elephants are grey; normally grey things are hard to see at dusk; therefore, normally elephants are hard to see at dusk. Here, and henceforth, the expression "Normally A are B" is intended to include the possibility that all A are B. In schema (5.1), statistical information about a population, B, is used to infer statistical information about a sub-population, A. The term *direct inference* to describe schema (5.1) is due to the logician Rudolf Carnap, and is intended to contrast it with the so-called *inverse inference*, in which statistical information about a population is inferred from statistical information about a sub-population (typically a random sample).

A slightly different form of this inference pattern, also sometimes called direct inference, is

$$w \text{ is a } B$$
$$\underline{\text{Normally, } B \text{ are } C}$$
$$w \text{ is a } C.$$

(5.2)

where w is not a property, but an individual. Thus: Clyde is an elephant; normally elephants are grey; therefore, Clyde is probably grey.

The inference schemas (5.1) and (5.2) differ in a number of respects, and must not be confused. In particular, notice that the first premise in (5.1), namely "A are normally B", concerns a statistical relationship between two properties. By contrast, the first premise in (5.2), namely "w is a B" concerns a non-statistical relationship between an individual and a property. Corresponding remarks apply to the conclusions of these inferences. Despite these differences, however, both inferences can be thought of as involving the inheritance of properties in exactly the same way. That is: property inheritance proceeds along a-kind-of links in just the same way as it does along is-a links. Since, then, this distinction does not affect the subject of this chapter, we can ignore it for the sake of brevity. Accordingly, when we speak of inference schema (5.1), our remarks should be taken as applying also to inference schema (5.2) as well. (For a discussion of the relationship between these two kinds of inference, see further reading.)

Of course, we know that schema (5.1) is, logically speaking, invalid: the premises can be true whilst the conclusion is false. (See exercise 1.) But that may not be a problem if the conclusion is *usually* true when the premises are true, that is, if *usually*, when A are normally B and B are normally C, A are normally C. For in real-world reasoning, as defenders of schema (5.1) would be quick to point out, the best we can standardly hope for are patterns of inference that usually work.

We now turn to an intuition which many people have (or think they have) about property-inheritance: that more specific information overrides less specific information. To be sure, animals in general, and elephants in particular, do not wear clothes. But if I tell you that elephants in Billy Smart's Circus normally wear sequin-covered robes, and that Jumbo is in Billy Smart's circus, you would guess, I take it, that Jumbo does indeed wear clothes. More formally, and more generally, if B' is a more specific category than B (i.e. if B' are normally B but not vice versa), then the inference

$$\frac{\text{Normally, } A \text{ are } B'}{\text{Normally, } B' \text{ are not } C}$$
$$\text{Normally, } A \text{ are not } C.$$

overrides or *defeats* the inference

$$\frac{\text{Normally, } A \text{ are } B}{\text{Normally, } B \text{ are } C}$$
$$\text{Normally, } A \text{ are } C.$$

The direct inference schema and the principle that more specific generalizations override less specific ones are the fundamental ideas behind property inheritance.

Given the use of a network such as figure 5.2 to encode knowledge, how do we find out whether a given type of object A has a given property C? It turns out that the procedure is straightforward. First, see if there is an arrow (plain or crossed-out) from A to C. If so, you have your answer (yes or no); if not, look at the parent of A – i.e. the type of object B in the network such that there is a plain arrow from A to B – and see if there is an arrow (plain or crossed-out) from B to C. If so, take that answer to be the answer to the original query; if not, look at the parent of B, and so on. If you ever reach the top of the network without finding a link to C, then the network does not know the answer to the question. Thus, the basic principles of property inheritance are simple to program for networks such as that of figure 5.2. The procedure `inherit(A, C)`, shown below will work in this case. Here, and in the sequel, we write A → B to mean "there is a plain arrow from node A to node B in the network" and we write A $\not\rightarrow$ B to mean "there is a crossed-out arrow from A to B in the network."

begin inherit(A,C)
  if A $\rightarrow$ C **then**
    return "normally"
  else if A $\not\rightarrow$ C **then**
    return "normally not"
  else if A $\rightarrow$ B **then**
    return inherit(B,C)
  else if A has no parent **then**
    return "Don't know"
  end if
end inherit

This procedure will always return an unambiguous answer so long as each node in the network has only one parent which itself has a parent.

Notice that, in the network of figure 5.2, not all the a-kind-of links between properties have the same English reading. For example, the link between "robin" and "bird" is read as "normally robins are birds", but the link between "animal" and "breathes" does not quite have this reading: for we cannot say "normally animals are breathes". The difference is, of course, that "bird" is a substantive in English, whereas "breathes" is a predicate. However, we can always turn these latter nodes into the former kind by relabelling. For example, we can relabel the node "breathes" as "breathing thing", in which case the link from "animal" to "breathing thing" could be taken to have the standard reading: "normally animals are breathing things". In fact, the distinction between substantives and predicates is not important if we are using the inheritance procedures discussed below; therefore, we will not make it, and we will continue to label nodes with words like "breathes," "grey," rather than "breathing thing," "grey thing," etc.

5.2 Problematic cases

In real-world situations, objects and object-categories have more than one parent in the inheritance hierarchy. The classic example is the so-called Nixon-diamond of figure 5.3. That is, the network of is-a links is multiply connected. Accordingly, inheritance in such networks is called multiple inheritance; and this is what we shall examine now.

Another intuition many people have about the network of figure 5.3 is that we cannot conclude anything about whether Nixon is or is not a pacifist, since we have competing inheritance paths between the nodes nixon and Pacifist. Sensible as this intuition seems at first sight, it is not difficult to construct networks for which its prescriptions are either indeterminate or counterintuitive. Consider the following example, due to Touretzky, shown in figure 5.4(a). This network states that elephants are normally grey, but that royal elephants (presumably some kind of

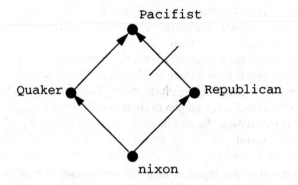

Figure 5.3   The 'Nixon-diamond'

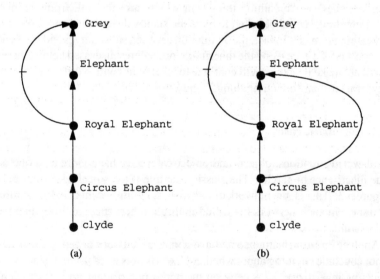

Figure 5.4   An inheritance network with a redundant link added

elephant) are normally not grey, and that, in addition, circus elephants are normally royal elephants, and hence are, by schema (5.1), normally not grey. (I cannot believe that this is true; but factual accuracy concerning circuses is not at issue here.) So far, so good; by the principles allegedly intuited in the previous section, we can infer, amongst other things, that Clyde, a circus elephant, is (probably) not grey.

But notice that we can also infer from this network that circus elephants are elephants. That is fair enough too: so they are. But if we add to the network an arrow pointing from *circus elephant* to *elephant* (which merely encodes the conclusion we just drew), we obtain the network depicted in figure 5.4(b). Now this network contains the path `clyde` → `Circus-elephant` → `Elephant` → `Grey`. And it is difficult to see therefore why the previous conclusion (that Clyde is not grey) which was based on the fact that Clyde is a royal elephant is not defeated by the inference corresponding to this new path. After all, once the link between `Circus-elephant` and `Elephant` is added, you can get from `Circus-elephant` to `Grey` as well as being able to get from `Royal-elephant` to not-`Grey`; and `Circus-elephant` is more specific than `Royal-elephant`. Thus, adding a true but redundant link compromises the intuitions adduced above for reasoning with inheritance networks. This would correspond to a situation in logic where the addition of a theorem to a set of premises causes other previously derivable theorems to cease to be derivable. (In fact, this situation was noted in the system of modal nonmonotonic logic developed by Drew McDermott, which we discussed briefly in chapter 4; he thought it a very bizarre and counterintuitive consequence of his system.) Indeed, we can make matters worse. For we may without contradiction suppose that the links between `Circus-elephant`, `Royal-elephant` and `Elephant` can be made strict: thus, *all* circus elephants are royal elephants, and *all* royal elephants are elephants. In that case, the redundant link is a *logical consequence* of the information already at hand. Thus, adding logical consequences of the premises encoded in the network compromises the intuitions of the previous section.

Touretzky has developed an inheritance procedure which yields the intuitively correct conclusion that Clyde is not grey. First, we need some notation. Let Γ be an inheritance network. We can think of Γ as simply being a set of positive links $x \rightarrow y$ and a set of negative links $x \not\rightarrow y$. As in the diagrams, when x and y are properties (or classes of entities), a positive link has the intuitive interpretation "x's are normally y's", whereas the negative link has the intuitive interpretation "x's are normally not y's". When x is an individual, then these positive and negative links have the intuitive interpretations "x is a y" and "x is not a y", respectively. Touretzky's idea is that inheritance along a path

$$x \rightarrow u_1 \rightarrow \ldots \rightarrow u_n \not\rightarrow y$$

(where all the links are positive except for the last) is *not* defeated by a contrary inheritance path

$$x \rightarrow v_1 \rightarrow \ldots \rightarrow v_m \rightarrow y$$

(where all the links are positive) if the latter path is *intercepted*. This happens, according to Touretzky, if x can inherit v_m in the network through a node z which has a direct negative link to y in the network (i.e. with $z \not\rightarrow y$ in Γ).

We get a feel for how this rather difficult idea is supposed to work by looking at the case of figure 5.4(b). There is a 'good' potential inheritance path

clyde $\rightarrow$ Circus-elephant $\rightarrow$ Royal-elephant $\not\rightarrow$ Grey.

according to which Clyde is not grey. This good path is in danger of being defeated by the bad path

clyde $\rightarrow$ Circus-elephant $\rightarrow$ Elephant $\rightarrow$ Grey.

which says that Clyde is grey. Touretzky observed, however, that this bad path is intercepted. For its penultimate node is Elephant, which can be inherited by clyde through the node Royal-elephant; and of course Royal-elephant has a direct negative link to Grey. So the unwanted inheritance path caused by adding the redundant link is ruled out. By contrast, no analogous interception happens with the good path. So the good path is left unaffected, and the inference that Clyde is not grey is saved.

More formally, we define a *path* through Γ to be a sequence of the nodes of Γ, $x_1 \rightarrow x_2 \rightarrow \ldots \rightarrow x_{n-1} \rightarrow x_n$ or $x_1 \rightarrow x_2 \rightarrow \ldots \rightarrow x_{n-1} \not\rightarrow x_n$, where all the links are positive except possibly the last, which may be positive or negative. The specification of the inheritance procedure then takes the form of specifying the conditions under which a given path σ is *supported* by Γ, written $\Gamma \models \sigma$. If Γ supports the path $x_1 \rightarrow x_2 \rightarrow \ldots \rightarrow x_{n-1} \rightarrow x_n$, then x_1 inherits the property x_n; if, on the other hand, Γ supports the path $x_1 \rightarrow x_2 \rightarrow \ldots \rightarrow x_{n-1} \not\rightarrow x_n$, then x_1 inherits not-x_n.

The definition is recursive. We use Roman letters $x, y, z, \ldots$ to denote nodes and Greek letters $\sigma, \tau, \ldots$ to denote sequences of nodes connected by positive links.

Case I: Single links

1. $\Gamma \models x \rightarrow y$ if $x \rightarrow y$ is in Γ
2. $\Gamma \models x \not\rightarrow y$ if $x \not\rightarrow y$ is in Γ

Case II: Compound sequences

1. $\Gamma \models x \rightarrow \sigma_1 \rightarrow u \rightarrow y$ if
    (a) $\Gamma \models x \rightarrow \sigma_1 \rightarrow u$
    (b) $u \rightarrow y$ is in Γ
    (c) $x \not\rightarrow y$ is not in Γ
    (d) for all v st. $\Gamma \models x \rightarrow \tau \rightarrow v$ with $v \not\rightarrow y \in \Gamma$, there exists a z ($\neq v$) such that $\Gamma \models x \rightarrow \tau_1 \rightarrow z \rightarrow \tau_2 \rightarrow v$ and $z \rightarrow y \in \Gamma$
2. $\Gamma \models x \rightarrow \sigma_1 \rightarrow u \not\rightarrow y$ if
    (a) $\Gamma \models x \rightarrow \sigma_1 \rightarrow u$

(b) $u \mathrel{\not\to} y$ is in Γ

(c) $x \to y$ is not in Γ

(d) for all v such that $\Gamma \models x \to \tau \to v$ with $v \to y \in \Gamma$, there exists a z ($\neq v$) such that $\Gamma \models x \to \tau_1 \to z \to \tau_2 \to v$ and $z \mathrel{\not\to} y \in \Gamma$.

It is not immediately obvious that the recursion in this definition terminates. That is, in order to apply the above procedure to tell whether

$$\Gamma \models x \to \sigma_1 \to u \to y,$$

we first have to determine whether Γ supports the other paths mentioned in clauses 1a and 1d: and it is not immediately obvious that, when we recursively apply the procedure to decide these cases, we will not eventually be led round in circles. In fact, however, a simple observation shows that the recursion will always terminate. Given a path σ from x to y through Γ, we can define the *degree* of σ to be the length of the longest path in Γ from x to y. It is easy to see that all the sequences referred to in clauses 1a–1d have a strictly smaller degree than σ. This guarantees non-circularity. Similar remarks apply to clauses 2a–2d. The degree of a path σ from x to y – that is, the length of the longest path from x to y – is called the *inferential distance* between x and y. For this reason, the above method of property-inheritance is called *inferential-distance* inheritance.

As explained above, inferential-distance inheritance correctly handles the cases of figure 5.4. But here is another case. Suppose A are normally C, and that is because A are normally B and B are normally C (actually, we could strengthen this last link to insist that all B are C). If w is an A with the exceptional property of not being B, then, intuitively, we cannot conclude that w is a C. Figure 5.5(a) shows a property inheritance system describing this situation. And it is straightforward to check that Touretzky's inferential distance system displays the correct behaviour.

But suppose that we add the true but redundant link from A to C, which says that A are normally C (figure 5.5(b)). (If the link from B to C is strict, then this redundant link is a *logical consequence* of the premises directly encoded in the network.) Again, we do not want to conclude, as a result of adding this logical consequence to the network, that w is (probably) C. But this time, Touretzky's inferential distance system does not yield the correct result. It can easily be seen from the above definitions that the path

$$w \to A \to C$$

is supported by the network of figure 5.5(b). So the value of Touretzky's definition, and the claim that it resolves problems due to true-but-redundant links must be open to doubt.

5.3 Default logic

In sections 5.1 and 5.2, we have examined one formalism – property inheritance – for making inferences about what is normally the case. And we have outlined

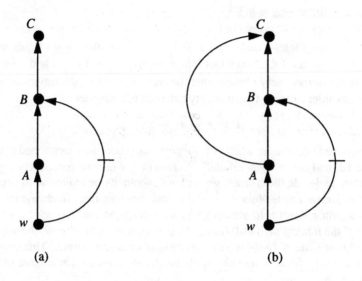

Figure 5.5   Another inheritance network with a redundant link added

some of its problems. In this section we examine an alternative formalism: *default logic.*

5.3.1   *Modelling uncertain inference with default logic*

The basic idea behind default logic revolves around so-called *defaults* of the form:

$$\frac{\alpha \;\; ; \;\; \beta_1, \ldots, \beta_m}{\omega}.$$

Such a default licenses the inference to ω provided that: (i) α can be inferred, and (ii) for each of the β_i, the negated formula $\neg\beta_i$ cannot be inferred. For example, the default

$$\frac{\text{bird}(\text{tweety}) \;\; ; \;\; \neg\text{ab}(\text{tweety})}{\text{flies}(\text{tweety})}$$

licenses the inference that Tweety flies if it can be shown that Tweety is a bird and if it cannot be shown that Tweety is abnormal. It is convenient to introduce variables into default rules, such as, e.g.:

$$\frac{\text{bird}(x) \;\; ; \;\; \neg\text{ab}(x)}{\text{flies}(x)} \tag{5.3}$$

with the intuitive interpretation that birds which cannot be shown to be abnormal can fly, or, in plainer English: birds normally fly. Thus, default rules are tailor made for expressing what is *normally* or *mostly* the case.

Before looking at the formal details of default logic, it will help to consider a simple example. Default rule (5.3) expresses a general assumption about flying. Given the formulae:

$$\text{bird(tweety), bird(oscar), ab(oscar)} \qquad (5.4)$$

it licenses the conclusion flies(tweety) but not the conclusion flies(oscar), since Oscar is known to be abnormal. Moreover, we can combine such a default rule with *general* facts about abnormal birds. For example, given the additional formulae:

$$\forall x(\text{penguin}(x) \rightarrow \text{ab}(x))$$
$$\forall x(\text{emu}(x) \rightarrow \text{ab}(x)) \qquad (5.5)$$
$$\text{emu(tweety)}$$

we would be able to prove that Tweety is abnormal (even though it is not stated directly), and so would no longer be able to conclude that Tweety can fly. Indeed it is even possible (in general) to encode information about abnormality using defaults. (After all, perhaps most penguins do not fly, but jet-assisted penguins, or whatever, do.)

More generally, default logic envisages a collection of interacting default rules which supplement a regular predicate calculus theory to allow the derivation of additional conclusions. Default logic is nonmonotonic, since additional premises can make it possible to derive the negations of some β_i in a default, so causing a previously derivable conclusion ω no longer to be a theorem. Very roughly, the default (5.3) corresponds to the predicate calculus formula

$$\forall x((\text{bird}(x) \& \neg \text{ab}(x)) \rightarrow \text{flies}(x))$$

under the circumscription of the predicate ab(x), allowing flies(x) to vary: it allows us to conclude that birds fly unless we can show that they are abnormal. But beware of over-hasty comparisons. In general, naively translating default rules into conditionals involving circumscribed predicates does not yield the same set of derivable formulae. The relationship between default logic and circumscription is fraught with complications, and there is certainly not the space to go into this topic here. (See further reading.)

5.3.2 Making inferences with default logic

Formally, we define derivability in default logic as follows. A *default theory* Δ consists of a set W of first-order predicate calculus formulae, and a set D of defaults. The critical idea is that of an *extension* of a default theory Δ. Intuitively, an extension of Δ is a 'minimal' set of predicate calculus formulae which: (i) contains all of the premises in W, (ii) contains all of its own logical consequences, and (iii) respects the defaults in D.

One piece of notation will be useful in the following discussion. If T is any set of formulae, we write $Th(T)$ (read: the *theory* of T) to denote the set of formulae derivable (by standard predicate calculus) from T. Now for the definition of extension.

Definition Let $\Delta = \langle D, W \rangle$ be a default theory. We first define an operator $\Gamma(S)$ as follows: if S is any set of formulae, then $\Gamma(S)$ is the smallest set of formulae satisfying the following properties:
1. $W \subset \Gamma(S)$
2. $Th(\Gamma(S)) \subseteq \Gamma(S)$
3. For each default:

$$\frac{\alpha \ ; \ \beta_1, \ldots, \beta_m}{\omega}$$

in D, if α is in $\Gamma(S)$ and none of the formulae $\neg\beta_i$ is in S, for $i = 1 \ldots m$, then ω is in $\Gamma(S)$. (Note, for these purposes, a default containing variables is simply treated as being equivalent to its set of instances obtained by substituting values for those variables.)

We then define an extension of Δ to be any set E which is a fixed point of Γ, that is, a set E such that $E = \Gamma(E)$.

Finally, if a formula ϕ is in all of the extensions of a default theory Δ, we say ψ is derivable from Δ, or, as we shall write:

$$\Delta \vdash_{default} \psi$$

The above definition of an extension is a little opaque; but it does provide intuitive results in simple cases. For example, if W is the collection of formulae (5.4), and D contains the single default rule (5.3), then we have

$$\langle D, W \rangle \vdash_{default} \text{flies(tweety)}.$$

Moreover, if W consists of the formulae (5.4) together with the formulae (5.5), we have, as expected,

$$\langle D, W' \rangle \nvdash_{default} \text{flies(tweety)}.$$

The following lemma provides an equivalent, and perhaps more intuitive characterization:

Lemma Let $\Delta = \langle D, W \rangle$ be a default theory and E a set of formulae. Then E is an extension if and only if the following holds:

There exists a sequence of sets $E_0, E_1, E_2, \ldots$ such that:
1. $E_0 = W$
2. For $i \geq 0$:

$$E_{i+1} = Th(E_i) \cup \left\{ \omega \ \middle| \ \frac{\alpha \ ; \ \beta_1 \ldots \beta_m}{\omega} \in D \ \ \alpha \in E_i \text{and} \ \beta_j \notin E \ (j = 1, \ldots, m) \right\}$$

and $E = \cup_{i=0}^{i=\infty} E_i$.

Very roughly, the idea is that an extension is a set E which can be built up by alternating bouts of (standard) theorem proving and applying default rules. First, use standard theorem proving to infer as much as possible; then see if any default rules can be applied; if so, that may make more theorem proving possible, which in turn might yield consequences that enable more default rules to apply; and so on. If the process stabilizes, so that no more defaults apply, and no more theorem proving is possible, then we have an extension.

But beware! The above lemma does not provide a recipe for computing extensions of Δ by iteration. The snag is that, when the default rules are used to construct E_{i+1} from E_i, we have to check that that the β_j are not members of the whole extension E – not merely that they are not members of the so-far-constructed E_i. Thus, given a proposed extension E, the lemma gives us an iterative procedure (at least in finite cases) for *checking* whether E really is an extension, but it does not tell us how to guess E in the first place.

Default theories can have zero, one or more than one extension. For example, the theory

$$\left\langle \left\{ \frac{; \neg p}{p} \right\}, \{\} \right\rangle \qquad (5.6)$$

has no extensions; the theory

$$\left\langle \left\{ \frac{; p}{p} \right\}, \{\} \right\rangle \qquad (5.7)$$

has exactly one extension, namely $Th(\{p\})$; and the theory

$$\left\langle \left\{ \frac{; p}{p}, \frac{; q}{q} \right\}, \{\neg(p \& q)\} \right\rangle \qquad (5.8)$$

has exactly two extensions, namely $Th(\{p\})$ and $Th(\{q\})$. As an example of the kind of reasoning required to determine the extensions of default theories, we show that the default theory (5.6) has no extensions. Suppose that (5.6) did have an extension E. Then $\Gamma(E) = E$ where Γ is the operator defined above. Now, either E contains the proposition p or it does not. Suppose, first, that p is in E. Then $\Gamma(E)$, the smallest set satisfying the closure conditions given above, is the empty set $\emptyset$, whence $\Gamma(E) \neq E$, contradicting the assumption that E is an extension. Suppose, secondly, that p is not in E. Then neither is $\neg \neg p$, so that the conditions of the only default rule are satisfied, which forces p to be in $\Gamma(E)$. Thus, again, $\Gamma(E) \neq E$, contradicting the assumption that E is an extension. So the default theory (5.6) cannot have any extensions. (For the corresponding proofs concerning theories (5.7) and (5.8), see exercise 5.)

5.4 Property inheritance and default logic

Any system of property inheritance with exceptions is clearly a kind of nonmonotonic logic: properties which are inheritable in one network, Γ, may no longer be inheritable in an augmented network, Γ', in which additional links have been added. (In fact, as we have seen, properties may even cease to be inheritable if Γ' differs from Γ only in the addition of links which Γ supports!) And it is instructive to look at the connection between property-inheritance and other types of nonmonotonic logics.

For example, we can translate inheritance networks into default theories. A positive link between two properties $X \rightarrow Y$ can be mapped to the default:

$$\frac{X(x); Y(x)}{Y(x)},$$

and a negative link between two properties $X \not\rightarrow Y$ to the default:

$$\frac{X(x); \neg Y(x)}{\neg Y(x)}.$$

Links from individuals to properties – $a \rightarrow Y$ and $a \not\rightarrow Y$ – are mapped to the formulae $Y(a)$, $\neg Y(a)$, respectively.

Suppose, then, an inheritance network Γ is translated in this way into a default theory Δ. Under this translation, it turns out that Δ has some extension E such that: (i) if Γ supports a path $b \rightarrow \ldots \rightarrow X$ then the formula $X(b)$ is in E; (ii) if Γ supports a path $b \rightarrow \ldots \not\rightarrow X$ then the formula $\neg X(b)$ is in E. So inferential distance inheritance is, in some sense, conformable with default logic.

However, a default translation of an inheritance network will in general have a large number of extensions which do not correspond to inheritance as we understand it. For example, the network of figure 5.6 corresponds to the default theory Δ:

$$D = \left\{ \frac{A(x); B(x)}{B(x)}, \frac{B(x); C(x)}{C(x)}, \frac{A(x); \neg C(x)}{\neg C(x)}, \right\}$$
$$W = \{A(w)\}.$$

And Δ indeed has, as an extension:

$$Th(\{A(w), B(w), \neg C(w)\})$$

containing the conclusion $\neg C(w)$ corresponding to the inheritance path $w \rightarrow A \not\rightarrow C$. However, Δ *also* has, as an extension:

$$Th(\{A(w), B(w), C(w)\})$$

containing the opposite conclusion. And property-inheritance does not license the inference to $C(w)$ because it is defeated by the more specific information that B are normally not C. Thus, property inheritance in effect selects between competing extensions of the associated default theory on the basis of specificity.

Of course, this last observation should not come as a surprise. The guiding idea of property inheritance is the precedence of the specific over the general –

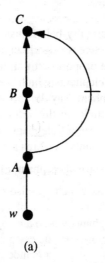

(a)

Figure 5.6   An inheritance network to be translated into a default theory

an idea which has no counterpart in default logic. Still, the connections between property inheritance and various forms of nonmonotonic logic are of considerable interest when it comes to understanding the relative power of these logics (and of property-inheritance), and has been studied widely. The results of this study belong to ongoing research, and will not be replicated here. See, for example, Brewka [2] for an account of the relationship between property inheritance and circumscription. Other results in this area are to be found in Etherington [6] and Brewka [3].

One last point concerning the translation of inheritance networks into default logic. It is sometimes claimed that such translations provide inheritance networks with a 'clear semantics'. The thought seems to be that translating inheritance networks into some logic such as default logic or circumscription gives us a clear sense of what these inheritance networks mean. But of course such translations do no such thing. As we saw in chapter 4, the 'semantics' for circumscription, while it may provide useful alternative characterizations of the theorems, does not constitute an assurance that the formalism captures our intentions, or that these theorems correspond to sensible inferences. Technically interesting as these translations may be, they do not – or at least do not obviously – constitute an explanation or clarification of the meanings of inheritance networks; and they do not – or at least do not obviously – sanction any inheritance method as a sensible inferential policy.

5.5 Gerrymandered categories

The system of reasoning with normally-beliefs just outlined will at least have to be modified, for, as it stands, it will license clearly unacceptable inferences. Suppose that you have no view as to the proportion of circus elephants that are grey, but that you do believe that circus elephants which are royal elephants are normally not grey. Take any circus elephant, say Jumbo which is not a royal elephant. You should *not* be able to conclude on this information that Jumbo is not grey. However, consider the predicate "royal* elephant", defined to hold of all and only those things which are royal elephants or which are identical with Jumbo.

royal*-elephant(x) ≡ (def) royal-elephant(x) or x = Jumbo.

If there are many royal elephants which are also circus elephants, it will be the case that, normally, things which are circus elephants and royal* elephants are not grey (simply because circus elephants which are royal elephants are normally not grey), so that, since there is no more specific category into which Jumbo falls than the category of royal* elephants, we can conclude that Jumbo is not grey. This is absurd.

Clearly, the trick of fiddling with honest-to-goodness categories such as royal elephant to produce mutants like royal* elephant (i.e. is-a-royal-elephant-or-is-identical-to-Jumbo), will wreck the system of defeasible inference just sketched. (Compare the situation here with the discussion of the predicate fridgeon(x) at the end of chapter 3, and with the *grue*-problem of chapter 9.)

Perhaps the most striking thing about the category of royal* elephant is its relative syntactic complexity. Can syntactic complexity be used to eliminate the unwanted inference? No. For the syntactic complexity in question pertains to the *definition* of "royal* elephant" in terms of "royal elephant", and that complexity can be mirrored in a definition of "royal elephant" in terms of "royal* elephant" as follows:

royal-elephant(x) ≡ (def) royal*-elephant(x) and x ≠ Jumbo.

This suggests that a syntactic criterion will not serve to eliminate inferences mediated by generalizations about categories such as royal* elephant.

To what extent are categories like royal* elephant a problem for *practical* property inheritance systems? Well, they are no problem so long as the language we allow the system to use – its repertoire of concepts – is fixed (as they are in all present-day AI applications). However, problems can be expected to arise in systems able to invent terms for new categories, for the principles determining what count as a sensible categories are not at present understood.

5.6 The reliability of property inheritance

The ever-nagging problem with all proposals for defeasible inference is that, since defeasible inference is, by its very nature, logically invalid, it is never entirely clear what the justification for making it is. Since the conclusion of schema (5.1) does not follow logically from its premises, then inferring according to that schema will sometimes lead us from true premises to true conclusions, but will also sometimes lead from true premises to false conclusions. A defender of schema (5.1) will no doubt reply that the inferences it recommends work *most of the time*. But who's counting? Logically speaking, it is just an invalid inference: so what real evidence do we have for the claim that it works most of the time?

First, the good news. There is, it turns out, an argument to show that if we choose three properties, A, B and C at random such that the premises of schema (5.1) are true, then, with high probability, the conclusion of (5.1) will also be true. In other words, schema (5.1) must hold *normally*, though not without exception, and its use in inference will prove to be *reliable*, though not infallible. Since the details of this argument are rather technical and require some statistical background, so it will be omitted here. (See further reading for a discussion of the justification of this sort of inference.)

Now the bad news. By way of breaking it gently, we begin with a digression on probability and causation. (We will return to this subject in considerably more detail in chapter 8.) Frequently, 'normally-statements' are associated with patterns of causation. Thus: normally, if someone is shot in the head, he dies; here, the shooting causes the dying. Or again: normally, if someone angers the mob, he gets shot in the head; here, the angering causes the shooting. But the direction of causation need not necessarily run from antecedent to consequent: normally if a patient exhibits symptom B, he has infection C; here the infection C (consequent) causes the symptom B (antecedent). In this section, we shall see how the correctness of schema (5.1) can depend on the underlying pattern of causation.

Suppose that, in a certain clinic, patients occasionally arrive complaining of symptom B. Now, symptom B can be the result of a dread disease A; in fact, if a patient has disease A, it is almost certain that this will lead to symptom B. Happily, however, symptom B, though it *can* be caused by A, is normally the result of a harmless infection, C. Hence:

Normally, if a patient has A, then he has B.
Normally, if a patient has B, then he has C.

Thus, the premises of schema (5.1) obtain (in slightly rewritten form). In addition, let it be given that we have no other information about the statistical relationships between A, B and C. Finally, let w be a patient whom we know (on independent grounds) has dread disease A.

In this case, it would be unreliable to conclude, as the advocates of property inheritance would apparently have us do, that w probably has harmless infection C. And it would be unreliable to conclude, as schema (5.1) would have us do, that normally, patients with disease A also have infection C. A and C, being alternative causes of B, may well be statistically independent. That is, the fact that someone has A may have no effect on the probability that he has C, and vice versa. So it will certainly not be true that people with A normally have C.

In fact, it is a general truth that, if A, B and C are properties such that having property A and having property C are alternative possible causes of having property B, then A and C can be statistically independent even if A are normally B and B are normally C. That is: it will *quite often* be the case that the conclusion of schema (5.1) will be false even if its premises are true. And this casts doubt on the claim that schema (5.1) is generally reliable. You have been warned.

5.7 A sceptical solution

This conclusion may seem at odds with the obvious expediency of inheritance-based knowledge representation schemes. For it seems both efficient and harmless to record the facts that aardvarks, baboons and crocodiles all do not wear clothes by recording the fact that (most) members of a more inclusive class – the class of animals – have that property, and by allowing inheritance of properties by sub-types. But this would be to miss the point of the argument of this chapter. That argument does not show that we should not store information in the efficient format such networks provide. What it does show is that, *if* we do so, we may not interpret the mechanism of property inheritance as a mechanism for performing inferences according to schema (5.1), and we may not interpret the links in an inheritance network as conveying *only* information of the form "Normally A are B", "Normally C are D", etc.

The point is one about the admissible semantics for inheritance networks. If we do store information in the form of an inheritance network, then we should recognize that, in allowing the network to be used in this way, we are encoding more information than the 'normally-statements' corresponding to the links: we are, in addition, *implicitly* encoding the information that, in the particular domain in question, our inheritance mechanism is reliable. And it goes without saying that if inheritance networks are so interpreted, the use of schema (5.1) to retrieve information from the network is trivially vindicated. To repeat: there is no reason why the inheritance method employed should not be made to apply by fiat, provided the result is that the system comes out with beliefs that we wanted it to have anyway. What we must not do is represent whatever property inheritance mechanism we employ as some sort of general inference mechanism for reasoning about conditionals of the form "Normally A's are B's".

This conclusion has important consequences for some of the recent work on property inheritance in complex networks. Authors disagree about how exactly to inherit properties in some of these cases; some speak of a 'clash of intuitions' (e.g. Horty, Thomason and Touretzky [7]) between the leading experts. But we have argued that even the simplest paradigms of property inheritance cannot be consistently represented as an inference mechanism for dealing with statements of the form "Normally, A are B". Whence we conclude that all inheritance networks – even the simplest – only make sense if they are considered implicitly to encode the additional information that the inheritance mechanism in question is reliable in the relevant domain. That being so, none of these mechanisms can be said to be *correct* or *incorrect* independent of a particular domain of application: doubtless, many different inheritance schemes will be correct in various different domains; but none will be correct in general.

Thus, it makes no sense to talk about 'clashes of intuitions' concerning the correct property inheritance mechanisms for complicated networks: there is nothing to intuit. *Either* (i) property inheritance is considered as a general method of reasoning with beliefs of the form "Normally *A* are *B*", *or* (ii) property inheritance is considered as a mechanism for efficiently encoding information in certain restricted domains where the particular inheritance strategy finds reliable application. On the first view, it makes sense to ask whether a given method of property inheritance is reliable, in the sense that the conclusion is *usually* true when the premises are true; and the answer is: sometimes. But it is difficult to see what general guidelines might exist for knowing under what conditions a given method of property-inheritance is reliable. On the second view, the particular property-inheritance method is correct by fiat; the information encoded in the network is simply defined to be that collection of facts which can be extracted by the particular inheritance mechanism being used. Thus, on this second view, property-inheritance is better seen as data-decompression than inference. It is not that the links and nodes in our network have an independent semantics which *justifies* the use of the chosen inheritance procedure. Rather, the network is just an efficient way of storing that information which our chosen inheritance procedure will generate.

Exercises

1. (To think about before reading section 5.6) It was claimed in section 5.1.1 that the direct-inference schema

    Normally, *A* are *B*
    Normally, *B* are *C*
    Normally, *A* are *C*.

    is invalid. Taking "normally" to mean "in 90% or more of the cases", construct an instance of the direct inference schema where the premises are true and the conclusion false.
2. Implement the procedure `inherit(A,C)` of section 5.1.1. Design a data-structure to encode the inheritance network of figure 5.2 and show that your inheritance procedure yields sensible results.
3. Implement a procedure `all-pos-paths(A,C)`, which returns a list of all the positive paths (i.e. paths whose final link is positive) from node A to node C in a network with multiple inheritance. Hence, or otherwise, implement the Touretzky inferential-distance inheritance procedure. Design data-structures to encode the network of figure 5.7, and try your inheritance procedure out.

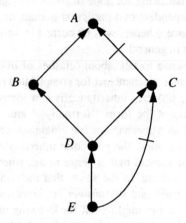

Figure 5.7   A problematical inheritance network

You should notice that E inherits A, but that neither C nor D (E's only parents in the network) inherits A. Do you think this behaviour reasonable?

4. It is proposed to modify the inferential-distance inheritance procedure as follows:

Case I: Single links

    1. $\Gamma \models x \rightarrow y$ if $x \rightarrow y$ is in Γ

    2. $\Gamma \models x \nrightarrow y$ if $x \nrightarrow y$ is in Γ

Case II: Compound sequences

    1. $\Gamma \models x \rightarrow u \rightarrow \sigma_1 \rightarrow y$ if

        (a) $\Gamma \models u \rightarrow \sigma_1 \rightarrow y$

        (b) $x \rightarrow u$ is in Γ

        (c) $x \nrightarrow y$ is not in Γ

        (d) for all v such that $\Gamma \models x \rightarrow \tau \rightarrow v$ with $v \nrightarrow y \in \Gamma$, there exists a z ($\neq v$) st. $\Gamma \models x \rightarrow \tau_1 \rightarrow z \rightarrow \tau_2 \rightarrow v$ and $z \rightarrow y \in \Gamma$

    2. $\Gamma \models x \rightarrow u \rightarrow \sigma_1 \nrightarrow y$ if

        (a) $\Gamma \models u \rightarrow \sigma_1 \nrightarrow y$

        (b) $x \rightarrow u$ is in Γ

        (c) $x \rightarrow y$ is not in Γ

        (d) for all v st. $\Gamma \models x \rightarrow \tau \rightarrow v$ with $v \rightarrow y \in \Gamma$, there exists z ($\neq v$) such that $\Gamma \models x \rightarrow \tau_1 \rightarrow z \rightarrow \tau_2 \rightarrow v$ and $z \nrightarrow y \in \Gamma$

Note the subtle alteration: whereas the original method chains forwards from a node to its ancestors in the network, this modified version chains backwards from a node to its descendants.

Show that, in the network of figure 5.7, the original version and the modified version yield *different* results. Is one method better than the other? How would you decide which method to use?

5. Consider the default theory $\langle D, W \rangle$ with

$$D = \left\{ \frac{;\, p}{p} \right\}$$
$$W = \emptyset$$

Let S be any collection of formulae. Show that, for the above default theory, if $\neg p$ is in S, $\Gamma(S) = \emptyset$, and if $\neg p$ is not in S, $\Gamma(S) = Th(\{p\})$. (Remember: $Th(\{p\})$ is the set of all sentences derivable from p.) Hence show that this default theory has just one extension, namely $T = Th(\{p\})$. Similarly, show that the default theory $\langle D, W \rangle$ with

$$D = \left\{ \frac{;\, p}{p}, \frac{;\, q}{q} \right\}$$
$$W = \{\neg(p \& q)\}$$

has exactly two extensions, namely $T_1 = Th(\{p\})$ and $T_2 = Th(\{q\})$.

6. Consider the default theory $\langle D, W \rangle$ with

$$D = \left\{ \frac{;\, \neg p(x)}{p(x)} \right\}$$
$$W = \{p(a), a \neq b\}.$$

The naive translation into a circumscriptive theory would then yield the theory $\{\forall x(\neg p(x) \rightarrow p(x)), p(a), a \neq b\}$, where $p(x)$ is the predicate to be minimized. This latter is of course just equivalent to the theory $\{\forall x p(x), a \neq b\}$. Show that, when $p(x)$ is minimized, this latter theory has minimal models, and that, in all of these minimal models, $p(a)$ and $p(b)$ are true; show also that the original default theory has no extensions.

7. Suppose that a reasoning system believes initially that birds normally fly, and that Tweety is a bird, but that Tweety does not fly. Model this knowledge using circumscription, and show that the system can conclude that Tweety is abnormal.

Consider the default theory $\Delta = \langle D, W \rangle$, where

$$D = \left\{ \frac{\mathrm{bird}(x)\,;\, \neg \mathrm{ab}(x)}{\mathrm{flies}(x)} \right\}$$
$$W = \{\mathrm{bird}(\mathrm{tweety}), \neg \mathrm{flies}(\mathrm{tweety})\}$$

The only sensible candidate extensions are:

$$Th(\{\text{bird(tweety)}, \neg\text{flies(tweety)}\})$$
$$Th(\{\text{bird(tweety)}, \neg\text{flies(tweety)}, \text{ab(tweety)}\})$$
$$Th(\{\text{bird(tweety)}, \neg\text{flies(tweety)}, \neg\text{ab(tweety)}\})$$

Verify that none of these sets of formulae is an extension of Δ, so that Δ has no extensions.

What conclusions do these results enable you to draw about the relationship between circumscription, default logic and defeasible reasoning?

8. In section 5.4, it was claimed that the default theory $\Delta = \langle D, W \rangle$ with:

$$D = \left\{ \frac{A(x); B(x)}{B(x)}, \frac{B(x); C(x)}{C(x)}, \frac{A(x); \neg C(x)}{\neg C(x)}, \right\}$$
$$W = \{A(w)\}.$$

has one extension containing

$$A(w), B(w), \neg C(w)$$

and another containing

$$A(w), B(w), C(w).$$

Using the lemma of section 5.3.2, verify this claim.

Further reading

For those interested in the technical aspects of property inheritance and its relation to other nonmonotonic inference systems, see Etherington [5] and Touretzky [9] and [10]). A good, recent overview of this material can be found in Brewka [3]. Another good source of up-to-date research is the recent conference proceedings of the AAAI and IJCAI; these contain a large number of papers on property inheritance. Readers more interested in the philosophical aspects of this type of reasoning (in particular, in the question of how statistical premises license uncertain but nonstatistical conclusions) is referred to Pollock [8] and Bacchus [1]. The psychological validity of property inheritance was investigated in influential work by Collins and Quillian [4].

Bibliography

[1] Bacchus, Fahiem *Representing and Reasoning with Probabilistic Knowledge* Cambridge, MA: MIT Press, 1990.

[2] Brewka, G. "The logic of inheritance in frame systems", *Proceedings, IJCAI-87*, Milan (1987) pp. 484–488.

[3] Brewka, G. *Nonmonotonic reasoning: the logical foundations of common-sense*, Cambridge: CUP, 1991.

[4] Collins, A.M. and M.R. Quillian "Retrieval time from semantic memory", *Journal of Verbal Learning and Verbal Behaviour*, 8 (1969) pp. 240–247.

[5] Etherington, D. "Formalizing Nonmonotonic Reasoning Systems", *Artificial Intelligence* 31, (1987) pp. 41–85.

[6] Etherington, D. *Reasoning with Incomplete Information*, London: Pitman, 1987.

[7] Horty, J.F., R.H. Thomason and D.S. Touretzky "A Clash of Intuitions: The Current State of Nonmonotonic Multiple Inheritance Systems", *IJCAI-87*, Milan (1987) pp. 476–482.

[8] Pollock, J. "Foundations for Direct Inference", *Theory and Decision*, 17 (1984).

[9] Touretzky, D.S. "Implicit Ordering of Defaults in Inheritance Systems", *Proceedings, AAAI-84*, Austin, Texas (1984) pp. 322–325.

[10] Touretzky, D.S. *The Mathematics of Inheritance Systems*, London: Pitman, 1986.

6 Reason Maintenance

6.1 The idea of reason maintenance

In previous chapters, we examined various attempts to formalize *defeasible* reasoning, that is, reasoning in which a previously derivable conclusion must be abandoned when the system's knowledge-base is augmented with some new premise. The modelling of defeasible reasoning is important in AI, since, in general, the acquisition of new information can have various effects on what one believes, causing not only new beliefs to be adopted, but also old ones to be abandoned. For example, a detective investigating a murder may, upon discovering a new clue, change his mind about who the culprit is, or a scientist investigating some natural phenomenon may, upon reading about a new experiment, modify or abandon previously held theories.

However, it is not sufficient, when modelling this sort of reasoning, simply to give the reasoning system some nonmonotonic proof-rules and leave it at that. For suppose the system's original knowledge-base T is augmented with some new premise ϕ. Then, the system needs to know *which* of its conclusions, previously drawn from T, are likely to be affected by coming to learn ϕ. It is important to realize that nonmonotonic logic does not give us any easy way of tackling this problem: so far as nonmonotonic logic is concerned, there is simply a knowledge-base (a set of premises) T; and its job is to determine whether a given formula ψ is nonmonotonically derivable from T. Augment the knowledge-base and all previous conclusions are, potentially, invalidated. In this sense, nonmonotonic logic furnishes no *incremental* means to manage accumulating evidence. Yet in practice, no reasoner can simply rub out all previously derived conclusions and start from scratch every time a new piece of information arrives. Evidently, a system is called for in which the arrival of new information leads only to changes in those beliefs that are likely to be affected. Other beliefs can be left alone.

A natural response to this demand for incremental changes in response to new information is to see an agent's beliefs as not just an unordered bag of propositions, but rather, a structure held together by relationships of *justification* or *support*. The underlying idea is that a belief is challenged only when one's reasons for it are invalidated. Of course, revising one belief will in general invalidate the reasons for others, thus leading to a chain of belief-revision. But many beliefs, whose reasons are unaffected by these changes, will remain undisturbed at no cost. A structure of reasons within a knowledge-base thus acts as a series of conduits, chanelling the attention of the belief-updating process to where it is needed. The task of updating belief systems in this way is called *reason maintenance* or, sometimes, *belief revision*, and in this chapter we shall be examining some approaches to this task within AI.

There is more than one way in which a previously derivable conclusion can be defeated by the arrival of new information. The following distinction will be important in the rest of this chapter. Suppose that a reasoning system has the premise

$$\forall x (\mathrm{bird}(x) \ \& \ \neg \mathrm{ab}(x) \to \mathrm{flies}(x)),$$

and is circumscribing $\mathrm{ab}(x)$ (allowing $\mathrm{flies}(x)$ to vary) to encode the assumption that things are normal unless there is reason to believe otherwise. As long as the system has no reason to infer $\mathrm{ab}(\mathrm{tweety})$, we can suppose that it will draw, as a conclusion, $\mathrm{flies}(\mathrm{tweety})$. However, as soon as new information arrives from which it follows that Tweety is abnormal, the system should then give up its belief that Tweety can fly. We might say that the arrival of the new information has *undermined* the conclusion $\mathrm{flies}(\mathrm{tweety})$, because it has invalidated the reasoning supporting it. Notice that, in this case, the system will not then in general know whether Tweety can fly or not.

Here is a different case. Suppose the system has derived the (defeasible) conclusion $\mathrm{flies}(\mathrm{tweety})$. Now new information arrives, that Tweety does not fly: $\neg \mathrm{flies}(\mathrm{tweety})$. Here again, the original conclusion must be given up – and the reasoning that led to it retracted. But this time, that reasoning has not so much been undermined, as *rebutted*, in that it is flatly contradicted by the additional information. In the sequel, we shall investigate frameworks for modelling the revision of beliefs by undermining and rebuttal.

6.2 Doyle's TMS

In this section, we present an influential approach to modelling reason maintenance proposed in Doyle [1], based on the notion of a *truth maintenance system*, or *TMS*. The name *truth*-maintenance is, as most people now agree, misleading, since what is maintained – if anything – is not *truth*, but at best something like *justifiedness* or *reasonableness*. Nevertheless, it is useful to reserve a special term for the particular formalism for reason maintenance which Doyle proposed. Accordingly, though we shall continue to speak of *reason* maintenance, we shall refer to instances of the Doyle's specific formalism as TMS's. In this book, we omit some of the more obscure and doubtful aspects of Doyle's formalism; however, those aspects that we do present illustrate the task of reason maintenance well. (See further reading.)

6.2.1   The framework of the TMS

In a TMS, there is a finite set N of *nodes*, each one of which represents a candidate belief – something the agent is able to consider believing. These nodes are, so far as the TMS is concerned, atomic, and have no internal structure. Of course, that does not mean that, for the reasoning system as a whole, its beliefs do not have internal structure. It is just that the internal structure of a belief such as, e.g.

$$(\text{penguin}(\text{tweety}) \lor \text{emu}(\text{tweety})) \rightarrow \neg\text{flies}(\text{tweety})$$

is invisible to the TMS. (The motivation for viewing beliefs in this way will become clear presently.)

The nodes, or potential beliefs, are linked together by a finite set J of *justifications*, which represent the system's views as to the dependencies between these potential beliefs. Each justification is written formally as:

$$\langle l_1, \ldots, l_i \mid m_1, \ldots, m_k \rightarrow n \rangle, \tag{6.1}$$

and has the intuitive interpretation

> if I accept the beliefs at nodes $l_1, \ldots, l_i$ and I have no reason to accept
> the beliefs at nodes at $m_1, \ldots, m_k$ then I should accept the belief at
> node n,

It is common, in the context of reason maintenance, to speak of nodes being assigned a status *in* (= believed) or *out* (= not believed). Hence, the nodes $l_1, \ldots, l_i$ are collectively known as the *in-list* of the justification (6.1) and the nodes $m_1, \ldots, m_k$ as its *out-list*; the node n is known as the *consequent* of the justification. If j is a justification such that all the nodes in the in-list of j are *in* and all the nodes in the out-list of j are *out*, then j is said to be *valid*. A node n should be made *in* if it is the consequent of one or more valid justifications.

TMS's can be pictured graphically as in figures 6.1 and 6.2. Figure 6.1 shows the graphical notation for a single justification and its associated nodes: the justification is represented by the square, and the nodes that it involves by circles. The consequent of the justification is identified by the outgoing arrow, and the nodes in the out-list distinguished by the crossed-out lines. The in-lists and out-lists may contain any finite number of nodes (including zero). Figure 6.2 shows how justifications and nodes can combine to form a structure of reasons. Nodes may be the consequent of any number of justifications, (including zero) and may participate in the in- and out-lists of any number of justifications (again, including zero). In general, there is no reason why a node should not be in its own in- or out-list; we shall investigate this possibility in detail later. Formally, a TMS, $\langle N, J \rangle$ is simply a set N of nodes paired with a set J of justifications of the form (6.1).

We said at the beginning of this chapter that the motivation for reason maintenance systems is the need to manage the updating of beliefs as new information arrives. We distinguished two sorts of revision due to the acquisition of new

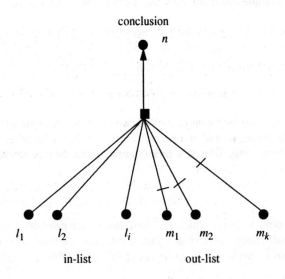

Figure 6.1 A single TMS justification and its associated nodes

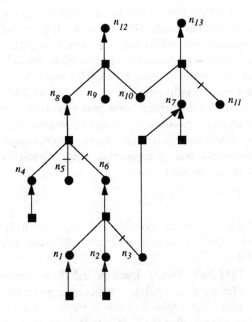

Figure 6.2 A TMS

premises: undermining versus rebuttal. Both of these sorts of revision can occur in a TMS.

In a TMS, the arrival of new information is modelled by the addition of new members to the set J of justifications. To model the acquisition of a new premise by the system, we simply add a justification of the form

$$\langle \quad | \quad \rightarrow n \rangle$$

where n is the node corresponding to the new belief. The empty in- and out-lists force the node in question to be unconditionally *in*. If, on the other hand, we want to model the acquisition of a new premise which may later be retracted, we might add a justification of the form

$$\langle \quad | \quad m \quad \rightarrow n \rangle$$

where m is some node for which no justifications are provided. So long as there remain no justifications with m as consequent, m will be *out*, so n will be *in*. But the system can be made to retract its belief in n by adding a suitable justification for m.

When, following the addition of a new justification, the status of a node changes from *out* to *in*, that may affect the validity of other justifications, so affecting the status of other nodes, and so on, thus bringing about a series of changes in the status of many other nodes in the TMS. Notice that, as a result of this process, some previously accepted beliefs can be abandoned, because their supporting justifications become invalidated. Here, then, we have defeat by *undermining*. This process of updating the status of the nodes in N is the first main function of the TMS. (We will explain in detail how the procedure works below.)

The previous paragraph explained how TMS's model the undermining of previously acceptable inferences by new information. But what of rebuttal? To model this phenomenon, TMS's distinguish some nodes as *contradiction* nodes – nodes which must be made out if possible. For example, suppose that l_1 and l_2 are nodes in a TMS corresponding to beliefs which the system decides are mutually contradictory – e.g. flies(tweety) and ¬flies(tweety). This contradiction can be expressed in the TMS with the justification

$$\langle \ l_1, l_2 \ | \ \rightarrow c \rangle \tag{6.2}$$

where c is marked as a *contradiction node*. If l_1 and l_2 are both marked *in*, so will c be, a situation the TMS wants to avoid. The TMS responds to this situation by trying to make c *out*.

The way the TMS does this is to trace through the reasons supporting c to see if they can be challenged at any point. For example, given the justification (6.2), the only way to make c *out* is to make either l_1 *out* or l_2 *out* (or both). How might this be done? Well, suppose that the TMS also includes the justification

$$\langle \quad | \quad m \ \rightarrow l_1 \rangle.$$

and that there are no justifications for m. Then, one way to make c *out* is to construct a new justification for m, for example the justification

$$\langle \quad | \quad \rightarrow m \rangle$$

with empty in- and out-lists. If this justification were added to the system, m would be made *in*, allowing l_1 and c to be made *out*. More generally, in response to a contradiction c, the TMS traces back through the reasons supporting c, looking for a point where adding a new justification will force c to be *out*. (In fact, the added justification will be more complicated than in this example, as we will see below.) This process is called *dependency-directed backtracking*, and is the second main function of a TMS.

We now turn to the details of the functions of a TMS. Sections 6.2.2–6.2.4 look at the problem of incrementally determining a labelling for the nodes of a TMS (in which each node is assigned the label *in* or *out*) as new justifications arrive. Section 6.2.5 explains how dependency directed backtracking allows the TMS to respond to contradictions.

6.2.2 Determining a set of justified beliefs

Let us assume, then, that we are given a set N of nodes and a set J of justifications of the form (6.1). Our task is to find a subset E of the nodes which are *in* – i.e. believed by the system. We shall begin by confining our attention to TMS's in which there are no circular justifications (i.e. when the graph of the TMS contains no cycles); that way, we encounter all the important ideas without some of the awkward complexities that arise when circular justifications are present.

Recall that, if j is a justification in J, and if, for a given labelling of the nodes in N, all the nodes in the in-list of j are labelled *in* and all the nodes in the out-list of j are labelled *out*, then j is said to be *valid*, and its consequent should be labelled *in*. Accordingly, one condition that a labelling must fulfil is that it must be closed under the application of the justifications in J in the following sense.

Definition *Let $\langle N, J \rangle$ be a TMS and $E \subseteq N$. We say that E is closed with respect to $\langle N, J \rangle$ if, for every $j \in J$, with*

$$j = \langle l_1, \ldots, l_i \mid m_1, \ldots, m_k \rightarrow n \rangle,$$

if $l_1 \ldots, l_i \in E$ and if $m_1, \ldots, m_k \notin E$ then $n \in E$.

We shall insist that the set E of *in*-labelled nodes be closed with respect to $\langle N, J \rangle$.

Of course, closure by itself is not a very useful constraint on E. To see why not, notice what happens if $E = N$. It is easy to check from the definition that N is always closed with respect to $\langle N, J \rangle$; thus, a sure-fire way to guarantee closure is simply to believe everything! True: we want E to include those propositions that we can justify, but we just as much want E not to include those propositions that we cannot justify.

What is required is that every node that is labelled *in* has some valid justification to support it. Accordingly, we define:

Definition   *Let* $\langle N, J \rangle$ *be a TMS and* $E \subseteq N$. *We say that* E *is supported with respect to* $\langle N, J \rangle$ *if, for every* $n \in E$, *there exists a*

$$j = \langle l_1, \ldots, l_i \mid m_1, \ldots, m_k \to n \rangle \in J$$

with $l_1 \ldots, l_i \in E$ *and* $m_1, \ldots, m_k \notin E$.

We shall insist that the set E of *in*-labelled nodes be supported with respect to $\langle N, J \rangle$.

Together, the two requirements of closure and supportedness produce sensible behaviour in TMS's where there are no cycles in the structure of justifications. For example, let $\langle N, J \rangle$ be the network depicted in figure 6.2. Consider the node n_1. This node has a single justification with an empty in-list and and empty-out list. (That is, n_1 is one of the system's foundational beliefs, resting on no other evidence.) It follows that this justification is trivially valid, and n_1 must be made *in* if the set E of in-nodes is to be closed. Similar considerations apply to n_2, which must also be *in*. Node n_3, however, is different. The TMS of figure 6.2 has *no* justifications with n_3 as consequent, and so n_3 must be made *out* if the set E of in-nodes is to be supported.

Now consider n_6. This node has one justification, with in-list consisting of n_1 and n_2, and out-list consisting of the single node n_3. Since we have already argued that n_1 and n_2 must be *in*, and n_3 *out*, it follows that this justification is valid, and n_6 must also be *in*. Moreover, n_8 must now be *out*, since there is only one justification with n_8 as its consequent, and that justification has n_6 in its out-list. Proceeding in a similar fashion, it is straightforward to assign a status to all of the nodes in the TMS of figure 6.2.

The same idea can be generalized to get a procedure for assigning a status to the nodes of any TMS (with no circular justifications). We proceed in stages. First, we define a procedure `get-validity-if-poss(just,part-assign)` whose job is to try to determine the validity of a single justification, `just` in the TMS. The second argument, `part-assign`, is a data-structure which assigns to each node in the TMS the status of *in*, *out* or *undecided*. Intuitively, `part-assign` is a *partial* specification of the final assignment we eventually want to reach. The procedure works as follows. First, it gets the in-list and out-list of the justification `just`. If all the nodes in the in-list are assigned the status *in* by `part-assign`, and all the nodes in its out-list have been assigned the status *out* by `part-assign`, then `just` is valid and so the procedure returns the value `valid`. If, however, `part-assign` assigns some node in the in-list the status *out*, or some node in the out-list the status *in*, then `just` must be invalid and so the procedure returns the value `invalid`. If neither of these conditions holds, then `part-assign` does not contain enough information to decide the validity of `just` and so the procedure returns the value *undecided*.

begin get-validity-if-poss(just,part-assign)
    let in-list be the in-list of just
    let out-list be the out-list of just
    if all nodes in in-list are in in part-assign **and**
      all nodes in out-list are out in part-assign **then**
      return valid
    else if some node in in-list is out in part-assign or
      some node in out-list is in in part-assign **then**
      return invalid
    else
      return undecided
    endif
end get-validity-if-poss

We now define get-status-if-poss(j-set,node,part-assign), a procedure whose job is to try to determine the status of a single node, node in the TMS, given the partial assignment part-assign. The first argument, j-set is the set of justifications in the TMS. The procedure returns one of three values: (i) *in*, if there is definitely at least one valid justification with node as consequent, (ii) *out*, if there are definitely no valid justifications with node as consequent, and (iii) *undecided*, if part-assign does not contain sufficient information to determine the status of node.

begin get-status-if-poss(j-set,node,part-assign)
    let current-j-set be the set of justifications in j-set
      whose consequent is node
    foreach justification just in current-j-set **do**
      call get-validity-if-poss(just,part-assign)
    end for each
    if some of these calls returned valid **then**
      return in
    else if all of these calls returned invalid **then**
      return out
    else
      return undecided
    end if
end get-status-if-poss

We are now in a position to assign a status to every node of a TMS (with no circular justifications). The basic procedure is propagate-justifications, which takes a partial status-assignment and finds nodes whose status can be determined from the information already in that partial status-assignment using the procedure get-status-if-poss. The result is another partial assignment in which fewer nodes are undecided. The procedure propagate-justifications then keeps on calling get-status-if-poss in this way until no more nodes can be assigned a status. Assuming that there are no circular justifications, the returned value will always be a complete status-assignment (i.e. a status-assignment in which all nodes are marked as *in* or *out*.)

```
begin propagate-justifications(j-set,part-assign)
    let no-action-flag be false
    until no-action-flag = true do
        let no-action-flag be true
        for all nodes node do
            if status of node in part-assign is undecided and
              get-status-if-poss(j-set,node,part-assign)
              is not undecided then
                modify part-assign so as to set status of node to
                  get-status-if-poss(j-set,node,part-assign)
                let no-action be false
            end if
        end for all
    end until
    return part-assign
end propagate-justifications
```

To compute a status-assignment from scratch, we simply construct the partial status-assignment in which *every* node is marked as undecided (call it null-assign) and we call propagate-justifications on null-assign. If $\langle N, J \rangle$ is a TMS containing no circular justifications, there is a unique set of nodes E which is both closed and supported with respect to $\langle N, J \rangle$, and the algorithm propagate-justifications will find it. (See exercise 1.)

6.2.3   Incremental changes to node labelling

We now turn to the all-important question of making the labelling procedure *incremental*. Remember: the original motivation for the development of a theory of reason maintenance was the need to manage the updating required by the arrival of new information, without having to recompute everything from scratch.

Suppose that additional information arrives in the form of a new justification j. If j is valid, then its consequent, say, node n, must be *in*. If n was already in before the addition of j, then j can have no immediate effect on the status-assignment, and nothing more needs to be done. If, on the other hand, n was previously *out*, then the change to n may have ramifications throughout the network. Suppose j' is another justification in J, which mentions n in its in-list; it is possible that the change in status of n makes j' valid, so making its consequent *in*, which may in turn affect the status of other nodes. Or suppose j'' is a justification which mentions n in its out-list; it is possible that the change in status of n makes j'' invalid, so making its consequent *out*, which again may affect the status of other nodes.

To determine the nodes that may possibly be affected by the new justification j, the procedure prop-uncert(changed-nodes,j-set,part-assign) suffices. This procedure takes, as its arguments, a set of nodes, changed-nodes, whose status has changed, the set of justifications in the TMS, j-set, and a partial status-assignment, part-assign. First, part-assign is modified so as to make all nodes in changed-nodes undecided. Next changed-nodes is reset to be the set of nodes whose status *could have been affected* by this modification, given that the justifications of the TMS are those in j-set. The process repeats until no new nodes are found which could have been affected. Calling the procedure with set-of-nodes set to contain the consequent of the new justification *j* as its only member, will then mark as undecided all nodes which could possibly have been affected by the addition of *j*.

> **begin** prop-uncert(changed-nodes,j-set,part-assign)
>   **until** changed-nodes is empty **do**
>   **for each** node in changed-nodes **do**
>   modify part-assign so that status of node is undecided
>   **end for each**
>   **let** next-nodes be the empty list
>   **for each** justification just in j-set **do**
>   **if** changed-nodes has one or more nodes in common
>   with the in-list or the out-list of just and
>   the consequent of just is not undecided
>   according to part-assign **then**
>   add the consequent of just to next-nodes;
>   **end if**
>   **end for each**
>   **let** changed-nodes be next-nodes;
>   **end until**
>   **return** status-assignment
> **end** prop-uncert

Once prop-uncert has been applied, propagate-justifications can be run on the partial status-assignment that it returns. Doing so will result in a correct status-assignment, taking into account the new justification. (See exercise 2.)

6.2.4 A simple example

We can illustrate the way in which a TMS guides the updating of beliefs in response to new information, by considering the case of Tweety. Suppose that a reasoner believes that birds normally fly, unless they are abnormal, that penguins and emus are abnormal birds, and that Tweety and Oscar are birds. These beliefs might naturally give rise to the structure of reasons shown in the TMS of figure 6.3. (For clarity, the nodes in the diagram of figure 6.3 are labelled with the propositions expressing the beliefs they correspond to.) As long as the system has no grounds for believing that Tweety and Oscar are abnormal, the TMS labelling process will

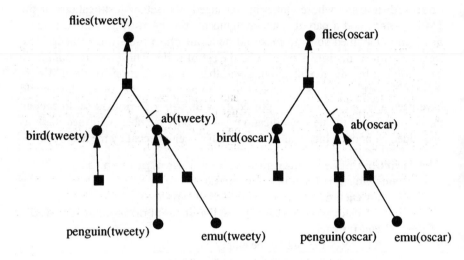

Figure 6.3   Incremental updating in a TMS

make the nodes corresponding to these beliefs *out*, so that the nodes corresponding to flies(tweety) and flies(oscar) will be *in*.

Suppose now that new information arrives that Oscar is a penguin. This will be modelled by adding a new justification for the node penguin(oscar). Running the procedure prop-uncert will then change the status of the nodes ab(oscar) and flies(oscar) to *undecided*, but will leave all other nodes unaffected. The procedure propagate-reasons can then be used to compute the new status-assignment, in which penguin(oscar) and ab(oscar) will be *in* and flies(oscar) will be *out*. Again the nodes corresponding to the other propositions are not affected, and their status stays the same. (See exercise 3.)

6.2.5   *Dependency-directed backtracking*

We have seen in detail how the revision of beliefs by undermining is implemented in a TMS. We now turn to the details of the revision of beliefs by rebuttal.

The goal of dependency directed backtracking (DDB) in a TMS is to make sure that nodes marked as contradictions are not *in*. This goal is achieved by finding a node or nodes which, if made *in*, would cause the contradictions to go *out*: extra justifications are then constructed to force these latter nodes to be *in*, thus saving the system from believing the contradictions.

Consider, for example, the TMS of figure 6.2, and suppose that the system decides that nodes n_6 and n_7 cannot be true together. This decision is expressed by adding a contradiction node – call it c – together with the justification:

$$\langle n_6, n_7 \mid \; \rightarrow c \rangle.$$

Ordinarily, n_6 and n_7 would have the status *in*, which, given the new justification, would force c to be *in* as well. The task of DDB is to find a way of adding a justification to the TMS so that c is *out*.

If c is to be made out, one of n_6 and n_7 must be made out. Since n_7 has a justification with an empty in- and out-list, there is no way of making that node out. But n_6 rests on a justification containing n_3 in its out list. If n_3 became *in* then n_6 would go *out*, and with it, the contradiction c. So the DDB process constructs a new justification for n_3.

What should this new justification look like? Well, there are various possibilities, about which we shall have something to say presently. But one that would certainly work in this case is the justification with n_3 as consequent and with empty in- and out-lists:

$$\langle \; \mid \; \rightarrow n_3 \rangle. \tag{6.3}$$

By adding justification 6.3, we would force out the contradiction node c as required.

In general, DDB can make a node – e.g. a contradiction node – *out* by tracing back along the justifications as follows. If a certain node n is to be made *out*, DDB finds a valid justification j for n and tries to make j invalid. If j has a nonempty out-list, then one of the nodes in the out-list of j is selected and made *in* by constructing a new justification. If there are no nodes in the out-list of j, DDB tries to make one of the nodes in the in-list of j *out* (this involves a recursive application of DDB on the nodes of the in-list). If the in-list of j is empty, or if none of the nodes in the in-list of j can be made out, then DDB returns with failure. If, on the other hand, DDB succeeds in invalidating j, the labelling of the TMS is updated to take account of the newly added justification (using the algorithms described above). If n had only one valid justification in the original TMS, then n will now be *out*. If it had other valid justifications, DDB may have to be applied again to try to invalidate them as well. Again, it is important to see how the changes to the system's beliefs are made by tracing along the justifications linking them together. DDB encounters only those beliefs that could be relevant to the revision of the contradiction.

Before giving the algorithm for DDB, we turn to the question of what justifications it should construct to make nodes *in*. Clearly, a justification with an empty in- and out-list will achieve the desired effect. But we might be able to do a little better.

To see what is at issue here, consider the fragment of a TMS shown in figure 6.4, where c is a contradiction node. This time, there is more than one way to remove the contradiction, since either n_6 or n_7 can be made *out* by adding suitable justifications. Faced with a choice of nodes to make *out*, DDB simply chooses the first one it comes across, returning to the others only if it cannot make the first

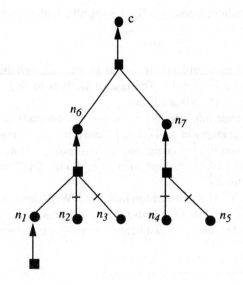

Figure 6.4   A fragment of a TMS with contradiction node c

choice *out*. Suppose that n_6 is chosen for being made *out*. One way to achieve this is to add a new justification for n_3. And, one possible justification for n_3 is justification (6.3), above, with empty in- and out-list. Since this justification will certainly be valid, it will lead to c's being assigned *out* as required.

Suppose however that, later on, the system acquires new information in the form of an additional justification which causes n_4 to become *in*. In that case, n_7 will become *out*, and the contradiction node c will be forced *out* whatever the status of n_3. Thus, when the new justification for n_4 arrives, there will no longer be any point in making n_3 *in*, since its only valid justification was added to the network expressly to avoid making c *in*. So it would be much better if the justification for n_3 were so constructed that, if new information arrives which makes c *out* anyway, that new information also invalidates the justification for n_3. That would avoid a situation in which n_3 was believed unnecessarily.

To construct such a justification, it is only necessary to look at the other nodes in the in- and out-lists of the justifications linking n_3 and c, and to include all of those nodes in the in- and out-lists of the new justification for n_3. Referring to figure 6.4, we see that n_3 is linked to c via one intermediate node, n_6. Looking first at the link from n_6 to c, we find that that justification has n_7 in its in-list: so we should put n_7 in the in-list of the new justification we construct for n_3. Turning now to the link from n_3 to n_6, we find that the justification has n_1 in its in-list and

n_2 in its out-list; so we should put n_1 and n_2 in the in-list and out-list, respectively, of the new justification we construct for n_3. The additional justification that DDB devises is therefore:

$$\langle\, n_7, n_1 \mid n_2 \rightarrow n_3 \,\rangle \tag{6.4}$$

If any new information arrives which forces c to be *out* anyway, that information will also invalidate the justification added by DDB for n_3, so that n_3 is not believed unnecessarily.

Generalizing from the above example, an algorithm for DDB is given below in the procedures makeout (set-of-nodes, ins, outs) and makein (set-of-nodes, ins, outs). One word of caution: this algorithm for DDB should be seen as an example of the kind of reason maintenance that *might* be used to model defeat by rebuttal in a TMS. (Even then, it is as it stands limited to TMS's in which there are no cycles present.) There are doubtless other ways of constructing additional justifications to force out contradictions.

The procedure makeout (set-of-nodes, ins, outs) takes a set of nodes (all presumed to be *in*) as its first argument and tries to add a justification to the TMS so as to make one of these nodes *out*; the procedure makein (set-of-nodes, ins, outs) takes a set of nodes (all presumed to be *out*) as its first argument and tries to add a justification to the TMS so as to make one of these nodes *in*. The additional arguments, ins and outs, form the in-list and out-list of any new justification created: that is, they represent alternative ways in which the contradiction node can fail to be *in*. As nodes further and further away from the contradiction node are examined, these lists grow. A call to makeout (set-of-nodes, ins, outs) can fail, since it can be impossible to make any node in set-of-nodes *out*; by contrast, a call to makein (set-of-nodes, ins, outs) only fails if set-of-nodes is empty.

To force out a contradiction node, c, in a TMS, we call makeout (set-of-nodes, ins, outs) with set-of-nodes containing the single element c and with ins and outs both empty. If this call returns failure, then c cannot be removed. If some nodes in the network have more than one valid justification, it may be necessary to repeat the process a number of times until c is finally made *out*.

The procedure makein (which is called by makeout) is relatively straightforward:

```
begin makein(set-of-nodes,ins,outs)
    if set-of-nodes is empty then
      return failure
    else
      let chosen be any element of set-of-nodes
      let set-of-nodes1 be set-of-nodes with chosen removed
      let outs1 be set-of-nodes1 together with outs
      add new justification ⟨ ins | outs1 → chosen ⟩
```

          to the justifications of TMS
        return success
      end if
end makein

The procedure makeout is a little more complicated:

begin makeout(set-of-nodes,ins,outs)
    if set-of-nodes is empty **then**
      return failure
    else
      until all nodes in set-of-nodes have been tried
      or success has been returned **do**
        let chosen be any element of set-of-nodes
        let ⟨ in-list | out-list → chosen ⟩ be any valid justification
          for chosen
        let set-of-nodes1 be set-of-nodes with chosen removed
        let ins1 be set-of-nodes1 together with ins and in-list
        call makein(out-list,ins1,outs)
      end until
      if success has been returned by any of above calls **then**
        return success
      else
        until all nodes in set-of-nodes have been tried
        or success has been returned **do**
          let chosen be any element of set-of-nodes
          let ⟨ in-list | out-list → chosen ⟩ be any valid
            justification for chosen
          let set-of-nodes1 be set-of-nodes with chosen removed
          let ins1 be set-of-nodes1 together with ins
          let outs1 be outs together with out-list
          call makeout(in-list,ins1,outs)
        end until
        if success returned by any of above calls **then**
          return success
        else
          return failure
        end if
      end if
    end if
end makeout

The detailed implementation of dependency-directed backtracking is, admittedly, difficult to follow. But the above procedures can be better understood by tracing through their operation with a simple example such as the TMS of figure 6.5. This TMS includes nodes for the beliefs flies(tweety) and ¬flies(tweety). These

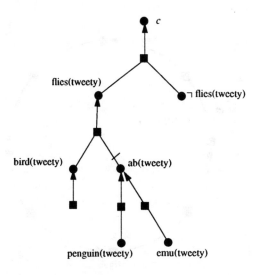

Figure 6.5   Backtracking in a TMS

beliefs are of course inconsistent, which is recognized in the TMS by the fact that they form the in-list of a justification for a contradiction node. As things stand, the TMS will label the nodes bird(tweety) and flies(tweety) *in*, and everything else as *out*.

Suppose now that new information arrives that Tweety cannot fly. This will be modelled by adding a new justification for the node ¬flies(tweety). The usual updating processes (as described above) will cause the contradiction node c to become *in*, thus triggering DDB. DDB will then trace through the reasons for c, looking for a way of adding a justification that would save it from having to believe the contradiction. In this case, the additional justification found would be

$$\langle \text{bird(tweety)}, \neg\text{flies(tweety)} \mid \rightarrow \text{ab(tweety)}\rangle.$$

After updating the status of all the affected nodes, ab(tweety) will be *in*. The reader might like to verify this observation. Notice that the nodes penguin(tweety) and emu(tweety) need never be accessed during this process. (See exercises 4 and 5.)

6.3   Circular justifications

6.3.1   *Groundedness and extensions*

In many applications of TMS's, cycles of justification can arise quite naturally. Suppose, for example that node n_1 represents a proposition of the form $\neg p \lor \neg q$,

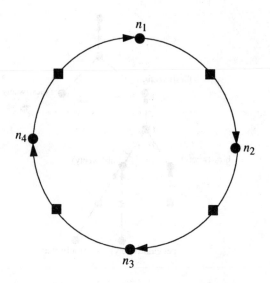

Figure 6.6   A circular TMS

and node n_2, the corresponding proposition $\neg(p \ \& \ q)$: then it would be natural for the system to have justifications to the effect that n_1 is a reason to believe n_2, and that n_2 is a reason to believe n_1. So, for some applications of TMS's, we need to know what to do when cycles arise.

The requirement that E be closed and supported with respect to $\langle N, J \rangle$ may lead to undesirable results when the graph of justifications contains cycles. For example, consider the TMS depicted in figure 6.6, in which each node is justified, ultimately, in terms of itself. For this TMS, there are two possible sets of nodes E which are closed and supported (according to the definitions of section 6.2.2), namely $E = \emptyset$ and $E = \{n_1, n_2, n_3, n_4\}$. (It is straightforward to verify that these sets are closed and supported.)

That the TMS should make no nodes *in*, given the circle of justifications in figure 6.6, is intuitively reasonable; that the TMS should make all nodes *in*, however, is not. It seems wrong that beliefs should be able reciprocally to justify one another in this way. Evidently, if we are going to rule out this sort of case, we need a characterization of non-circularity in the application of justifications. (See exercise 6.)

The standard approach in dealing with this problem is to jettison the notion of *supportedness* and replace it by that of *groundedness*, thus:

Definition *Let $\langle N, J \rangle$ be a TMS and $E \subseteq N$. We say that E is grounded with respect to $\langle N, J \rangle$ if, for every $n \in E$, there exists a sequence of nodes*

$$n_0, \ldots, n_h = n$$

also in E such that, for every g, $0 \leq g \leq h$, there is a justification

$$l = \langle l_1, \ldots, l_i \mid m_1, \ldots, m_k \rightarrow n_g \rangle \in J$$

with $l_1 \ldots, l_i$ among the $n_0, \ldots, n_{g-1}$, and with $m_1, \ldots, m_k \notin E$.

That is, a grounded subset E of N is one in which every node n lies at the end of a chain $n_0, \ldots, n_{h-1}, n$ of nodes such that each node in the chain is supported by a valid justification whose in-list consists only of nodes *earlier in the chain*. (Thus, the first element in the chain must be justified by a justification j whose in-list is empty). However, the notion of groundedness imposes no corresponding 'chain'- condition on the out-lists of the supporting justifications: the only condition is that the nodes in their out-lists not appear in the final extension E. Thus, if the node $n = n_h$ at the end of such a chain is justified by $j \in J$, then the in-list of j can contain at most the nodes $n_0, \ldots n_{h-1}$, but the out-list can contain nodes which do not appear in the chain. Finally we define:

Definition *Let $\langle N, J \rangle$ be a TMS and $E \subseteq N$. We say that E is an extension of $\langle N, J \rangle$ if E is closed and grounded with respect to $\langle N, J \rangle$.*

The intended interpretation of an extension of a TMS $\langle N, J \rangle$ is that it is a set of beliefs (from among the possible beliefs in N) which are justified by the reasons in J.

When no cycles are present, a set E of nodes is grounded if and only if it is supported. Thus, in this special case, the new notion of groundedness conforms to the intuitions developed in section 6.2.2. However, the notion of groundedness allows us to avoid some of the difficulties that arise when cycles are allowed. For example, it is not difficult to check that the TMS of figure 6.6 has the empty set $\emptyset$ as its only extension. To see that $\emptyset$ is an extension, observe that $\emptyset$ is closed for the TMS of figure 6.6 and, being empty, trivially grounded. To see that $\emptyset$ is the only extension, observe that any extension E of this TMS must be closed, and so must either contain no nodes or all of them. Thus: $E = \emptyset$ or $E = N$. To see that N is not an extension, we note that there is no node in N with a valid justification which does not mention other nodes in N. This fact alone is sufficient to show that $E = N$ is not grounded.

6.3.2 Computing the extensions of a TMS

It is not immediately obvious from the definition of extension given in section 6.3.1 how to compute the extensions of a TMS. However, it turns out – somewhat surprisingly – that a slight modification to `propagate-justifications` is all that is required.

First of all, we are helped by the following lemma, which gives an alternative characterization of extensions.

Lemma *Let $\langle N, J \rangle$ be a TMS and $E \subseteq N$ a closed set of nodes. Then E is an extension of $\langle N, J \rangle$ if and only if there exists a sequence of sets $E_0, E_1, \ldots E_N$ such that:*

1. $E_0 = \emptyset$

2. For $i \geq 0$:

$$E_{i+1} = E_i \cup \{n | \langle l_1, \ldots, l_h \mid m_1, \ldots, m_k \to n \rangle \in J,$$
$$l_1, \ldots, l_h \in E_i \text{ and}$$
$$m_1, \ldots, m_k \notin E\}$$

3. $E = E_N$.

What is significant for present purposes is that this lemma enables us to check, for a given set $E \subseteq N$ of nodes, whether E is an extension of a TMS $\langle N, J \rangle$. We simply start off with $E_0 = \emptyset$ and generate the successive E_i by applying as many justifications as possible (as prescribed in the lemma). Since the set of nodes is finite, the process must eventually stop, with $E_{N+1} = E_N$ for some N. There are then two possibilities: (i) $E = E_N$ and so, by the lemma, E is an extension, (ii) $E \neq E_N$ and so E is not an extension. (See exercise 7.) Note that the lemma does not directly provide us with a means of *finding* extensions of a TMS, since we have to know the final extension E to generate the E_i which ultimately make it up. This is where the slight modification to the algorithm propagate-justifications comes into play.

We can proceed as follows. First, we construct the partial status-assignment in which *every* node is marked as *undecided* – call it null-status-assign. Then we call propagate-justifications (j-set, null-status-assign), where j-set is the set of justifications in the TMS. In general, the resulting status-assignment will contain some undecided nodes. (If not, we have the unique extension and are done.) We take any node n which is still undecided in the resulting status-assignment and work separately on two different assumptions: first, that n has the status *in* in the final extension, and secondly that n has the status *out* in the final extension. Once we have assumed a status for n, we can apply the algorithm propagate-justifications again to see if we can make any more assignments on that basis. We can be sure the new assignments will be correct for any extension in which n has the assumed value. Again, if there are still unassigned nodes, we again choose one of them, say, m and work separately on two different assumptions: first, that m is *in*, and secondly that m is *out*, repeating the above procedure. Eventually, we will reach a stage where all nodes in N have been assigned a status. At this point, the set of *in*-nodes E will form our candidate extension, and we can then check to see if it really is an extension using the criterion of the above lemma.

The procedure is as follows:

begin find-extensions (j-set, node-set)
    let init-assign be the status-assignment in which all
      nodes in node-set have status undecided
    let assign-queue be the 1-element list containing init-assign
    let found-extensions be the empty list
    until assign-queue is empty **do**

let first-assign be the first assignment in assign-queue
let new-assign be the result of
  propagate-justifications(j-set,first-assign)
if there are nodes which are undecided in new-assign **then**
  select any node node which is undecided in new-assign
  form two new assignments from new-assign by giving node
    the status in and out, respectively
  delete first-assign from assign-queue
  add the new assignments to front of assign-queue
else
  check whether new-assign is an extension using the above lemma
  if new-assign is an extension **then**
    add new-assign to found-extensions
  end if
  delete first-assign from assign-queue
  end if
end until
return found-extensions
end find-extensions

The algorithm find-extensions correctly finds all of the extensions of a TMS. The critical observation is that the application of propagate-justifications completes all the status assignments forced by the justifications, given the assumptions already made about an extension. Efficiency improvements are possible (see further reading); unfortunately, however, these tend to make the algorithm difficult to understand, and we have avoided them here. (See exercise 8.)

Of course, merely being able to compute extensions given a set J of justifications is not enough: we must be able to re-compute extensions *incrementally* when new information arrives in the form of additional justifications. Subject to the provisos made below in section 6.3.3, this task can be accomplished by marking as undecided all those nodes whose status might be affected by a new justification (along the lines specified in prop-uncert) and using the resulting partial assignment as the starting point for find-extensions, rather than the status-assignment in which all nodes are undecided.

6.3.3 Multiple extensions

The possibility of circular justifications in TMS's opens a Pandora's box of complications and difficulties. In particular, it is not difficult to construct TMS's which have any finite number of extensions (including zero). For example, the TMS

$$N = \{l\}$$
$$J = \{\langle \mid l \rightarrow l \rangle\}$$
(6.5)

shown in figure 6.7(a), has no extensions; and the TMS

$$N = \{m, n\}$$
$$J = \{\langle \;|\; m \to n\rangle, \langle \;|\; n \to m\rangle\} \qquad (6.6)$$

shown in figure 6.7(b), has exactly two extensions, namely, $\{m\}$ and $\{n\}$. (See exercise 10.) The first of these TMS's is an example of an *odd-loop* – a circle in the justifications which is unsatisfiable. If l is *in* then it has no valid justification and so it should be made *out*; but if l is *out* it has a valid justification and so should be made *in*. The second of these TMS's is an example of an *even-loop* – a circle in the justifications which is satisfiable, but in more than one way. It is not clear what a reason maintenance system should do in such cases. (Remember: the function of reason maintenance is to decide which things to believe in the face of a given set of reasons.) Intuition does not give any clear guidance.

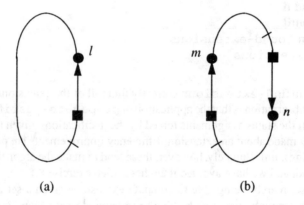

(a)   (b)

Figure 6.7   Circular TMS's with (a) no extensions, and (b) two extensions

Whatever, exactly, the TMS does when faced with zero or multiple extensions, the possibility of odd- and even-loops complicates the process of updating a TMS as new justifications arrive. The TMS pictured in figure 6.8 illustrates the sort of difficulty that can occur. This TMS is basically a combination of the TMS's (6.5) and (6.6) above. The node l participates in a potential odd-loop, much as in (6.5); the only difference here is that the justification for l has an in-list one of whose nodes, k, cannot be *in* (since k has no justifications). Thus, the absence of justifications for k serves to switch off the odd-loop involving l. The nodes m and n form an even-loop as in (6.6); the only difference here is that m is in the in-list of the justification for l. Since m and n form an even-loop, one of them must be in, but both may not be in together. Since k is out, the justification for l is unproblematically invalid, and l is also out. We can see, then, that this TMS has exactly two extensions, namely $\{m\}$ and $\{n\}$.

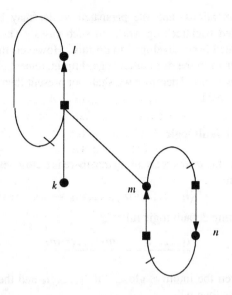

Figure 6.8   A problematical TMS

Suppose, then, that the system has opted for the former extension, and has assigned the status *in* to m and *out* to everything else. What happens if a new justification arrives for k, making k in? Suppose that, following the procedure of section 6.3.2, we mark all of the nodes whose status might depend on k as undecided. This is a simple matter of chaining through the justifications: the only node that depends on k is l. And suppose that, next, we run find-extensions on the resulting partial status-assignment. Now there is a problem. Since m and k are *in*, the dormant odd-loop involving l is activated, and there is now no consistent status-assignment for l. However, the new TMS (i.e. with the new justification for k) does have an extension – namely, $\{k, n\}$. It is just that the procedures suggested above for incrementally updating a TMS will not work.

It is not difficult to see where the problem lies. The original TMS of figure 6.8 has two extensions, $\{m\}$ and $\{n\}$, of which the former vanishes when a justification for k is added. The problem is that, if the system has chosen to use the former extension, it has no way of easily (i.e. incrementally) flipping to the latter when the new justification arrives. Unless it has stored the latter extension already, the arrival of the justification for k will mean that, basically, everything must be re-computed from the start. Thus, incremental updating is not possible unless the system stores all the possible extensions given its current set of justifications. Of course, the system could simply respond by marking everything as undecided and start from scratch, thus finding the unique extension. But that would rather destroy the point of reason maintenance systems.

We have discussed incremental computation of status-assignments in TMS's with circular justifications; and the persistent reader may be wondering how dependency-directed backtracking works in such cases. The answer is that algorithms have indeed been developed to do this. However, these algorithms are complicated, suffer from the difficulties regarding incrementality just mentioned, and involve no new ideas. Therefore we shall not present them here. (See further reading, and exercise 11.)

6.4   TMS's and default logic

It may have come to the reader's attention that there is a close resemblance between a TMS justification
$$\langle l_1, \ldots, l_i \mid m_1, \ldots, m_k \to n \rangle$$
and the corresponding default logic rule:
$$\frac{l_1, \ldots, l_i \; ; \; \neg m_1, \ldots, \neg m_k}{n},$$
since both are given the intuitive gloss: "if $l_1, \ldots, l_i$ and there is no reason to believe $m_1, \ldots, m_k$ then n."

Moreover, the definition of an extension for a TMS in section 6.3.1 is similar to the definition of a default logic extension given in chapter 5. Accordingly, we define:

Definition   *Let $\langle N, J \rangle$ be a TMS. The default theory constructed from $\langle N, J \rangle$ is the default theory $\langle D, W \rangle$ where*

1. *the individual nodes in N are treated as proposition letters in the language of $\langle D, W \rangle$*
2. *for each $\langle l_1, \ldots, l_i \mid m_1, \ldots, m_k \to n \rangle \in J$, D contains the default rule*
$$\frac{l_1, \ldots, l_i \; ; \; \neg m_1, \ldots, \neg m_k}{n}.$$
3. *W is the empty set.*

Thus, the set of defaults D is taken to be the set of translations of justifications in J, while the set of monotonic axioms W is taken to be empty. Notice, incidentally, that the above translation will yield defaults with empty in- and out-lists. We could instead have translated the justification $\langle l_1, \ldots, l_i \mid \to n \rangle \in J$ (with non-empty in-list and empty out-list) by the implication $(l_1 \& \ldots \& l_i) \to n$, and the justification $\langle \mid \to n \rangle \in J$ (with empty in- and out- lists) by the fact n, putting both in the monotonic component W. But doing so would have made no difference, and we will ignore this complication here.

Having set up a standard translation from TMS's into default theories, we can give the following correspondence result.

Lemma   *Let $\langle N, J \rangle$ be a TMS and $\langle D, W \rangle$ the default theory constructed from $\langle N, J \rangle$. Then a subset E of N is an extension of the TMS $\langle N, J \rangle$ if and only if $Th(E)$ is an extension of the default theory $\langle D, W \rangle$.*

We have seen how to construct a default theory corresponding to a given TMS, but what of the reverse direction? Suppose that $\langle D, W \rangle$ is a default theory. Can we construct a TMS such that the extensions of the TMS correspond one-to-one with the extensions of the original default theory? The answer is yes, but with some difficulty. The problem is that, in general, default theories involve logically complex (i.e. nonatomic) formulae, between which relations of implication obtain; and these relations must be constructed explicitly in the TMS. To take a trivial example, suppose the default theory contains the default

$$\frac{p \; ; \; \neg q \vee q}{r},$$

and suppose we construct a TMS having nodes n_p, $n_{\neg q \vee q}$ and n_r, corresponding to the formulae p, $\neg q \vee q$ and r, respectively. Then we could certainly translate the above default rule as

$$\langle n_p \quad | \quad n_{\neg q \vee q} \rightarrow n_r \rangle,$$

but we would also have to add a justification of the form

$$\langle \quad | \quad \rightarrow n_{\neg q \vee q} \rangle$$

to encode the fact that $\neg q \vee q$ is derivable. In general, it transpires that the translation of the default theories into TMS's is a difficult, though soluble, problem. However, it is at present unclear what the significance of such a translation is. (See further reading.)

6.5 Assumption-based TMS's

So far in this chapter, we have examined one model of reason maintenance – that provided by the notion of a TMS. A simpler and in many ways more elegant model is based on the notion of an *assumption-based truth maintenance system*, or *ATMS*, devised by de Kleer [5]. It is to this alternative model that we now turn.

6.5.1 Basic ideas

An ATMS, like a TMS, is a collection of nodes and justifications. In the simplest version of the ATMS (which is the only version we shall be concerned with here), all justifications are monotonic – that is, they have empty out-lists. Justifications in an ATMS are therefore of the form

$$l_1, \ldots, l_i \rightarrow n$$

with the intuitive interpretation that the belief corresponding to node n would be justified by the beliefs corresponding to $l_1, \ldots, l_i$. Thus, from a logical point of view, justifications are, in effect, ordinary conditionals. The nodes $l_1, \ldots l_i$ are called the justification's *antecedents*, and n its *consequent*. In addition, an ATMS distinguishes certain nodes as *assumptions*. Intuitively, the assumptions represent the changeable data on which the rest of the system's beliefs are based.

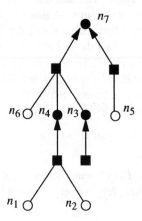

Figure 6.9   An ATMS: the white circles represent assumptions

Figure 6.9 shows an ATMS (notice that the justifications have no out-lists) with the assumptions, n_1, n_2, n_5 and n_6, marked as white circles.

The basic function of the ATMS is to *label* each of the nodes with those sets of assumptions which, according to the system's justifications, would support the belief corresponding to that node. The idea is that each node n should be tagged with a data- structure of the form

$$\{\{a_1, a_2, \ldots, \}, \{b_1, b_2, \ldots\}, \ldots\}$$

where $\{a_1, a_2, \ldots, \}$ is a set of assumptions which would support the belief in n, $\{b_1, b_2, \ldots, \}$ is another set of assumptions which would support the belief in n, and so on. A set of assumptions in an ATMS is called an *environment*. Thus, the basic function of an ATMS is to label each node with a set of environments which would justify that node.

We can get an idea of what this process entails by examining the nodes n_3, n_4 and n_7 in the ATMS of figure 6.9. Consider first n_3. This node has only one justification, which has no antecedents. Thus, n_3 is supported even if none of the assumptions is believed, and so gets the label $\{\emptyset\}$ – that is, the set containing just one environment: the empty set. Second, consider n_4. This node also has just one justification, which has assumptions n_1 and n_2 as its antecedents. Thus n_4 is supported if the assumptions n_1 and n_2 are believed, and so gets the label $\{\{n_1, n_2\}\}$ – that is, the set containing the single environment consisting of nodes n_1 and n_2. Third, consider n_7. This node has *two* justifications, one with antecedents n_3, n_4 and n_6, the other with antecedent n_5. Thus there are two sets of assumptions which would support n_7, namely, $\{n_1, n_2, n_6\}$ and $\{n_5\}$, and so n_7 gets the label $\{\{n_1, n_2, n_6\}, \{n_5\}\}$. In computing the label for each node – that is, a set of environments which support the corresponding belief – the ATMS is making explicit the dependencies implicit in its justifications.

Notice that, since n_4 is derivable from the environment $\{n_1, n_2\}$, it must also be derivable from any larger environment (remember: we are dealing only with monotonic justifications here) – in particular, the environment $\{n_1, n_2, n_5\}$. However, it would not be very useful for the system to associate with n_4 environments containing assumptions which are redundant as far as the derivability of n_4 is concerned, and so $\{n_1, n_2, n_5\}$ is not included in the label of n_4. More generally, the criterion is that labels contain only *minimal* environments, in the following sense: if E is an environment in a label, then that label does not contain any environment F such that E is a proper subset of F.

We can now state the job of the ATMS more precisely. Given a set of nodes (including a distinguished subset of assumptions) together with a set of monotonic justifications, the job of the ATMS is to determine, for each node, a label (i.e. a set of environments) such that: (i) the node is derivable from every environment in the label, given the justifications; (ii) no environment in the label is a subset of any other; (iii) if the node is derivable from some environment E, given the justifications, then the label contains some environment E' such that $E' \subset E$.

Before we go on to give the algorithm for computing labels for nodes, we need to explain how *revision* of beliefs is modelled in an ATMS: that is, after all, the whole point of reason maintenance. Since the justifications in an ATMS are monotonic, undermining of inferences by new information is impossible: once a node is derivable from an environment E, the addition of new justifications can never prevent that node being derivable from E. However, a form of rebuttal *is* modelled, by distinguishing a *contradiction node*, $\perp$, and using it to declare environments to be inconsistent.

The idea is as follows. To declare a set of nodes $\{n_1, n_2, \ldots\}$ to be inconsistent, an ATMS is given a justification

$$\langle n_1, n_2, \ldots \rightarrow \perp \rangle.$$

By finding a label for $\perp$ in the normal way, the ATMS is able to find environments that must also be inconsistent. An environment that is found to be inconsistent in this way is called a *nogood*. Belief revision then takes place in the ATMS as follows: once an environment is found to be a nogood, it, together with any of its supersets, is removed from every label in the ATMS. Thus, the ATMS only tags nodes with *consistent* environments from which they can be derived. In the presence of contradiction-nodes, the arrival of new justifications can cause nodes to have fewer environments in their labels.

Figure 6.10 shows the same ATMS as figure 6.9, but with the node $\perp$, together with one justification for it, added. Here, $\perp$ has just one justification:

$$\langle n_1, n_6 \rightarrow \perp \rangle.$$

So the environment $\{n_1, n_6\}$ is declared to be a nogood, and it, together with all its supersets are removed from all labels in the ATMS. Consider node n_7. Before

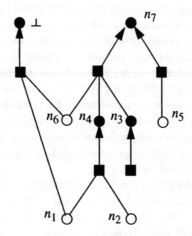

Figure 6.10   An ATMS with the contradiction node ⊥

the addition of the justification for ⊥, this node had the label $\{\{n_1, n_2, n_6\}, \{n_5\}\}$. But now that $\{n_1, n_6\}$ is declared nogood, the first of these environments must be deleted, leaving $\{\{n_5\}\}$ as the label for n_7. The labels of all other nodes are unaffected by the contradiction.

6.5.2   Computing labels for an ATMS

The algorithm for recomputing the labels of a node when a new justification is added is straightforward. Suppose that the new justification in question is
$$l_1, \ldots, l_i \to n$$
with consequent n. This new justification will in general cause additional environments to be inserted into the label of n. To calculate these new environments, we take the labels for the l_i in the ATMS. Let us suppose that these are:

$$
\begin{array}{ll}
l_1 & E_{1,1}, E_{1,2}, \ldots \\
l_2 & E_{2,1}, E_{2,2}, \ldots \\
& \ldots \\
& \ldots
\end{array}
$$

where each of the E's is an environment – i.e. a set of assumptions, from which the corresponding node is derivable. Then, to make a new environment for n, it suffices to select, for each of the l_i, an environment E_{i,j_i} from its label, and to collect all of the resulting assumptions together: $E_{1,j_1} \cup E_{2,j_2} \cup \ldots$. Of course, there will be many ways of selecting the E_{i,j_i} for each i; each such way produces an environment supporting n.

Once all of these new environments supporting n have been constructed, they are added to the existing label for n. It is then a straightforward matter to remove those environments which are supersets of some other environments, and also those environments which are supersets of a nogood. The result will be a correct label for n, taking account of the new justification.

The procedure for adding a justification is then as follows. First, a new label is computed for n as described above. Next, those justifications involving n as an antecedent are reprocessed resulting in new labels for their consequents. Next, justifications involving these consequents as antecedents are processed leading to new labels for *their* consequents, and so on. In this procedure, a node may have its label updated more than once (there is no ban on circular justifications), but the process is guaranteed to come to an end eventually, with correct labels for all the nodes. The only exceptional case is the node ⊥. When a justification for this node is processed, the nogood environments are removed from the labels of every node. The details are routine and need not be spelled out here.

6.5.3 Applications

The sort of reason maintenance performed by a TMS can help a computer make inferences by telling it how to revise its beliefs as new information arrives. However, it does not help much if the computer has the inverse problem of deciding under what circumstances a given belief would be justified. To get this sort of information from a TMS, it would have to *try out* all possible combinations of assumptions, and see under which of these combinations the belief in question was accepted.

Yet this sort of question is sometimes important. In particular, if an intelligent agent makes a surprising observation, it might well want to know what possible assumptions, singly or in combination, could explain it. The sort of reason maintenance performed by the ATMS is tailor made for answering questions of this kind. The conditions under which a belief can be accepted can be read off from the label of the corresponding node; and this label is updated incrementally as new observations arrive.

One application of this sort of reasoning is trouble-shooting in complex systems. Consider, for example, a computer program whose task is to locate malfunctioning components in electronic circuits. The program has a description of the circuit, together with a set of rules specifying how each component device ought to behave if it is functioning correctly. Now suppose that the program is provided with various observations concerning the actual inputs and outputs of the device. (These will in general disagree with the desired input-output pairings.) The task of the program is to say which components might, singly or in combination, be malfunctioning so as to explain these observations.

This inferential task can be viewed as a matter of reasoning backwards from a set of beliefs to the assumptions that would consistently explain them. If implemented using an ATMS, the nodes of the ATMS would correspond to propositions about the inputs and outputs of various components of the circuit, and its justifications, to the program's rules describing the typical behaviour of these components. These rules would have, in their antecedents, assumptions to the effect that the relevant components are functioning correctly (or, perhaps, that they are malfunctioning in certain specified ways). The task of deciding, on the basis of a collection of observations, which of these assumptions can be consistently believed so as to account for these observations, is then one which the techniques of the ATMS can be used to perform. (See further reading.)

6.6 Conclusion: defeasible reasoning and reason maintenance

The central insight underlying work on reason maintenance is that a belief-system should be thought of as a structure of reasons, by means of which belief-revision is controlled. Of course, this insight was not *invented* by AI researchers; on the contrary, it belongs to our commonsense conception of inference. In particular, the notion that an intelligent agent should retract beliefs based on discredited inference, or that it should revise its beliefs in the light of a contradiction, are paradigms of rationality. And the achievement of work in reason maintenance in AI is to have helped to articulate these notions and to investigate their computational consequences.

It helps to see this achievement in the light of the question we asked in chapter 1: what sorts of complexity must a device exhibit before we can sensibly describe it as *inferring* or *deciding* on the basis of its *beliefs* and *desires*? We argued in chapter 1 that part, though not all, of the answer lies in our ability impose a certain structure on the device according to which its computations are seen as heuristically guided movement through a space of possible inferences. The observations of this chapter suggest another kind of structure that may be fundamental to our ability to conceive of a device as making inferences: it must display the ability to revise its beliefs in the light of new evidence in accordance with the paradigms of rationality alluded to in the previous paragraph.

Yet it is important to realize that reason maintenance – at least as modelled by TMS's or ATMS's – also omits important inferential phenomena. Interestingly, it *disregards* the heuristic nature of inference, of which so much play was made in chapter 1. There are no heuristics involved in TMS's, because, ignoring the troublesome phenomenon of multiple extensions, everything is compulsory. While logics – including nonmonotonic logics – define a tree of possible inference sequences through which it is the job of the system's heuristics to navigate, a TMS leaves no freedom of choice, no latitude for individual preferences.

In a real inference system, both these aspects of reasoning must be included: on the one hand, a mechanism for directing inference so as to bypass beliefs unlikely to need revision, and on the other, a set of heuristics for choosing among the myriad possible inference sequences. But it is not at the time of writing clear how these phenomena are best combined into a single framework. The ideas described in this and the preceding chapters constitute advances along the path towards understanding the complex structure of inference. But the relationships between logic, reason maintenance and inference are still not fully understood.

Exercises

1. (Programming) Implement the algorithm `propagate-justifications` of section 6.2.2 and test it out on the TMS of figure 6.2. You will need to devise data-structures (in whatever language you are programming) to represent nodes and justifications, in such a way that the information required by `propagate-justifications` and `get-status-if-poss` is available. You may also find it convenient to write some programs to help you enter the nodes and justifications when setting up a TMS.

   Actually, the algorithm `propagate-justifications` is very inefficient, because it causes all justifications to be scanned every time the status of a node changes. Suggest some more efficient (but equivalent) way of propagating justifications.

2. (Programming) Implement the algorithm `prop-uncert` of section 6.2.2 and test it out on the TMS of figure 6.2 by adding some new justifications. Make sure you test justifications which cause nodes which were previously *in* to become *out*, and vice versa.

   Actually, the algorithm `prop-uncert` is very inefficient, because it marks as undetermined many nodes whose status cannot change as a result of j. Suggest some more efficient (but still correct) way of picking out the nodes whose status might change.

3. (Programming) Try out your implementations of `prop-uncert` and `propagate-justifications` on the example of figure 6.3. Make sure that the implementations are such that only those nodes are accessed that really need to be accessed.

4. In section 6.2.5, we described how DDB might force the contradiction node c in the TMS of figure 6.4 *out* by making n_3 *in* (and hence n_6 *out*). An alternative, of course, would be to make n_4 *in* (and hence n_7 *out*). We also described in section 6.2.5 how to construct justification (6.4) for n_3, which causes c to become *out*, but which has the property of becoming invalid if some other justification arrives forcing c *out* regardless of n_3. Construct a justification for n_4 which has the property of becoming invalid if some other justification arrives forcing c *out* regardless of n_4.

5. (Programming) Implement the algorithm DDB of section 6.2.5, and test it on the TMS of figure 6.4. Extend this algorithm so that it copes with the case where nodes have more than one valid justification supporting them.

6. In section 6.2.2, we presented a procedure, `propagate-justifications`, capable of computing, for a TMS with no cycles, a closed and supported set of nodes to be labelled *in*. What would happen if this procedure were executed on the circular TMS of figure 6.6?

7. (Programming) Using the lemma of section 6.3.2 as a basis, write a computer program which, when given a TMS, $\langle N, J \rangle$, and a set $E \subseteq N$ of propositions, determines whether E is an extension of $\langle N, J \rangle$.

8. (Programming) Implement the algorithm find-extensions and try it out on the problematical TMS of figure 6.8.

9. Suppose $\langle N, J \rangle$ is a TMS with extensions E_1 and E_2. Show that E_1 cannot be a proper subset of E_2.

10. It was claimed in section 6.3.2 that the TMS

$$\langle \{l\}, \{\langle \mid l \rightarrow l \rangle\} \rangle$$

has no extensions. Show that this is so. (Hint: if E is an extension of this TMS, then $E = \emptyset$ or $E = \{l\}$. Verify that $\emptyset$ is not closed and $\{l\}$ is not grounded.

It was further claimed that the TMS

$$\langle \{m, n\}, \{\langle \mid m \rightarrow n \rangle, \langle \mid n \rightarrow m \rangle\} \rangle,$$

has exactly two extensions. Show that $\{n\}$ and $\{m\}$ are both extensions. Show that the only other possibilities, namely $\emptyset$ and $\{m, n\}$ are not extensions.

11. Actually, the algorithm DDB given in section 6.2.5 can generate new justifications which, when added to the network, lead to circularities in the structure of justifications. Find an example where this happens. Suggest ways of extending the algorithm so that it can cope with cycles of justification.

Further reading

The presentation of TMS's in this chapter is simplified in one important respect: we have omitted any mention of CP ("conditional proof") justifications, which form a part of Doyle's original system. It turns out that CP justifications are messy to deal with, and do not add any important ideas. However, the reader interested in pursuing this topic is referred to Doyle [1]. We also simplified the account of backtracking in TMS's by confining ourselves to the case where no cycles can arise. For a more general (if not entirely easy-to-follow) account, see Petrie [11]. On the subject of the correspondence between default theories and TMS's: see Junker and Konolige [4]. For a selection of recent papers on TMS's, see Martins and Reinfrank [9]. De Kleer's ATMS is presented in the three papers: de Kleer [5], [6] and [7]. For an treatment of diagnosing faults in electronic circuits, see de Kleer and Williams [8].

A general theory of belief revision and theory change is presented in Gärdenfors [2]; at present, there is much interest in understanding the relationship between models of reason maintenance proposed in AI and the more abstract approach taken by Gärdenfors.

The models of reason maintenance presented here are extremely rationalistic, in that they pay no regard to the computational cost of following the recommended updating procedures. There is a certain amount of psychological evidence to show that humans follow nothing like the patterns of belief-revision prescribed by these models. In particular, there are some robust experiments which show that people often do not retract beliefs when their original reasons for those beliefs are abandoned. For an account of these experiments, see Nisbett and Ross [10], ch. 8. For an alternative approach to belief-revision based on the idea of *explanation*, see Harman [3].

Bibliography

[1] Doyle, J. "A Truth maintenance system", *Artificial Intelligence*, 12 (1979) pp. 231–272.

[2] Gärdenfors, Peter *Knowledge in Flux: Modelling the Dynamics of Epistemic States*, Cambridge, Mass: MIT Press, 1988.

[3] Harman, G. *Change in View*, Cambridge, Mass: MIT Press, 1986.

[4] Junker, U. and K. Konolige "Computing the extensions of autoepistemic logic and default logic with a TMS", *Proceedings, AAAI-90*, Boston, MA (1990).

[5] De Kleer, Johan "An assumption-based TMS", *Artificial Intelligence*, 28 (1986) pp. 127–162.

[6] De Kleer, Johan "Extending the ATMS", *Artificial Intelligence*, 28 (1986) pp. 163–196.

[7] De Kleer, Johan "Problem Solving with the ATMS", *Artificial Intelligence*, 28 (1986) pp. 197–224.

[8] De Kleer, Johan and Brian C. Williams "Diagnosing multiple faults", *Artificial Intelligence*, 32 (1987) pp. 97–130.

[9] Martins, J.P. and M. Reinfrank (eds.) *Truth Maintenance Systems*, Lecture notes in Artificial Intelligence no. 515, Berlin: Springer-Verlag, 1991.

[10] Nisbett, R. and L. Ross *Human Inference: Strategies and Shortcomings of Social Judgement*, Englewood Cliffs, NJ: Prentice Hall, 1980.

[11] Petrie, Charles J. "Revised dependency-directed backtracking for default reasoning", *Proceedings, AAAI-87*, Seattle, Washington (1987) pp. 167–172.

7 Memory Organization

Imagine that, while looking out of the window, you notice a distinctive sports car drive by. Seeing the car may cause you to think of other, related things. For example, you might be reminded of unusual cars you have seen, or recall the last time you were at a garage, or wonder about the vehicle's likely value. But your thoughts are not so likely to turn to unrelated subjects such as – say – toothbrushes or nuclear war. More generally – and this is surely an uncontentious observation – people's thoughts do not occur completely at random, but rather, in apparently regular or semi-regular sequences.

What function might this phenomenon of reminding have? One possibility is the following. Any system with a level of intelligence comparable to human beings must possess a vast store of knowledge on all manner of subjects, of which, on any given occasion, only a small part will be needed. If that knowledge is to be used efficiently, the system will need some mechanism for focusing attention on those parts of that knowledge most likely to be relevant to its current concerns, and for ignoring those parts likely only to lead to fruitless branches in its search spaces and to slow its thought-processes down. The question then arises as to how such a system's memory should be organized so that, as far as is possible, only useful information is recalled. In building a memory only part of which can be usefully processed at any time, what principles should control the way information is retrieved from it? This is the question we shall address in this chapter.

7.1   The need for memory organization

An example will help us to get a clear idea of the issues involved. Consider the following story:

> John went into a restaurant. He ordered a hot dog. The
> waiter said they didn't have any. He asked for a ham-
> burger. When the hamburger came, it was burnt. He left
> the restaurant.
> (7.1)

Anyone who understands this story must be able to answer the following questions:

1. Did John sit down?
2. Did John eat a hot dog?
3. What did the waiter serve John?
4. Why didn't John eat the hamburger?

$$(7.2)$$

Notice that these questions are not settled directly by the text, but must be inferred from the information given. Thus, we must infer that John did not eat a hot dog, because the restaurant didn't have any; or again, we must infer that the waiter served John a hamburger, because a hamburger came. Making these inferences depends on general background knowledge about restaurants: for example, the knowledge that customers in restaurants only eat things that the restaurant has, or that food is served by waiters in restaurants.

Clearly, then, understanding simple stories such as 7.1 relies, in general, on bringing to bear relevant background knowledge and combining it with the details given in the text. It follows that the ability to understand stories about a variety of subjects – restaurants, car crashes, VIP visits, earthquakes, terrorist incidents, etc. – requires that the reasoner have at his disposal bodies of knowledge relating to each of these subjects. Now consider the problem of getting a *computer program* to understand stories such as story (7.1), in the sense of being able to answer simple comprehension questions such as (7.2). Presumably, such a program would have to be endowed with the requisite background knowledge to support the inferences expected of it. And the question therefore arises as to how might we represent all this background knowledge.

The central insight underlying work on memory organization in AI is that this background knowledge must be structured in a way which facilitates recall of useful information. To take an extreme case, simply regarding a system's memory as a big bag of facts (represented, say, using predicate calculus formulae) about restaurants, car crashes, VIP visits, terrorist incidents, etc. all jumbled up together in no particular order, is not a sensible memory for a story-understanding program. For there is not usually much point in recalling just *one* fact about restaurants: if *some* piece of knowledge about restaurants is relevant to understanding a given situation, it is likely that other pieces are too. Much better, then, to organize the program's knowledge into *packets* of propositions that are likely to be useful together, and which can somehow be activated by appropriate cues. Thus, for example, we would expect the system to have a packet of information about restaurants – in particular, about the kinds of things and events typically associated with restaurants – so that all of the stored propositions could be retrieved together, in one go. That way, the program would not have to wade through oceans of irrelevant knowledge in its search for islands of useful information.

It is worth noting that there is another, older, name for such a packet of related items in memory: it is called a *concept*. A person may be said to possess the concept *restaurant* if he can recall and deploy, in a connected way, a suitable array of facts about restaurants and what happens in them. The nature of concepts forms a major topic in the cognitive sciences generally, but especially in philosophy, cognitive psychology and cognitive linguistics. (See further reading.) It is not clear to what extent the concerns of these disciplines mesh with those of AI, but theories of memory organization in AI can be viewed as theories of concepts. In the following sections, we shall be examining two proposals for memory organization. The advantages and disadvantages of these proposals are difficult to evaluate, and are still the subject of current debate. But the best way to get an overview of the general issues is first to look at some examples.

7.2　Scripts

7.2.1　A simple script-applier

We begin with a simple but influential proposal for a memory structure due to Roger Schank and his colleagues, designed to facilitate processing of stories about *stereotypical* situations, such as the story (7.1) of the previous section.

A *script* is a data-structure whose function is to encode knowledge about a stereotypical situation or sequence of actions such as a meal in a restaurant, the purchase of an article in a shop, a bus or train ride, a vehicle accident, and so on. For example, the information a story-understanding program would need concerning restaurants might include such details as:

> In a restaurant, the following sequence of events takes place.
> Some customers go into a restaurant, sit down at a table
> and wait. When a waiter comes, the customers order food.
> The customers then wait again until the waiter brings the
> food. The customers eat the food. Then, the waiter comes
> and gives the customers a bill for some amount of money.
> The customers give the waiter the money, and leave the
> restaurant.
> $$(7.3)$$

How might this information be encoded in a data-structure that a computer could process? An early answer to this question was provided in the program SAM (Script Applier Mechanism), by Richard Cullingford (Schank and Riesbeck [10]). SAM processes stories about stereotypical situations: restaurants, car crashes, VIP visits, and so on, combining its background knowledge about these events with the details of the story being processed. As a result of this processing, SAM can answer simple questions about these stories; for example, given the story (7.1) in the previous section, SAM can answer the questions (7.2). (In addition, SAM can précis the stories in English and Spanish). Since SAM is a somewhat complicated program, we shall, in this chapter, describe a much more basic procedure, `simple-script`, for applying scripts to process stories. Our procedure will lack much of the flexibility of SAM, of course. However, it will have the advantage of perspicuity.

First, we need to make some decisions about how to represent the story. SAM represents stories as lists of events written in an influential knowledge-representation language called CD (conceptual dependency) notation. (See further reading.) However, we need not concern ourselves with the details of this language, since knowledge-representation at the level of individual events is not at issue. We will suppose, therefore, that the story to be processed is a list of events represented using predicate-argument combinations of the kind familiar from earlier chapters. Consider the following restaurant 'story':

John went into Leone's, ate a Hamburger and left.   (7.4)

We will use the following data-structure to represent this story:

```
story(
    name(restaurant-1),
    events([enter(john,leones),          (7.5)
            orders(john,hamburger),
            leaves(john,leones)])).
```

Of course, for a story-understanding program to be useful, it must have access to a program which translates stories in natural languages like English into the requisite internal representations. In particular, SAM uses a program called ELI, which parses English sentences into CD notation. However, the processing of natural language and the many difficult issues concerning the way such processing interacts with reasoning processes lie outside the scope of this book, and we shall simply assume that the story has been processed into the format of (7.5).

We now turn to the restaurant-script, the data-structure used to store the knowledge in (7.3). Since the components of this data-structure must be matched against the story events, we shall employ a compatible notation. We therefore take the following data-structure to be our restaurant script. (Note: we here revert to the convention of indicating variables with initial capital letters.)

```
script(
    name(restaurant-script)
    variables(Customers,Restaurant,Table,Waiter,
              Food,Money),
    events(
      [enters(Customers,Restaurant),
       sits-at(Customers,Table),
       waits(Customers),goes(Waiter,Table),       (7.6)
       orders(Customers, Food),waits(Customers),
       places(Waiter,Food,Table),
       eats(Customers,Food),
       gives(Waiter, Customers, bill(Money)),
       gives(Customers,Waiter,Money),
       leaves(Customers,Restaurant)])).
```

The correspondence between data-structure (7.6) and the English version (7.3) should be clear. It should furthermore be clear that it is straightforward to store (7.6) in a computer. We shall assume that the script-applier has access to a collection of such scripts, one for each stereotypical situation that it knows about.

We now outline our script-applier procedure, `simple-script`. The first job of the script-applier, when processing a story, is to decide which of its scripts to apply. In SAM, a script for a certain type of event is activated when the story either (i) asserts directly that an event of that type has occurred, (ii) mentions another event which is spatially connected with a location in a script, (iii) makes a statement about the way an event of that type is a means to a goal, or (iv) asserts that some precondition of that type of event has been achieved. For example, the sentence "John went into a restaurant" would activate the restaurant script, while the sentence "Enver Hoxha, the premier of Albania, arrived in Peking" would activate the VIP-visit script, and so on. However, in `simple-script`, we shall avoid these details and simply scan the story for predefined trigger-words. For example, we might decide that the words "Leone's" (the name of a restaurant) and "hamburger", amongst others, should cause the system to access its knowledge about restaurants. This can be implemented using data-structures

```
        trigger(leones,restaurant-script)
        trigger(hamburger,restaurant-script)
```

to ensure that mention of Leone's or of hamburgers triggers the restaurant script.

Having decided to apply a particular script, the script applier then steps through the story, fitting the sentences it finds to the events in the script. Thus, the first event, `enter(john,leones)` matches the first script event `enter(Customers,Restaurant)` by assigning `john` to `Customers` and `leones` to `Restaurant`. As the sentences in the story are matched to the events in the script, the variables are bound consistently throughout the entire script.

In general, the story will contain sentences matching only some of the events in the script, with the remaining events being inferred. For example, when `simple-script` encounters the second event in the story (7.5), i.e. `orders(john,hamburger)` it finds that the next event in the script (7.6) which it matches is `orders(Customers,Food)`. The omitted events, namely,

```
    sits-at(john,Table),waits(john),goes(Waiter,Table)
```

are then *inferred to have occurred.* (Notice also that `john` has been substituted for the variable `Customers` here.) Similarly, `simple-script` will match the final event in (7.5), namely, `leaves(john,leones)` to the final event in (7.6), namely `leaves(Customers,Restaurant)` again leaving the intermediate events

```
  waits(john),places(Waiter,hamburger,Table),
  eats(john,hamburger),gives(Waiter,john,bill(Money)),
  gives(john,Waiter,Money).
```

to be inferred.

The resulting, partially instantiated version of the restaurant script will then be

```
script(
  name(restaurant-script)
  variables(john,leones,Table,Waiter,hamburger,Money),
  events(
    [enters(john,leones),
     sits-at(john,Table),
     waits(john),goes(Waiter,Table),
     orders(john,hamburger),waits(john),
     places(Waiter,hamburger,Table),
     eats(john,hamburger),
     gives(Waiter,john,bill(Money)),
     gives(john,Waiter,Money),
     leaves(john,leones)])).
```

Thus, the processed version of the story is:

$$
\begin{array}{l}
\texttt{[enter(john,leones),sits-at(john,Table),}\\
\texttt{waits(john),goes(Waiter,Table),}\\
\texttt{orders(john,hamburger),waits(john),}\\
\texttt{places(Waiter,hamburger,table),}\\
\texttt{eats(john,hamburger),gives(Waiter,john,bill(Money)),}\\
\texttt{gives(john,Waiter,Money),leaves(john,leones)].}
\end{array}
\tag{7.7}
$$

where the uninstantiated variables are taken to be existentially quantified. As a result, `simple-script` will be have made the inferences required to answer questions such as "Did John sit down?" "Did John give anyone any money?", etc.

The two operations just illustrated with reference to `simple-script`, namely the consistent binding of individuals mentioned in the story to variables in the script, and the filling in of events appearing in the script but not in the story, form the core of SAM's inference mechanism.

7.2.2   Some extensions of the script idea

The restaurant script just presented allows the processing only of the simplest possible restaurant scenarios. In particular, the story (7.1), in which the protagonist needs two goes to order, and then walks out in disgust, will be beyond its scope. But it is not too difficult to see how scripts could be made more flexible by some additional structure. Consider, for example, the data-structure depicted in figure 7.1, which incorporates branch-points and a loop. This data-structure might be used to represent the possibility that an attempt to order food fails because the requested items are unavailable, or that the customer rejects the food and leaves without paying. A program using such a data-structure as a basis for understanding scenes in restaurants would then be able to trace out several possible courses of

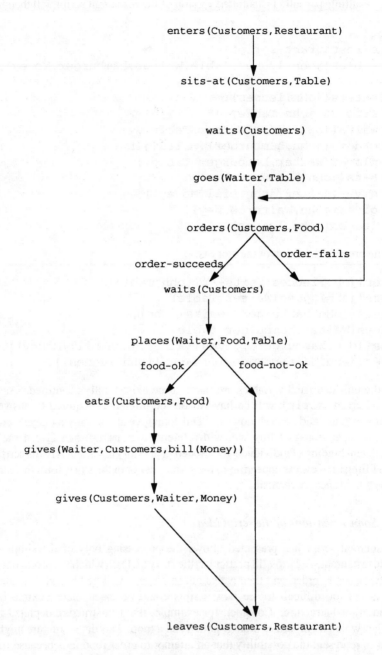

Figure 7.1   A more complex restaurant script

events. (Actually, the presence of the loop in the script of figure 7.1 implies that there are *infinitely many* such courses of events contained in the script.) Part of the script matching process would involve making decisions as to which of the possible courses of events best fit the given story.

Before we proceed, a word of warning. The restaurant script of figure 7.1 is set-out graphically; such diagrams are often used when discussing knowledge-representation in AI, because they are easier (for the human reader) to see at a glance, at least, as long as they do not become too big. But it is important not be misled by such graphical notations. The links in the diagram simply represent pointers which a program can follow, and any implementation in a computer language inevitably involves translating such a diagram into a data-structure looking much more like the script (7.6), except that there will be special constructs indicating branches and loops. Moral: what is important and distinctive in the data-structure of figure 7.1 is not the possibility of graphical depiction, but the structure of pointers linking the various component representations into a package.

We have discussed in some detail the idea that, in an intelligent system, knowledge about stereotypical situations should be bundled together into scripts. But how are these bundles to be organized in memory? Should a system's memory be an unordered bag of scripts, or should scripts themselves be organized into higher-level structures? In fact, the need for higher-level organization of such knowledge-packets has long been recognized. Firstly, many scripts will share important features, thus leading to duplication if scripts are treated as completely self-contained pieces of knowledge. Thus, much of what transpires in restaurants is shared with other sorts of dining events – e.g. sitting at tables and using knives and forks – and with other kinds of services provided on a commercial basis – e.g. not paying if the service is unsatisfactory. Ideally, we would like scripts sharing common elements to be linked together in such a way that they both pointed to some more partial or more abstract memory packet – e.g. memory packets containing information about *meals* or *commercial services*. Secondly, the organization of scripts into higher-level structures would aid the acquisition of scripts, since experiences gained in one situation could be applied to others. Thus, if the system acquires additional knowledge about the way meals are conducted, we would want it to apply that knowledge to its understanding of restaurants. Or again, if the system learns that unsatisfactory commercial services sometimes result in customers' refusing to pay, we would want it to be able to use that information to explain what happens in a restaurant when the food is inedible. One well-known program to tackle this problem is Dyer's BORIS system (Dyer, [1]). BORIS uses data-structures which are generalized notions of scripts called MOP's (Memory Organization Packets), devised to overcome the limitations just mentioned. Another, more recent, system is the CHEF program (Hammond [3]), in which the MOPs are recipes in Chinese cookery. CHEF builds and maintains a structured memory of recipes, which it uses to devise new recipes by modifying old ones. (See further reading.)

7.2.3   The logical content of scripts

The proposal that memory should be organized into script-like packets, perhaps linked together so as to permit the sharing of common elements, certainly has a great deal of intuitive plausibility. However, it is not without its difficulties, as we shall see in this section.

It helps to think of scripts as fulfilling two quite different functions. The first function is to encode beliefs – specifically, those beliefs we have about restaurants, car crashes, VIP visits, etc. – needed to make useful inferences from stories involving stereotypical situations. The second function of scripts, however, is to *guide* the reasoner's attention. That is, after all, the point of having packets of knowledge in the first place: they function so as to help the reasoner decide what to think about. For example, the procedure simple-script will not normally make just *one* inference about a restaurant story: it will make a whole block of them at a time, and will do so, moreover, whenever the restaurant script is triggered. Following the approach set out in chapter 1, we shall call these two functions the *representational function* and the *heuristic function*, respectively. Thus, the representational function of scripts is to encode various pieces of information; the heuristic function, by contrast, is to guide the reasoner in choosing what to infer and when to infer it.

Let us consider first the representational function of scripts. Suppose an AI system contains the script (7.6). In practice, any system capable of serious inferences about restaurants would have to rely on a much more complex kind of script; however, this complication does not affect the following argument. The script (7.6) is supposed to encode the system's beliefs about what normally happens in restaurants. Very well, then: *what*, exactly, does a system endowed with the script (7.6) actually believe? Put another way: what do data-structures of this type *mean*?

One answer suggests itself immediately. The meaning of the script (7.6) is just the collection of facts expressed in English in (7.3). But this cannot be right. For, given the script (7.6) and the story-representation (7.5), simple-script makes certain inferences, namely, that the events represented by the processed story (7.7) occurred. Thus, if the meaning of the script (7.6) really is given by (7.3), simple-script must be seen as making the following inference.

Premise 1:   In a restaurant, the following sequence of events takes place. Some customers go into a restaurant, sit down at a table and wait. When a waiter comes, the customers order food. The customers then wait again until the waiter brings the food. The customers eat the food. Then, the waiter comes and gives the customers a bill for some amount of money. The customers give the waiter the money, and leave the restaurant.

Premise 2:   John went into Leones, ate a Hamburger and left.

Conclusion: The following events took place. John went into a restaurant, sat down at a table and waited. When a waiter came, John ordered a hamburger. John then waited again until the waiter brought the hamburger. John ate the hamburger. Then, the waiter came and gave John a bill for some amount of money. John gave the waiter the money, and left the restaurant.

But this inference is surely not valid in any known logic. (The matter is a little obscure because it is not completely clear how the above statements about restaurants are to be interpreted.) If (7.3) really is what the script (7.6) means, then the inferences made by simple-script are just invalid.

We have a choice: *either* we say that simple-script makes invalid inferences, *or* we say that the script (7.6) encodes beliefs over and above those given in (7.3). Assuming, then, that we do not want to opt for the former, the question remains: what, exactly, does the script (7.6) mean?

A more plausible answer to this question would be something along the following lines. We regard a script, in conjunction with whatever mechanism is used to activate scripts, as a sort of *flexible if-then rule* of the form:

> **If** a person x enters a restaurant r, or eats a meal in a restaurant r, or is served food f in a restaurant r or ... (or whatever the script-activation conditions are) ...
> **then** those events will be a sub-sequence of the following sequence of events: x goes into a restaurant, sits down at a table and waits; when a waiter, w, comes, x orders food f. ... (or whatever the body of the script is).

This is, of course, very rough and ready. In fact, the flexible way in which scripts are fitted to stories makes it extremely difficult to specify their meaning in terms of a list of if-then rules having the same inferential import as the original script.

Proponents of logical techniques in AI often complain that, since there is no clear account of the meanings of scripts (at least not one that would justify the inferences made with them), the whole thrust of this approach to memory organization is hopelessly flawed. For, without a clear account of the meaning of scripts, it is difficult to evaluate any given proposal as to how they should be used – that is, as to what inferences they should support. True, one can try a given script-application procedure on some stories and see if it gives apparently sensible results; but this is hardly scientific. Compare the situation here with reasoning using a logic such as the predicate calculus. There, the semantics are clearly defined, and so inferences can be assessed for their ability to preserve truth; nothing like this exists for evaluating methods of script application.

Turning now to the heuristic function of scripts, questions arise as to *what*, exactly, that heuristic function is supposed to be. So far, we have spoken of a memory packet relating to restaurants as functioning so as to cause the system's knowledge about restaurants to be recalled all in one go. But what, in terms of the way AI systems process information, does "recall" mean here? There is more than one possibility. One is that memory packets function so as to *define the search space of possible inferences*, in order to make reasoning more manageable. Thus, in searching for a possible conclusion, the system might be restricted to the memory packets which are currently being accessed. Another possibility is that the memory packets function so as to *gather inferences together.* (This is the way we assumed scripts to function when describing the procedure simple-script.) Thus, the presence in memory of the *restaurant* packet might mean that the system does not standardly infer that someone ate a meal in a restaurant unless it *also* infers that the person entered the restaurant, sat down and paid the bill afterwards, and so on. The issue of how best to understand the heuristic function of scripts is not one that we have space to resolve here. Rather, the point we need to understand is this. Just as with the representational function of scripts, so with the heuristic function: the absence of any clear specification of how the script is *supposed* to function in inference makes it difficult to evaluate any script-application procedures that might be suggested.

Many of those researchers in AI who stress the importance of memory organization – particularly in the area of story-processing – do not separate out the representational and heuristic functions of scripts (or of the other data-structures in which they traffic). Let us recall the distinction between beliefs and heuristics that we drew in chapter 1. There, we put forward the view that a reasoner's beliefs should be seen as defining a search space of *possible* inferences, through which it is the job of the reasoner's heuristics to navigate. Indeed, we took it to be of the essence of data-structures which encode beliefs, that the inferences to which they actually give rise must be seen as located within a larger search space of possible inferences which they license. Insofar as this merging together of the representational and heuristic functions of scripts is deliberate, it represents a challenge to the framework of chapter 1.

7.3 Frames

Data-structures containing packets of general knowledge concerning some central theme are not confined to representing sequences of events; they can also represent everyday *objects.* Consider our commonsense knowledge about cars:

> A car is a kind of motor vehicle. It is used for transportation.
> Its method of operation is driving. Its principal components are
> a chassis and a body. It also contains seats, wheels, an engine, a   (7.8)
> steering wheel and a dashboard. It normally has a maximum speed
> of less than 150 mph. . . .

Again, it seems sensible for an AI system to organize its memory so that important and general facts about cars (such as those given above) are stored together in a packet, rather than being scattered at random amongst everything else the system knows about.

How might these memory packets be encoded in a data-structure that a computer could process? The data-structure normally used is called a *frame.* The basic idea is the same as that of a script – i.e. it is a memory packet – except that frames do not contain temporally ordered sequences of events. For convenience of representation, frames coerce all beliefs within a given packet into so-

```
frame: car
   structural-components:[body, chassis]
   parts:[seat, wheel, dashboard, engine, steering-wheel]
   function:transport
   maximum-speed: 150mph
   method-of-operation: driving
   is-a: motor-vehicle
```

Figure 7.2   A frame encoding the concept car

called *slot-filler* form. Figure 7.2 shows a frame-representation of the concept *car*, containing the information in (7.8). The symbols `structural-component`, `parts`, etc. are called *slots*; the entries `[body, chassis]`, `[seat, wheel, dashboard, engine, steering-wheel]` next to them are called *fillers*. Again, there is noting special about the graphical notation: in practice, such a data-structure would be stored in a computer in something like the following form:

```
frame(name(car),
        structural-components([body, chassis]),
        parts([seat, wheel, engine, dashboard,
                steering-wheel]),
        function(transport),
        maximum-speed(150mph)
        method-of-operation(driving),
        is-a(motor-vehicle)).
```

Obviously, slot-filler form is somewhat limiting; for example, it does not give us a straightforward way of saying how many wheels a car has. However, we shall not concern ourselves with the problem of introducing more complex representations into frames here. The key idea is that a sensible organization of memory should group facts about cars into a packet of knowledge which could be accessed in one go. That is, a sensible organization of memory should contain the *concept* of a car.

Notice that the categories of objects mentioned in this frame – chassis, wheel, dashboard, etc. – are themselves things about which similar packets of memories might plausibly be stored. For example, commonsense knowledge of dashboards might be stored using the frame :

```
frame(name(dashboard),
      parts([speedometer,fuel-gauge,thermometer,
            warning-light]),
      function(convey-information),
      is-a(instrument-panel),
      is-part-of(motor-vehicle)),
```

and commonsense knowledge of motor-vehicles might be stored using the frame:

```
frame(name(motor-vehicle),
      structural-components([body,chassis]),
      parts([wheel,engine]),
      function(transport),
      is-a(vehicle)).
```

(Again, we need not worry too much about the details.) Similar frames might be given for the other things mentioned in the car-frame: engine, steering wheel, transport, driving, etc. There is no reason why frames need to be restricted to representing physical objects.

Since an AI system with a knowledge of cars may well need to retrieve its knowledge on one of these related categories, it is sensible to view the relevant memory packets as being linked together into some larger structure. To say that one memory packet is *linked* to another is to say that there is a pointer from the data-structure implementing the first memory packet to the data-structure implementing the second, so that a processing program accessing the first memory packet can efficiently retrieve (i.e. without a search through memory) the contents of the second. Intuitively, the motivation is that thoughts about cars should lead naturally to thoughts about – say – steering wheels, motor vehicles, and dashboards, but not so naturally to thoughts about – say – toothbrushes.

The idea of linking networks of such memory packets together suggests that the techniques of property inheritance, as discussed in chapter 5, can be used to store information more efficiently. Take, for example, the fact that cars are used for transportation. Being a central fact about cars, it would seem to warrant inclusion in the packet of commonsense knowledge that should be retrieved whenever the system needs to think about cars. However, another central fact about cars is that they are *motor vehicles*, and a central fact about motor-vehicles generally is that they are used for transportation. So it seems sensible to store this fact in the memory packet pertaining to motor vehicles (or at some memory packet still further up the hierarchy), and let memory packets pertaining to its subclasses – cars, vans, trucks, etc. inherit that information. This linking together of frames can be depicted graphically, as in figure 7.3. Here, the arrows from the slots of one frame to other frames represent pointers to the memory locations where the relevant data-structures are to be found. Of course, exceptional cases which do not inherit the values from the slots of more general concepts can be recorded by simply filling in the appropriate slot, with the convention that more specific information overrides more general information. As we pointed out in chapter 5, some convention needs to be adopted to resolve the ambiguities created by multiple inheritance.

Like scripts, then, frame systems fulfil a representational and a heuristic function. The representational function of frames is to *encode information*: thus, links between the frames of figure 7.3 encode the information in (7.8), and some more facts besides. The heuristic function of frames is to *direct knowledge-retrieval*: the program responsible for making inferences, once it has decided it needs to retrieve knowledge about cars, will then have ready access to the related packages

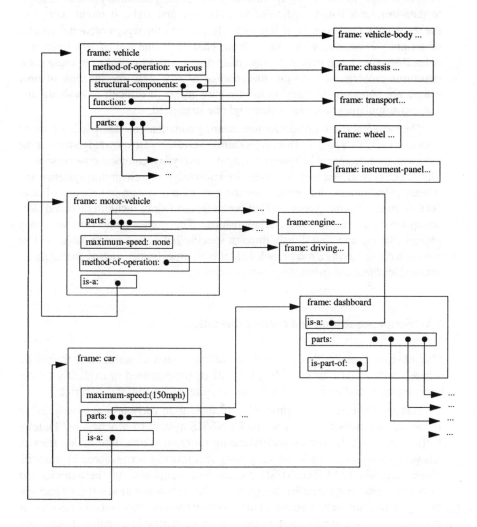

Figure 7.3   A collection of frames

of information by following the links from the car-frame to nearby frames. Of course, these frames will in turn contain pointers to still more frames. The further the links are followed, the less relevant to the original inferential task the retrieved knowledge is likely to be. The distinctive feature of frames – what sets them apart from knowledge-representation formalisms such as the predicate calculus, in which knowledge-bases are simply viewed as a bag of facts – is precisely that they are intended to support the kinds of reminding-functions just alluded to.

The remarks in section 7.2.3 concerning the importance of separating the representational and heuristic functions of scripts, and of a clear specification of both of these functions when evaluating the script-application procedure, apply to data-structures based on frames as well. At first sight, it might seem that the representational content of frames is clearer than the representational content of scripts. However, as we know from chapter 5, the use of is-a links for defeasible inheritance makes the task of giving the meanings of even these data-structures problematic. Again, the absence of any clear specification of how frames are supposed to function in inference makes it difficult to evaluate any frame-manipulating procedures that might be suggested.

The most ambitious project for representing commonsense knowledge in an AI system is the CYC project. This project aims to create a vast knowledge-base of the kind which its designers believe is essential to everyday, commonsense reasoning. The CYC system employs a variety of knowledge-representation systems and inference techniques; however, a central part of the system is network of over 5000 frames, containing over 4000 different types of slots, including *is-a* and slots for spatio-temporal part-whole relationships. The frames range from everyday objects like *car* and *toothbrush*, through specific but non-concrete 'objects' like *renting a car* or *buying a toothbrush*, to highly abstract frames such as *spatial thing*, *intangible object* and *event*. (See further reading.)

7.4   Script acquisition and concept formation

One obvious question that arises from the discussion of scripts and frames is: where do they come from? Must they all be programmed in explicitly by the programmer? And if not, how might an AI system form useful new scripts?

Perhaps the best way to proceed is to look at an early program designed to model the acquisition of scripts, the GENESIS system of Mooney and DeJong ([7]). GENESIS is a story-understanding program which, like SAM, tries to answer questions about a text by matching that text to a script stored in memory. However, unlike SAM, if GENESIS does not find a suitable script – i.e. a specialized knowledge-packet specifically designed for the current situation – it falls back on more general knowledge to connect the events of the story together. If GENESIS is successful in understanding a story using its more general knowledge, it may form a new script which can be used in future to process similar stories more quickly.

The following example illustrates the ideas underlying the script-formation policy adopted by GENESIS. Consider the following story:

> Ted is the father of Alice. He won $1 million in a lottery. Bob imprisoned Alice in his basement. Bob got $750,000 and released Alice.

Anyone who understands this story must be able to answer questions such as:

> Who gave Bob the money?
> Why did Bob lock up Alice?
> Why did Bob release Alice?

(though perhaps an intelligent agent could be forgiven for not being able to answer the last of these questions).

There are two quite different ways a computer program might go about this task. One way is to look for a predefined packet of knowledge – say, the *kidnapping script* – which could be applied to the story. Given the availability of such a packet, a large amount of commonsense knowledge about kidnapping becomes available to the program, in one shot, for making suitable inferences from the text. Thus it would be a simple matter for the program to instantiate the variables in the script and infer that Bob threatened Ted using Alice as a hostage, that Ted entered into a bargain with Bob in order to get Alice back, that this bargain involved money, and so on. This is, of course, the way SAM would tackle such a problem.

If, however, the program did not have any kidnapping script in its memory, there is another way it might still be able to make sense of the text, namely, by reasoning from general principles. Suppose, for example, that the program has access to rules such as:

> If x tells y that p, then y may believe that p.
> If x is the father of y, then x may love y.
> If x loves y and x believes that z is holding y captive, then x may want z to release y more than x wants $\$ m$

and so on. Such rules can allow the story-understanding-program to connect the events of the story in an explanatory chain. For instance, by supposing Bob tells Ted that he has imprisoned Alice, the program can use the events of the story to explain, by means of the rules just given (and others like them), how Bob achieved a presumed goal of acquiring money by means of imprisoning Alice. (There is no need to worry about the details of these rules here.)

However, the above story would be a difficult exercise for a program reasoning from first principles, because the explicitly provided details are sparse, and so the chains of inference connecting them are long. In particular, there is no indication in the story that Bob told Ted that he would release Alice if he gave him $750,000: the program is left to think up this crucial step on its own. This sparseness of the text would inevitably result in a very large search-space, and would consequently slow down the program's response.

An easier story for such a program to process is the following:

> Fred is the father of Mary, and a millionaire. John approached Mary.
> She was wearing blue jeans. John pointed a gun at her and told her
> he wanted her to get into his car. He drove her to his hotel and locked
> her in his room. John called Fred and told him he was holding Mary
> captive. John told Fred if Fred gave him $250,000 at Trenos then
> John would release Mary. Fred gave him the money and John released
> Mary.

Here, the search for connecting links between the propositions is much more constrained by the extra detail. For example, there is no need for the program to think up the crucial step that John told Fred that he would release Mary if he got the $250,000: that detail is mentioned in the text.

We can now describe the idea behind GENESIS. Given a story, GENESIS first tries to understand it by invoking a script (à la SAM). If this strategy fails, GENESIS falls back on general rules, and tries to chain these rules together to construct an explanation linking the events in the story together. But in the latter case, the amount of time GENESIS is prepared to spend is limited. In particular, the first (sparse) story above is so artificial that GENESIS gives up before it finds a solution, and so is unable to answer the above questions. However, when given the second (rich) story, GENESIS can connect all the critical sentences together in an explanation of such events as John's getting $250,000 and John's releasing Mary. Figure 7.4 shows part of the explanatory structure produced by processing the second story – specifically, that part which contributes to John's getting a quarter of a million dollars. Notice that some details of the story, for example, the fact that Mary was wearing blue jeans, being irrelevant to this explanation, are not mentioned.

At this point, GENESIS notices that a new explanation has been found for how an interesting goal is achieved (namely, acquiring money). GENESIS then takes this explanatory structure and generalizes it. The details of the generalization process will not be discussed here. (See further reading.) But the basic idea is that individuals in the explanation such as *Fred* and *Mary* are replaced in a consistent way by variables, and some of the specific properties and relationships involving them are replaced by more general properties and relationships that would serve the same explanatory roles (according to the causal rules which the systems knows about). The result of this generalization process is shown, in a somewhat simplified form, in figure 7.5. Finally, this generalized explanation is stored as a memory packet.

In effect, what GENESIS has done is to use its general knowledge to infer a novel plan for getting money, which we know by the name of *kidnapping*. (Obviously, GENESIS will not know this English word.) The stored plan can then be regarded as a script, much like the restaurant script (7.6), that can be invoked for story understanding by matching events in the story against events in the script,

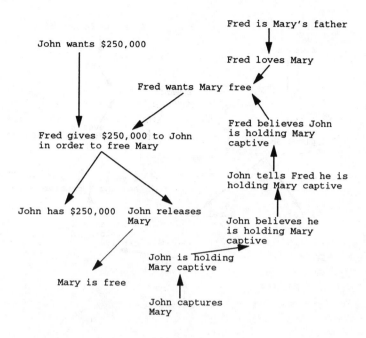

Figure 7.4   Explanation of the second story

inferring missing events and instantiating variables as required. Of course, there are some differences between GENESIS' kidnapping script and the restaurant script of section 7.2.1. Most obviously, the former contains an account not just of what happens in kidnapping, but of *why* it happens. However, the basic idea of a knowledge-packet of events that can be matched against events in a narrative is common to both sorts of script. Once GENESIS has built the kidnapping script, then, it is able to process the first story and answer the associated questions, without the need for extensive search. Thus, as a result of processing the second story and generalizing the result, GENESIS has created a new script which enables it to process stories that would otherwise have required prohibitive search.

We might describe the inference that GENESIS performs as acquiring or *learning* the concept of kidnapping. Notice that this kind of learning involves the packaging of existing knowledge into potentially useful chunks, rather than the acquisition of new information. The rules which GENESIS used to process the second story could, *in principle* (i.e. given enough time), have been used to process the first. What happened as a result of processing the second story was that certain of these rules were 'chunked' or 'compiled' into a single, one-step schema, which rendered practicable what was before merely possible.   The idea of learning as chunking or as compilation which results in increased efficiency of inference is a widespread theme, both in artificial intelligence and cognitive psychology. This

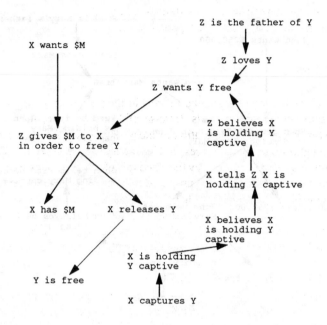

Figure 7.5   Generalization of the explanation of the second story

process is commonly studied within the context of rule-based systems. (See further reading.)

7.5 Conclusion

We began this chapter by arguing that a reasoner able to deal with a wide range of inferences about everyday situations must have recourse to some system of memory organization. In particular, we argued that pieces of knowledge about everyday situations and objects should be grouped together into packets, the contents of which can be retrieved all in one go. The underlying insight is simply that the facts stored in such packets are likely to be useful together. In particular, we examined two common types of memory packets: scripts and frames. In addition, we described work on the acquisition of scripts, and we saw how the formation of some concepts could be seen as the decision to generalize and store previous inferences. We pointed out the potential utility of this process in speeding up reasoning.

However, we also pointed out the difficulties associated with these data-structures. In particular, without a clear account of the representational and heuristic functions of these data-structures, it is difficult to evaluate AI systems that claim to make inferences with them. Important as the topic of memory organization is in AI, the theory surrounding it is still poorly developed.

Further reading

There is a long history of academic interest in the phenomenon of reminding. In 1739, David Hume published his *Treatise of Human Nature*, in which he propounded his theory of the *association of ideas*. Hume was fascinated by the way related thoughts follow in sequences, and his theory was supposed to account for it. The theory was very simple and, by the standards of modern cognitive psychology, hopelessly vague. Specifically, it proposed that the idea of one thing leads to the idea of something else which is either (i) *qualitatively similar*, (ii) *nearby in space or time*, or (iii) *causally related*. These three principles, according to Hume, were supposed to account for the way in which ideas follow on, one after the other, in human thought. It is instructive to compare Hume's theory with work on reminding in AI.

We mentioned in passing that, traditionally, much of the work on scripts has used a graphical form of knowledge-representation, called conceptual dependency notation. For an account of CD notation, see Schank and Riesbeck [10], ch 2. (Later chapters of the book contain an account of SAM.) There is a sizeable literature on the importance of different kinds of schemes for representing events, particularly concerning the relationship between "logic-like" representations (such as the predicate calculus) and "graphical" representations, such as CD. For an up-to-date survey of this topic, see Sowa [11].

The simplified script-application procedure, simple-script is very easily programmed in Prolog. See Sterling and Shapiro [12] for a version.

The best explanation of the use of structures of MOPs in reasoning is Hammond's CHEF system (Hammond [3]). CHEF is a planning program, where the plans in question are recipes for Chinese dishes. The program finds plans for new dishes by *modifying* plans for similar dishes which it knows have worked. This approach is sometimes called *case-based reasoning*, because of the heavy reliance on remembered cases. A good introduction to the techniques of case-based reasoning is Riesbeck and Schank [9]. Clearly, memory-organization is at the heart of this approach to reasoning. Again, however, this approach suffers from problem that, since the meanings of its data-structures are unclear, it is often difficult to evaluate the inferences made with them.

Progress on the CYC project, in which frames play a particularly important role, is described in Lenat and Guha [6] and Guha and Lenat [2].

The GENESIS system is described in detail in Mooney and DeJong [7]. This paper raises a number of issues which we have ignored here, in particular, the question of *when* to generalize pieces of reasoning to form new concepts. The idea that concept-formation proceeds by chunking together and storing inferences for future use has been championed by a number of psychologists and computer scientists. See, for example, Laird, Rosenbloom and Newell [4] and Newell [8]. These researchers claim that certain empirical results on human acquisition of cognitive skills, such as the so-called power law of learning, can be explained by taking such skill acquisition to be a matter of compiling chains of relatively general if-then rules into relatively special-purpose, single-step if-then rules.

For an interesting account of conceptual organization from the point of view of cognitive linguistics, see Lakoff [5].

Bibliography

[1] Dyer, M. *In-Depth Understanding: A Computer Model of Integrated Processing for Narrative Comprehension*, Cambridge, MA: MIT Press, 1983.

[2] Guha, R.V. and D. Lenat "CYC: A midterm Report", *AI Magazine*, Fall, 1990, pp. 32–59.

[3] Hammond, Kristian, J. *Case-Based Planning: Viewing Planning as a Memory Task*, Boston: Academic Press, 1989.

[4] Laird, J., P. Rosenbloom and A. Newell *Universal Subgoaling and Chunking: The Automatic Generation and Learning of Goal Hierarchies*, Dordrecht: Kluwer, 1986

[5] Lakoff, George *Women, Fire and Dangerous Things*, Chicago: Chicago University Press, 1987.

[6] Lenat, Douglas B. and R.V. Guha *Building Large Knowledge-Based Systems: Representation and Inference in the Cyc Project*, Reading, MA: Addison-Wesley, 1989.

[7] Mooney, R. and G. DeJong "Learning Schemata for Natural Language Processing", *Proceedings, IJCAI-85* (1985) pp. 681–687.

[8] Newell, A. *Unified Theories of Cognition*, Cambridge, MA: Harvard University Press, 1990.

[9] Riesbeck, C. K. and R.C. Schank (eds.) *Inside Case-based Reasoning*, Hillsdale, NJ: Lawrence Erlbaum, 1989.

[10] Schank, R. C. and C. K. Riesbeck (eds.) *Inside Computer Understanding: Five Programs Plus Miniatures*, Hillsdale, NJ: Lawrence Erlbaum, 1981.

[11] Sowa, John (ed.) *Principles of Semantic Networks: Explorations in the Representation of Knowledge*, San Mateo, CA: Morgan Kaufmann, 1991.

[12] Sterling, Leon and Ehud Shapiro *The Art of Prolog*, Cambridge, MA: MIT Press, 1987.

8 Probabilistic Inference

In previous chapters, we have seen how various nonmonotonic formalisms can be used to model uncertain reasoning. However, none of these formalisms gives us any way of representing *degrees* of uncertainty associated with beliefs or modes of inference. And it is not difficult to think of applications of artificial intelligence systems which require the ability to quantify uncertainty. The AI literature contains a variety of formalisms for representing degrees of uncertainty. Of these, one has by far the longest history (dating back to the 17th century) and the best theoretical motivation: probability theory. In this chapter, we shall discuss probability theory and the problems arising in developing computer systems which reason probabilistically.

The central problem which any formalism for representing degrees of uncertainty must address is that of how to *combine* uncertainties associated with information from different pieces of evidence. Consider, for example, a computer program designed to produce medical diagnoses given a range of symptoms exhibited by a patient. Each one of the symptoms is more or less indicative of various medical conditions. One problem which the designers of the program must solve is how to fuse a number of observations about the patient to obtain likelihoods for the various possible diagnoses. The key advantage of probability theory as a basis for representing uncertainty in such a system is that it provides a solution to this problem. In this chapter, we see how to build a program which reasons with uncertain information using probability theory as a theoretical basis.

The plan of the chapter is as follows. We begin by arguing the case for using probability theory: specifically, we claim that any method for representing uncertainty that is not in agreement with probability theory must exhibit certain undesirable features. Next, we show that using probability theory imposes problematic computational requirements on any inference system: specifically, we show that the use of probability theory in general requires storage of a large amount of data. Finally, we discuss methods of meeting these requirements, and show how these methods can be used to construct programs for probabilistic inference.

8.1 Subjective probability

We begin, then, with the argument for probability theory. Our approach will be to define probabilities in terms of the *betting* behaviour that they can be expected to induce. For example, suppose I offer you the following bet on a horse race: I pay you £x if *Red Rum* wins; you pay me £10 if *Red Rum* loses. Whether or not you accept this bet (for given winnings x) is a function of how likely you think *Red Rum* is to win the race. The better you think *Red Rum*'s chances are, the smaller the potential winnings x can be for which you will accept the bet. For example, if you are sure of Red Rum's victory, you will accept a bet in which the winnings are only, say, £1, since then you have an excellent chance of winning £1 and only a slim chance of losing £10. If you doubt that *Red Rum* will win, then you will not accept the bet unless the potential winnings are very high, say £100. To repeat: the *greater* your confidence that something will happen, the *worse* the odds you are prepared to accept when offered a bet.

This fact suggests the possibility of using betting dispositions (which we can observe) to quantify degrees of certainty (which we cannot). Thus:

Definition   *A bet on proposition a at odds m : n is a transaction between an agent and a bookie in which, for some $\lambda \neq 0$, the bookie agrees to pay the agent λm units of money should a turn out to be true, and the agent agrees to pay the bookie λn units of money should a turn out to be false.*

Definition   *Suppose that h is the smallest number such that an agent will accept a bet on a at odds h : 1. We may say that he thinks $\neg a$ is h times as likely a. On this basis, and so as to make the likelihoods of a and $\neg a$ add up to 1, we say that the subjective probability which the agent assigns to proposition a is*

$$p(a) = \frac{1}{1+h}.$$

This approach to probabilities is sometimes called *subjectivism*, because the probability of a proposition is defined in terms of the degree of belief which a particular agent (or subject) places in that proposition. Thus, subjective probabilities are agent-relative, since different agents may have different betting dispositions. Subjectivism contrasts with *objectivism*, in which probabilities are defined in terms of (objective) *frequencies* of occurrence. This is not the place to go into the debate between subjectivism and objectivism. (See further reading.) Henceforth, we shall assume the subjectivist approach and speak simply of *probability* when we mean subjective probability.

Probability, on the subjectivist approach, appears at first glance to be a very unconstrained affair. After all, who is to say what bets an agent may or may not be prepared to accept? So who is to say what probabilities he should assign to various propositions? However, as we shall now see, some combinations of degrees of belief exhibit some very undesirable features.

Let a and b be propositions, and suppose an agent adopts the following probabilities:

$$p(a) = 0.6, \quad p(b) = 0.5, \quad p(\neg(a \lor b)) = 0.25, \quad p(\neg(a\&b)) = 0.7. \qquad (8.1)$$

(Notice that probabilities may be assigned to logically complex propositions as well as to atomic propositions.) According to the definition of probability, the agent will then accept the following bets if they are offered to him (amounts in £'s)

bet 1:	40 to 60 on a
bet 2:	50 to 50 on b
bet 3:	75 to 25 on $\neg(a \lor b)$
bet 4:	30 to 70 on $\neg(a \& b)$

Let us look at the payoffs in the four situations that can arise:

a	b	bet 1	bet 2	bet 3	bet 4	net outcome
T	T	win 40	win 50	lose 25	lose 70	lose 5
T	F	win 40	lose 50	lose 25	win 30	lose 5
F	T	lose 60	win 50	lose 25	win 30	lose 5
F	F	lose 60	lose 50	win 75	win 30	lose 5

We see that the agent is logically guaranteed to lose £5 no matter what happens. Clearly, then, this combination of probabilities is one to be to avoided!

The question arises as to whether we can say anything more general about which combinations of probabilities are sensible and which are not. Let us make the following idealizing assumption:

> If an agent declines a bet on a at odds $m : n$, he will accept a bet on $\neg a$ at odds $n : m$.

This says, effectively, that probabilities are defined for all propositions. Obviously, it is an idealizing assumption, rather like the assumption of frictionless motion in physics problems. (After all, few people would bet their life savings on the toss of a coin, even with favourable odds.) However, this assumption is useful in thinking about what properties degrees of belief ought to have. For it can be shown that, if the agent's degrees of belief do not obey the axioms (8.2) given below, then it is possible to construct a so-called *Dutch book* against the agent:

Definition *A Dutch book is a sequence of bets, each of which the agent is disposed – given his degrees of belief – to accept, yet which taken together will cause the agent to lose money no matter what happens.*

The axioms are, for all propositions ϕ and ψ:

$$\text{(i)} \quad \text{if } \vdash \phi \text{ then } p(\phi) = 1$$
$$\text{(ii)} \quad \text{if } \vdash \neg\phi \text{ then } p(\phi) = 0$$
$$\text{(iii)} \quad \text{if } \phi \vdash \psi \text{ then } p(\phi) \leq p(\psi)$$
$$\text{(iv)} \quad p(\phi \lor \psi) = p(\phi) + p(\psi) - p(\phi \& \psi). \tag{8.2}$$

Notice that axiom (iii) guarantees that logically equivalent formulae have the same probability. (See exercise 1.)

The above sequence of bets is then a Dutch book constructed against an agent who has the subjective probabilities in (8.1), which is a violation of the axiom (iv).

To repeat: *any* violation of the axioms (8.2) leads to the possibility of a Dutch book, though we shall not prove the general result here. (See further reading.)

A *probability distribution* p over a language is an assignment to each proposition in the language of a real number in the range $[0, 1]$, such that the overall assignment obeys axioms (8.2) for all propositions ϕ and ψ. The above considerations suggest that degrees of belief for a rational agent can be captured, given certain idealizing assumptions, using a probability distribution. Notice that a probability distribution, being a mapping from propositions to their probabilities, will in general require a great deal of information. We will see presently how to specify probability distributions.

The foregoing argument is the basic rationale for the use of probabilities in quantifying uncertainty: if uncertainty is an aspect of mind that conditions, amongst other things, betting dispositions, then, under certain idealizing assumptions, that aspect of mind ought to admit of quantification as a probability distribution – i.e. an assignment of probabilities obeying the above axioms. (But see exercise 2.) However, it should be pointed out that the approach taken above is only one among several ways of justifying the above axioms and, in the sequel, we shall be focusing on the technical results of those axioms, which hold independently of the underlying philosophical motivation.

8.2 Conditional probability

It is obvious that degrees of belief ought in general to change in response to new information. Thus, a doctor may revise his confidence in a given diagnosis as new test results become available, or a meteorologist may change his forecast as he receives additional reports from weather stations. The question arises, if degrees of belief are represented in terms of a probability distribution, as to how those degrees of belief ought to be revised in response to new information.

We begin with a definition.

Definition *If ϕ and ψ are propositions over which the probability distribution p is defined, we say that the conditional probability of ϕ given ψ is the quantity*

$$p(\phi \mid \psi) = \frac{p(\phi \& \psi)}{p(\psi)} \tag{8.3}$$

Now, we adopt the following proposal:

Proposal *If an agent's current degrees of belief are given by the probability distribution p, and the agent later comes to accept proposition ψ as certain, where $p(\psi) \neq 0$, then his new degrees of belief should be given by the probability distribution p_ψ defined as:*

$$p_\psi(\phi) = p(\phi \mid \psi) \tag{8.4}$$

Note the different status of the two equations above: equation (8.3) is a definition of the expression "$p(\phi \mid \psi)$"; equation (8.4), however, makes a substantive claim about the way agents should revise their probabilities. This way of updating probabilities is called *conditionalizing*, or *Bayesian updating*.

Technically, we must show:

Lemma *For any probability distribution p, and any proposition ψ such that $p(\psi) \neq 0$, the function p_ψ, defined by equation (8.4), is also a probability distribution.*

That is to say, we must show that, if an agent's degrees of belief obey the axioms (8.2), and the agent then conditionalizes on a proposition ψ, his new degrees of belief will also obey the axioms (8.2). The proof is a matter of checking that the axioms hold for the new probability distribution. We illustrate in the case of axiom (i). Suppose that $\vdash \phi$. We must show that $p_\psi(\phi) = 1$. This means showing that

$$p_\psi(\phi) = p(\phi \mid \psi) = \frac{p(\phi\&\psi)}{p(\psi)} = 1.$$

That is, we simply need to show that $p(\phi\&\psi) = p(\psi)$. But if $\vdash \phi$, then $\psi \vdash (\phi\&\psi)$, and we certainly have $(\phi\&\psi) \vdash \psi$; so two applications of axiom (iii) suffice two show that $p(\phi\&\psi) = p(\psi)$ as required. (See exercise 3.)

Conditionalizing has a number of properties which one might expect any decent belief-revision methodology to exhibit. For example, suppose p is a probability distribution and ϕ, ψ and π are propositions. If we learn that π is true, then we should update our probabilities to reflect this new knowledge. This means changing from probability distribution p to probability distribution p_π. Suppose further that we subsequently learn that ψ is true. We should then again update the probability distribution to $(p_\pi)_\psi$. According to equations (8.3) and (8.4), the new probability of ϕ after learning first that π is true, and then that ψ is true is given by:

$$(p_\pi)_\psi(\phi) = p_\pi(\phi|\psi) = \frac{p_\pi(\phi\&\psi)}{p_\pi(\psi)} = \frac{p(\phi\&\psi\&\pi)/p(\pi)}{p(\psi\&\pi)/p(\pi)} =$$

$$\frac{p(\phi\&\psi\&\pi)}{p(\psi\&\pi)} = p(\phi|\psi\&\pi) = p_{\psi\&\pi}(\phi).$$

That is to say: learning π and then ψ always has the same effect on one's degrees of belief as learning the conjunctive proposition $\psi\&\pi$. And since $\psi\&\pi$ is logically equivalent to $\pi\&\psi$, it follows that learning π and then ψ always has the same effect on one's degrees of belief as learning ψ and then π. That is to say, the effect of various pieces evidence on one's degrees of belief does not depend on the *order* in which that evidence is considered. This seems intuitively correct.

8.3 Some basic results of probability theory

In this section we examine some simple results that follow from the axioms (8.2). First, some standard definitions:

Definition *Propositions $a_1, ..., a_n$ are mutually exclusive if at most one is true, i.e., if*

$$p(a_i \& a_j) = 0, \text{for } i \neq j.$$

Propositions $a_1, ..., a_n$ are jointly exhaustive if at least one is true, i.e.. if

$$p(a_1 \vee ... \vee a_n) = 1.$$

Propositions $a_1, ..., a_n$ form a partition if exactly one is true, i.e., if

$$p(a_i \& a_j) = 0, \text{for } i \neq j \quad \text{and} \quad p(a_1 \vee ... \vee a_n) = 1.$$

It is easy to show from the axioms that:

Lemma *If $a_1, ..., a_n$ are mutually exclusive, then*

$$p(a_1 \vee ... \vee a_n) = p(a_1) + ... + p(a_n).$$

If $a_1, ..., a_n$ form a partition, then

$$p(a_1) + ... + p(a_n) = 1.$$

The latter is sometimes written $\sum_{i=1}^{n} p(a_i) = 1$.

The above lemma tells us what information we need in order to compute the probability of an arbitrary proposition, ϕ. Suppose we are concerned with a language having N proposition letters $e_1, ..., e_N$, together with all the usual Boolean connectives. There are 2^N possible assignments of truth-values to the e_i (corresponding to the rows of a truth-table). The state of affairs represented by any such assignment of truth-values can be described by a formula of the form:

$$\epsilon_1 \& \epsilon_2 \& ... \& \epsilon_N \tag{8.5}$$

where, for $i = 1$ to n, ϵ_i is either e_i or $\neg e_i$. The 2^N distinct formulae of the form (8.5) are called *state descriptions*; let us denote them by $\sigma_1, ..., \sigma_{2^N}$. If ϕ is any formula in the language, then we can collect together those state descriptions (if any), $\sigma_{i_1}, ..., \sigma_{i_m}$ in which ϕ is true. Then we have

$$\phi \iff \sigma_{i_1} \vee ... \vee \sigma_{i_m}$$

where $\iff$ denotes logical equivalence. The disjunctive formula $\sigma_{i_1}, ..., \sigma_{i_m}$ is called the *disjunctive normal form* of ϕ. Since the σ_i are mutually exclusive, using the above lemma, we have

$$p(\phi) = p(\sigma_{i_1}) + ... + p(\sigma_{i_m}).$$

Thus, to compute the probability of any proposition ϕ, it suffices to know the probabilities of all the state descriptions.

However, it is also important to note what does *not* follow from our axioms. One important point is that, given values for $p(a)$ and $p(b)$, it is *not* in general possible to determine $p(a\&b)$ or $p(a \vee b)$. In fact there is nothing to stop $p(a\&b)$ taking any value between 0 and $\min(p(a), p(b))$. In particular, the probability of a state description σ cannot be computed from the probabilities of the ϵ_i that make it up. Thus, to specify a probability distribution over a propositional language using the proposition letters $e_1, \ldots, e_n$, we need to specify the probabilities of every *state description*, of which there are 2^N. (Actually, since the probabilities of all the state-descriptions add up to 1, we only need to specify $2^N - 1$ of them.) Thus, given N proposition letters, we need to know $2^N - 1$ probabilities to be able to calculate the probability of an arbitrary proposition ϕ. Even for modest numbers of propositions, this is impracticable: if $N = 30$, $2^N - 1 \approx 1$ billion.

Thus we are left with something of a dilemma. On the one hand, we have argued that, unless we want an agent to be open to Dutch book arguments, his degrees of belief must be such that they can be represented as a probability distribution. On the other hand, we have shown that probability distributions can be expensive in terms of storage. Our task, in the remainder of this chapter, will be to investigate conditions under which probability distributions can be stored more compactly, and how these more compact representations can be used for probabilistic inference in AI.

One final technical result before we proceed.

Lemma *Given two propositions ϕ and ψ with non-zero probabilities, one of the following three cases obtains:*
1. *the equations*

$$p(\phi\&\psi) = p(\phi)p(\psi)$$
$$p(\phi \mid \psi) = p(\phi) = p(\phi \mid \neg\psi)$$
$$p(\psi \mid \phi) = p(\psi) = p(\psi \mid \neg\phi)$$

all hold, in which case, ϕ and ψ are said to be independent;
2. *the inequalities*

$$p(\phi\&\psi) > p(\phi)p(\psi)$$
$$p(\phi \mid \psi) > p(\phi) > p(\phi \mid \neg\psi)$$
$$p(\psi \mid \phi) > p(\psi) > p(\psi \mid \neg\phi)$$

all hold, in which case, ϕ and ψ are said to be positively relevant;
3. *the inequalities*

$$p(\phi\&\psi) < p(\phi)p(\psi)$$
$$p(\phi \mid \psi) < p(\phi) < p(\phi \mid \neg\psi)$$
$$p(\psi \mid \phi) < p(\psi) < p(\psi \mid \neg\phi)$$

all hold, in which case, ϕ and ψ are said to be negatively relevant.

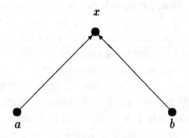

Figure 8.1   Two possible causes of x

This lemma implies that, if ϕ means that ψ is more likely, then the reverse is also true: ψ means that ϕ is more likely. Conversely, also, if ϕ means that ψ is less likely, then ψ means that ϕ is less likely. (See exercise 4.)

8.4   Probability, causation and Bayes networks

8.4.1   Probability and causation

Our conclusions so far are that, given certain idealizing assumptions, we should represent uncertainty by means of a probability distribution, and should update such a distribution by means of conditionalizing. Unfortunately, storing a probability distribution can require a great deal of space. Thus, we need to store probability distributions so that they (i) do not take up too much space; (ii) allow efficient conditionalizing. The key to the approach we take derives from certain observations concerning the relationship between probability and causation.

The philosopher Hans Reichenbach (Reichenbach [6]) made the following observations concerning the relationship between probability and causation. Suppose a, b and x are propositions such that a and b are alternative causes of x. That is: a's being true can cause x to be true, or, equally, b's being true can cause x to be true. Suppose in addition that these causal relationships are not certain, but hold only with a given probability. Figure 8.1 depicts this situation.   Then, claimed Reichenbach, the equation

$$p(a \ \& \ b|x) = p(a|x)p(b|x),$$

cannot hold. Another way of writing this equation is in terms of the probability distribution p_x that we would get after conditionalizing on x:

$$p_x(a \ \& \ b) = p_x(a)p_x(b). \tag{8.6}$$

Figure 8.2   Two possible effects of x

So we might express Reichenbach's claim as: "Causes cannot be independent given their effects". (Actually, this is a slight strengthening of Reichenbach's original claim; see further reading.)

The following example, from the domain of medical diagnosis, illustrates the point. Suppose x is the proposition: "patient has a positive chest x-ray", a the proposition "patient has tuberculosis" and b the proposition "patient has bronchitis". Then x can be (separately) caused by a or b. Now, let it be given that the patient has a positive chest x-ray: i.e. x is true. This information, by itself, *increases* the chance of both tuberculosis and bronchitis, for both are possible causes. But if we obtain the *further information* that the patient definitely has bronchitis (which would explain the chest x-ray by itself) then that leaves us with no special reason to believe that tuberculosis is present, and the probability of tuberculosis should be reduced to whatever it was before.

That is, if we have the positive chest x-ray as our evidence, the probability of tuberculosis is increased:

$$p_x(a) > p(a).$$

However, the probability of tuberculosis *given that the patient has bronchitis and has a positive chest x-ray*, may just be the same as the probability of tuberculosis before we knew anything at all:

$$p_x(a|b) \approx p(a).$$

Hence:

$$p_x(a|b) < p_x(a).$$

That is: a and b are negatively relevant given x. Therefore, equation (8.6) does not hold.

Suppose, however, that x, y and z are propositions such that y and z are possible *effects* of x, as in figure 8.2. Then, claimed Reichenbach, the equation

$$p(y \ \& \ z|x) = p(y|x)p(z|x),$$

can hold. In other words: "Effects can be independent given their causes".

As an example, suppose there is an infectious disease x which normally produces a variety of symptoms affecting the lungs and the brain. Let us suppose that, for a patient with disease x, there is a 50% chance of damage to the lungs and a 10% chance of damage to the brain. If we know for sure that a patient has the infection x, then we can infer that there is a 50% chance that his lungs are damaged (y) and a 10% chance that his brain is damaged (z). But if we find in addition that the patient's brain is definitely undamaged, that may well have no effect on the probability that his lungs will be damaged. That is, *given that the patient has infection x*, damage to the brain and damage to the lungs may well be probabilistically independent. Indeed, one would normally expect such independence if the causal mechanisms were quite different in the two cases. For example, if some property of the patient's brain determines whether disease x causes any damage to that organ, that property may well have no influence on whether there is any damage to his lungs.

8.4.2 Bayes networks

The observation that effects can be probabilistically independent given their causes, but that causes cannot be probabilistically independent given their effects, leads to the concept of a *Bayes network*.   A Bayes network is an acyclic, directed graph such as that of figure 8.3 in which the nodes represent propositions and the links causal connections between them. At each node x in the network, with causes c_1, ..., c_M, we store a matrix specifying the probability that x is true, given all the possible combinations of truth-values which the causes $c_1, \ldots, c_M$ can take. The key idea behind Bayes networks is that *effects are assumed to be independent given their causes: but causes are not assumed to be independent given their effects*. Clearly, this assumption is inspired by the observations of section 8.4.1.

Figure 8.3 shows a simple Bayes network. Here, the node x_6 ("Patient is complaining of coughing") can have two possible causes: x_3 ("Patient has lung cancer") and x_4 ("Patient has bronchitis"). Likewise, the node x_4 can have two possible effects: x_6 and x_7 ("Patient has positive chest x-ray").

Since x_6 has two causes in the network, x_3 and x_4, it must be tagged with a matrix specifying the conditional probability of x_6 given the possible combinations of truth-values that x_3 and x_4 can take. Such a matrix might look like:

	x_3	$\neg x_3$
x_4	0.4	0.25
$\neg x_4$	0.1	0.03

Here, the probability that a patient suffers from coughing given that he has bronchitis but not lung cancer is given as 0.25; the probability that a patient suffers from coughing given that he has neither bronchitis nor lung cancer is given as 0.03; and so on.

The node x_3, by contrast, has only one cause in the network, namely x_1 ("Patient smokes"), and so must be tagged with a matrix specifying the probability of x_3 given the two possible truth-values of x_1. Such a matrix might look like:

x_1	$\neg x_1$
0.2	0.004

Here, the probability that a patient has lung cancer given that he smokes is given as 0.2; and that the probability that a patient has lung cancer given that he does not smoke is given as 0.004. (The actual numbers here are of course not relevant here.)

The node x_1 has no causes in this network. Therefore we simply store at that node its (unconditional) probability $p(x_1)$.

It is worth pausing briefly to consider the size of these matrices. The node x_6 has two causes; therefore the matrix at that node needs to store four probabilities. The node x_3 has one cause; therefore the matrix at that node needs to store two probabilities. The node x_1 has no causes in the network; therefore we need to store just the one value, $p(x_1)$, at that node. More generally, if a node x has M causes in the network, its conditional probability matrix will have 2^M entries.

The critical point about Bayes networks is that, because of the assumed independence of effects given causes, the probability matrices stored at the nodes contain all the information required to store a complete probability distribution for

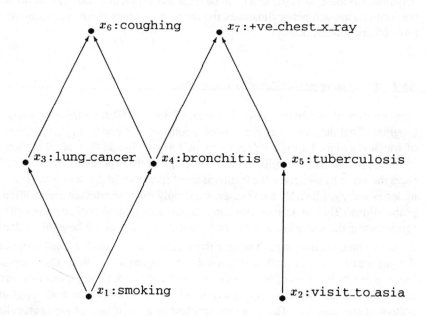

Figure 8.3   A simple Bayes network (after Lauritzen and Spiegelhalter)

the network. (We shall see presently how the probability of any given proposition can be computed.) Why is this fact so significant? Well, suppose that there are N nodes in the network. We can regard these N nodes as, effectively, N proposition letters $x_1, \ldots, x_N$; and we know that, in general, to store a probability distribution for N proposition letters, $2^N - 1$ numbers are required. Now, unless the network is highly connected, the amount of information stored at all of the nodes (2^M numbers for each node, where M is the number of causes of that node) will be far less than 2^N. So, the use of Bayes networks to represent probabilistic knowledge holds out the prospect of a much compressed encoding of a probability distribution. (See exercise 5.)

What makes this compression possible are the independence assumptions. Unfortunately, these independence assumptions are complicated to state in full generality, and a formal treatment lies beyond the scope of this book. (See further reading.) However, we can get a good intuitive grasp of how these independence assumptions work by describing how a Bayes network can be used to compute probabilities. It is to this, then, that we now turn.

8.5 Computing probabilities with Bayes networks

In this section, we present two approaches to computing probabilities with Bayes networks. Of these, only the latter can be regarded as practically useful. However, the former approach better illustrates the the way in which Bayes networks store probabilistic information.

8.5.1 Computing probabilities by simulation

Suppose then, we set up the network of figure 8.3 as a data-structure in a computer program. That data-structure consists of a collection of nodes, $x_1, \ldots, x_7$, each of which is assigned a truth-value, `true` or `false`. In addition, at each node is stored a conditional probability matrix, which gives the probability that that node takes the value `true`, given the truth-values of its causes in the network. (For the nodes x_1 and x_2, which have no causes, we simply store the relevant unconditional probabilities.) Then, it turns out, we can compute the probability of *any* proposition formed using the nodes of the network by *simulation*. Let us see how this is done.

Let us imagine that, to each node x in the network, we attach a small program, the purpose of which is to assign a truth-value, `true` or `false`, to x. This program looks at the truth-values of the causes of x in the network (if any), and then uses that input to decide which truth-value x should have. Consider the node x_1 at the bottom of the network. The program attached to x_1 will look at the probability $p(x_1)$ (remember, this is stored at the node), and will assign the value `true` with probability $p(x_1)$. The following piece of code would suffice:

```
begin code-for-x₁
  let p be a random number between 0 and 1
  let q be p(x₁)
  if p < q then
    let truth-value of x₁ be true
  else
    let truth-value of x₁ be false
  end if
end code-for-x₁.
```

The node x_2 would have a similar piece of code assigning the value true to it with probability $p(x_2)$.

Consider now the node x_3. The program attached to x_3 examines the causal input from x_1. This program comes into play as soon as x_1 has been assigned a value, true or false. If x_1 has been assigned true, then the program at x_3 randomly assigns a truth-value to x_3 in such a way that the chance of assigning the value true is $p(x_3 \mid x_1)$ (remember that this number is stored at the node x_3). If, on the other hand, x_1 has been assigned the value false, then the program at x_3 assigns to x_3 the value true with probability $p(x_3 \mid \neg x_1)$ (which is also stored at the node x_3). The following piece of code would suffice:

```
begin code-for-x₃
  if x₁ has been assigned a truth-value then
    let p be a random number between 0 and 1
    let q be p(x₃|x₁) or p(x₃|¬x₁)
       according to the truth-value assigned to x₁
    if p < q then
      let truth-value of x₃ be true
    else
      let truth-value of x₃ be false
    end if
  end if
end code-for-x₃.
```

The truth-value for x_4, which also takes a single input from x_1, can be assigned analogously by a program attached to it.

Once the values at x_3 and x_4 are assigned, the program at x_6 can now choose a value for x_6. Suppose that, say, x_3 has taken the value true and x_4 the value false. Then the program at x_6 randomly chooses a truth-value for x_6, assigning true with probability $p(x_6 \mid x_3 \& \neg x_4)$, which is stored at node x_6. (Other combinations of truth-values for x_3 and x_4 are handled similarly.) The following piece of code would suffice:

begin `code-for-`x_6
 if x_3 and x_4 have been assigned truth-values **then**
   let p be a random number between 0 and 1;
   let q be $p(x_6|x_3\&x_4)$, $p(x_6|\neg x_3\&x_4)$, $p(x_6|x_3\&\neg x_4)$
     or $p(x_6|\neg x_3\&\neg x_4)$
   according to the truth-values assigned to x_3 and x_4;
   if p < q **then**
     let truth-value of x_6 be `true`;
   else
     let truth-value of x_6 be `false`;
   end if
 end if
end `code-for-`x_6.

In this way, truth-values for all the nodes can be decided, starting at the bottom of the network, and working up to the top. Notice how we are using the assumed independence of effects given causes. For example, once truth-values have been assigned to nodes x_3, x_4 and x_5, the truth-values of their possible effects – x_6 and x_7 – are randomly assigned on the basis of their causes, *but without reference to each other*. That is, when assigning a truth-value to x_6, we do not need to look at what is happening to x_7, just at what has happened to x_3 and x_4.

So far, we have seen how to assign truth-values to the nodes in a Bayes network. We can think of the above process as a simulation of one possible scenario – what might happen to the patient (or whatever the network is about), according to our causal-probabilistic model. Now, consider any proposition ϕ formed (using the standard Boolean connectives) from the proposition letters x_1, ..., x_7 corresponding to the nodes in our network. For example, we can let ϕ be $x_3\&(\neg x_7 \vee x_2)$, with the intuitive interpretation: "The patient has lung cancer and either does not have a positive x-ray or has visited Asia." (Never mind why anyone would want to know this probability.) Once we have assigned truth-values to the nodes $x_1, \ldots, x_7$ as described above, we will have determined a truth-value for ϕ. (This can of course be computed using truth-tables in the normal way.) How does this help us calculate the probability of ϕ? Well, *in any one scenario*, ϕ will turn out to be either true or false, depending upon how the random assignment of truth-values has turned out. But *in a large number of scenarios*, we can count the proportion of times ϕ comes out true; and this proportion gives us an estimate of the probability $p(\phi)$ as determined by the network. Thus, to find $p(\phi)$, we run the network as described above, say, one million times, noting, for each run, whether ϕ comes out true or false. We then simply up count how many times ϕ was true, and divide by 1 million. That is of course only an estimate of $p(\phi)$, since we can always be unlucky and get an unrepresentative sample of random numbers. But the more times the network is run, the more likely it is that the result is close to the correct answer.

More formally, the procedure `find-prob-by-sim` is as follows. It takes two arguments: `query-proposition` and `number-of-sweeps`. Here, query-proposition is a Boolean combination of nodes in the network specifying the proposition ϕ whose probability we are computing, and number-of-sweeps is some arbitrary large number – say, 10,000 – specifying the number of times the nodes in the network are updated. The larger the number of sweeps, the more accurate the result, in general. The procedure returns the estimated probability of query-proposition.

begin find-prob-by-sim(query-proposition, number-of-sweeps)
  let counter be 0
  repeat number-of-sweeps times **do**
    set truth-value of all nodes to be undefined
    until all nodes have been assigned truth-values true or false **do**
      foreach node X with truth-value undefined such that
        none of the causes of X have truth-value undefined **do**
        run the code attached to node X
      end for each
    end until
    compute truth-value of query-proposition based on values
      assigned to nodes
    if query-proposition is true **then**
      let counter be counter + 1
    end if
  end repeat
  return counter divided by number-of-sweeps
end find-prob-by-sim

8.5.2 *Computing conditional probabilities by simulation*

So far, we have seen how to compute the probability of any proposition from the information stored in a Bayes network. For this to be useful, however, we must be able to compute *conditional probabilities*. For example, in the domain of medical diagnosis, what we usually want to know is the probability that a patient has a certain disease *given* the information that we have concerning him, e.g. that he does not smoke and has recently come back from a trip to Asia. How can we compute such conditional probabilities using causal simulations?

In order to compute a conditional probability, $p(\phi|\psi)$, using the method of simulation just described, the best we can do in general to is to compute the (non-conditional) probabilities $p(\phi\&\psi)$ and $p(\psi)$ and use equation

$$p(\phi|\psi) = \frac{p(\phi\&\psi)}{p(\psi)}.$$

To compute, e.g. $p(x_4\&\neg x_3 \mid x_1\&x_6)$ we run the network a large number of times, as described in the procedure find-prob-by-sim, except that we simultaneously obtain estimates of $p(x_4\& \neg x_3\& x_1\& x_6)$ and $p(x_1\& x_6)$. (The modification to the algorithm to enable simultaneous calculation of two probabilities is completely straightforward.) Given these quantities, we can compute:

$$p(x_4\& \neg x_3 \mid x_1\& x_6) = \frac{p(x_4\& \neg x_3\& x_1\& x_6)}{p(x_1\& x_6)}$$

(See exercise 6.)

8.5.3 *The accuracy of simulation*

Of course, the question arises as to how accurate the method of estimating probabilities by simulation is. And it turns out that this question can be answered easily by standard techniques in statistics. (Readers unfamiliar with such techniques may skip the indented argument.)

> Suppose we compute $p(\phi)$ by simulation. There is always a chance that we will be unlucky and get an answer very far from the true value (due to random fluctuations). But suppose that we want to be 95% certain that our answer is within ϵ of the true answer, p. Each run can be thought of as a sampling of a random variable Φ with distribution:
>
> $$p(\Phi = 1) = p$$
> $$p(\Phi = 0) = 1 - p$$
>
> It is a standard result of statistics that Φ then has mean p and variance $p(1-p)$. The point of thinking of runs in terms of sampling a random variable is that counting the proportion of N runs in which ϕ turns out true can be thought of as sampling the random variable Φ with sample size N, and then computing the mean of that sample.
>
> Now the mean of a sample (of size N) of a random variable Φ can itself be thought of as a random variable, $\overline{\Phi}$. Moreover, $\overline{\Phi}$ will be approximately *normally distributed* (for large N) with mean p and variance $p(1-p)/N$. In such a distribution, there is a roughly 95% chance of the value lying within two standard deviations of the mean. That is, there is a 95% chance of the value of $\overline{\Phi}$ lying within a distance $2(p(1-p)/N)^{1/2}$ of p. So to have a 95% chance of getting the answer within ϵ of the correct value, we must have
>
> $$N > \frac{4p(1-p)}{\epsilon^2} \qquad (8.7)$$

We have established, then, that if the result of our simulation is to have a 95% chance of being within ϵ of the correct answer, we must run the network at least $4p(1-p)/\epsilon^2$ times. And this leads to severe problems with low probabilities. For example, suppose we have to compute the probability that a patient has disease ϕ given that he has a symptom ψ – i.e. we want to compute

$$p(\phi \mid \psi).$$

To do this we must find $p(\phi \& \psi)$ and $p(\psi)$ and then divide. But even if the conditional probability $p(\phi \mid \psi)$ is quite high, the absolute probabilities $p(\phi \& \psi)$ and $p(\psi)$ tend to be extremely small – easily (in medical applications) of the order of 1 in a million. This means, that, if $p \approx 10^{-6}$, to get just *two significant figures of accuracy* in calculating the requisite probabilities, we must have $\epsilon \approx 10^{-8}$, so that, by equation (8.7),

$$N \approx \frac{10^{-6}}{10^{-16}} = 10^{10},$$

an impractically large number of network runs.

Obviously, we need a more efficient way to compute conditional probabilities in Bayes networks than simulation. And it is to such a way that we now turn our attention.

8.5.4 Pearl's relaxation method

The following algorithm, due to Pearl (Pearl [3]), uses a relaxation technique to compute the probability of one node in a Bayes network, given that the values of certain other nodes are known. The theoretical justification for this procedure lies beyond the scope of this book. However, it is relatively straightforward to implement, and its results can be compared with the simulation approach, of section 8.5.1.

The basic idea is as follows. The network is initialized by assigning truth values (true or false) to the nodes. Those nodes whose values are known – let us call them the *evidence nodes* – are set accordingly, and all other nodes – let us call them the *nonevidence nodes* – are assigned truth-values (true or false) at random. Note: in this algorithm, we never set truth-values to undefined.

Each nonevidence node x is taken in turn, and its truth-value is updated as follows. First, we calculate the probability that x takes the value true, *given the current truth-values of all the other nodes (evidence node and nonevidence nodes) in the network.* (We explain how to do this below.) Let this probability be p. Then, x is randomly assigned the value true (with probability p) or false (with probability $1 - p$). Once x has been updated, all the other nonevidence nodes in the network are processed in exactly the same way, until we have completed one entire sweep through the network. Notice that, if the truth-value assigned to x changes as a result of this assignment, then this will in general have an effect on the updating of the other nonevidence nodes. Once all the nonevidence nodes in the network have been updated, the whole process is repeated a large number of times. On each sweep, the nonevidence nodes have their truth-values updated one by one, based on the *current* truth-values of the other nodes in the network. We can think of the probability matrices as constraints on the truth-values which the nodes in the network 'like' to take; the updating process is then a matter of making the network more 'comfortable' by adjusting the truth-value of each node given the current truth-values of the other nodes.

In this way, the status of any nonevidence node x is recalculated many times, once during each sweep through the network. Sometimes, x will be assigned the value true, at other times, the value false. It turns out that the *proportion of times x is* assigned the value true gives an estimate of the probability that x is true given the known values of the evidence nodes. Thus, this relaxation method is like the simulation method described in sections 8.5.1 and 8.5.2, with the crucial difference that conditional probabilities can be directly computed by keeping the evidence nodes fixed at their known values throughout the whole computation. There is no need to compute two probabilities separately and then divide.

The procedure is set out formally below. Here, query-node is a node in the network, specifying the (atomic) proposition whose probability we are computing, and number-of-sweeps is some arbitrary large number – say, 10,000 – specifying the number of times the nodes in the network are updated. The larger the number of sweeps, the more accurate the result, in general. The procedure returns the estimated probability of query-node.

> **begin** find-prob-by-relax(query-node,number-of-sweeps)
>> **let** counter be 0
>> set truth-values of evidence nodes to known values
>> set truth-values of nonevidence nodes randomly
>> **repeat** number-of-sweeps times **do**
>>> **for each** nonevidence node node **do**
>>>> **let** p be a random number between 0 and 1
>>>> **let** q be the probability that node is true given
>>>> truth-values of other nodes in the network
>>>> **if** p < q **then**
>>>>> **let** truth-value of node be true
>>>> **else**
>>>>> **let** truth-value of node be false
>>>> **end if**
>>> **end for each**
>>> **if** truth-value of query-node is true **then**
>>>> **let** counter be counter + 1
>>> **end if**
>> **end repeat**
>> **return** counter divided by number-of-sweeps
> **end** find-prob-by-relax

We now return to the problem of calculating, for a given node x, the probability that x takes the value true given the current truth-values of all the other nodes in the network. This *looks* like a difficult problem. After all, we started off wanting to compute the probability of a node given the values of just a few evidence nodes;

and the procedure just given requires us to calculate the probability of a node given the current truth-values of *all* the other nodes in the network! In fact, however, the procedure for doing this is remarkably simple. Again, the justification of this procedure lies beyond the scope of this book; we simply confine ourselves to describing how to carry it out.

One preliminary detail before we do so. Recall that each node x in the network is tagged with a probability matrix specifying the probability that x is true, given the various possible combinations of the truth-values x's causes. For example, in the network of figure 8.3, the node x_6 has an associated matrix:

	x_3	$\neg x_3$
x_4	0.4	0.25
$\neg x_4$	0.1	0.03

So, if nodes x_3 and x_4 are assigned truth-values – say, true and false, respectively – we can always look up the probability that x_6 is true given the current values of its causes – in this case, 0.1. Let us call the procedure of looking up an entry in a probability matrix for node x, given the current truth-values of the causes,

$$\texttt{lookup}(x)$$

Implementing this procedure is of course trivial – it is merely a matter of table-lookup.

Now we can proceed. Remember: the relaxation procedure described above requires us to calculate the probability that a node x takes the value true given the current truth-values of all the other nodes in the network. To do this, we calculate two quantities, which we shall call q_x and $q_{\neg x}$. To calculate q_x, we *temporarily* set the node x to have the truth-value true, and then we set q_x to the product

$$q_x = \texttt{lookup}(x).\texttt{lookup}(e_1).\ldots.\texttt{lookup}(e_N)$$

where $e_1, \ldots e_N$ are the effects of x in the network. Likewise, to calculate $q_{\neg x}$, we *temporarily* set the node x to have the truth-value false, and then we set $q_{\neg x}$ to the product

$$q_{\neg x} = (1 - \texttt{lookup}(x)).\texttt{lookup}(e_1).\ldots.\texttt{lookup}(e_N).$$

Note that the $\texttt{lookup}(e_i)$ will not, in general, be the same in the two expressions above, for $\texttt{lookup}(e_i)$ depends on the truth-values of the causes of e_i, and one of these is x. Finally, the probability that x takes the value true given the other nodes in the network turns out to be:

$$p(x \mid \text{current values of other nodes in network}) = \frac{q_x}{q_x + q_{\neg x}}.$$

And this is the quantity we wanted. This completes the description of the relaxation process for estimating conditional probabilities in Bayes networks. (See exercises 8 and 9.)

Exercises

1. In the axioms (8.2), axiom (iii) is actually redundant, in that it can be proved from the other axioms. Show that this is so.
2. (To think about) Suppose you are given a series of numbers in the range from 1 to 1,000,000, and are asked to bet whether they are prime. That is, you are asked to bet on propositions such as
   "100,001 is prime."
   At what odds would you accept a bet on this particular proposition? Does any mathematical theorem help you decide the odds? What, according to the axioms (8.2), is the probability of the above proposition, and what bets does it make sense to accept? What does this tell you about Dutch book arguments?
3. Let p be a probability distribution and b a proposition such that $p(b) \neq 0$. Prove that p_b obeys the axioms (8.2).
4. Using the axioms (8.2), prove the lemma at the end of section 8.3.
5. Count how many numbers have to be stored in order to specify the Bayes network in figure 8.3. How many numbers would have to be stored to encode a general probability distribution involving 7 propositions?
6. (Programming) Write a computer program to simulate the network shown in figure 8.3. Hence obtain an estimate of the conditional probability $p(x_4 \& \neg x_3 \mid x_1 \& x_6)$. Remember to run your network for a large enough number N of times if you want a reasonable result.
7. Assess the extent to which the assumed independence of effects given their causes really holds of the network of figure 8.3. In particular, consider the implications of the fact that smoking is something which, if done at all, can be done to a greater or lesser extent. If the degree of smoking is (as seems plausible) connected with the likelihood of contracting smoking-related illnesses, what does that say about the conditional independence of these illnesses given that the patient smokes?
8. (Programming) Implement the relaxation method for computing conditional probabilities using the procedure `get-prob-by-relax`. Compare its performance with `get-prob-by-sim` on a number of networks.
9. (Programming) Having implemented `get-prob-by-relax`, write a program which plots a graph showing how the current estimate of the probability of a node in question changes as more and more sweeps through the network are made. How stable, exactly, is this process? How might you decide how many sweeps to carry out before you accept the output of the algorithm as your estimate of the desired probability?

Further reading

The most famous system for reasoning under uncertainty in medical domains is the program MYCIN (Shortliffe [8]). MYCIN uses a system of 'certainty-factors' to represent probabilistic connections, whose correct probabilistic interpretation did not become clear until some time after the program was written. Programs based on Bayes networks can be regarded as successors to these early systems. One such program, MUNIN, specialized for the domain of neurological disease diagnosis, is described in Lauritzen and Spiegelhalter [2].

Dutch book arguments and the foundations of probability theory are discussed in Jeffery [1]. For the philosophical issues surrounding the relationship between probability and causation, see Salmon [7]. For a comprehensive (though very difficult) account of probabilistic reasoning in AI, including a more rigorous treatment of the independence assumptions in Bayes networks, see Pearl [4]. More information on the relaxation algorithm for computing probabilities in Bayes networks can be found in Pearl [3]. A useful collection of papers on uncertainty in AI is to be found in Pearl [5].

Bibliography

[1] Jeffrey, R.C. *The Logic of Decision*, 2nd ed., Chicago: University of Chicago Press, 1983.

[2] Lauritzen, S.L. and D.J. Spiegelhalter "Local computations with probabilities on graphical structures and their application to expert systems", *Journal of the Royal Statistical Society*, B. 50, no. 2 (1988) pp. 157–224.

[3] Pearl, J. "Evidential reasoning using stochastic simulation of causal models", *Artificial Intelligence*, 32 (1987) pp. 245-257.

[4] Pearl, J. *Probabilistic Reasoning in Intelligent Systems: Networks of Plausible Inference*, San Mateo: Morgan Kaufmann, 1988.

[5] Pearl, J. (ed.) *Uncertainty in Artificial Intelligence*, San Mateo: Morgan Kaufmann, 1988.

[6] Reichenbach, H. *The Direction of Time* Berkeley, CA: California University Press, 1971.

[7] Salmon, W. *Scientific Explanation and the Causal Structure of the World*, Princeton, NJ: Princeton University Press, 1984.

[8] Shortliffe, Edward H. *Computer-based Medical Consultations: MYCIN*, New York: American Elsevier, 1976.

9 Induction

9.1 Introduction

Many instances of useful reasoning involve the application of generalizations to individual cases. For example, a doctor treating a patient might rely on diagnostic rules such as:

If the patient has jaundice, fever, pain in upper abdomen, pale stools and weight loss, then the patient (probably) has hepatitis.

If the patient has pain in central upper abdomen delayed after food, nausea, weight loss and no jaundice and no fever, then the patient (probably) has a duodenal ulcer.

If the patient has a cough, purulent sputum, fever, and if there are crackles and wheezes on listening to chest, then the patient (probably) has pneumonia.

(Actually, the above diagnostic rules have been simplified somewhat; but the medical details are not really important here.)

These diagnostic rules belong to an accumulated body of medical knowledge concerning the correlations between combinations of symptoms and diseases. But where did this knowledge *come from*? Somewhere along the line, someone must have had to *infer* these rules, since they are hardly knowledge we are born with. Ultimately, the basis of this knowledge must be the experience, over many years, of a large number of individual cases: patients who had this or that combination of symptoms and who turned out to have this or that disease. The inference of generalizations from facts concerning individual cases is known as *inductive inference* (or just *induction*), and is the subject of the present chapter. Specifically, we ask: how might we program an AI system to make such inferences?

In the middle years of this century, much effort was expended trying to formalize inductive inference, with the best-known example of this work being provided by the philosopher Rudolf Carnap. The aim was to produce an inductive logic which, when presented with a body of evidence and a suggested hypothesis, would prescribe the degree of belief (in terms of a probability) to be placed in the hypothesis, given the evidence. Inductive logic, which sometimes also passes by the more modest name of *confirmation theory*, seeks to do for induction what the predicate calculus has done for deduction, namely, to provide it with a rigorous codification. Unfortunately, as systems of inductive logic were investigated, severe difficulties appeared, as a result of which inductive logic never developed into anything comparable with the compelling account of deduction provided by the predicate calculus. Recently, however, the growth of *machine learning* as a topic in AI has led to a revival of interest in induction among the AI and computer science communities, and new approaches to induction are beginning to emerge. In this chapter, we will be surveying some techniques of inductive inference from the point of view of AI systems. We will also see how some of the difficulties that plagued inductive logic still pose a challenge to research on induction in AI.

9.2 A framework for inductive inference

9.2.1 A simple induction problem

Although medical examples illustrate the practical importance of inductive inference, they suffer from the disadvantage of being rather complicated. Simple combinations of symptoms are seldom sure-fire indicators of particular diseases. And some diagnostic rules have complicated logical forms; for example, they may require that a patient exhibit *more than a certain number* of symptoms from a given list, or specify some symptoms as being *more important* than others. Since induction is a difficult enough subject at the best of times, we need to confine ourselves to problems which illustrate the logical issues involved without these complications.

The following abstract induction task is adapted from a well-known series of psychology experiments (Bruner, Goodnow and Austin [2]). Figure 9.1 shows a sequence of five cards, on each of which is inscribed three shapes: a circle, a square and a triangle, always in that order. Each shape comes in two colours: black or white. All the cards are the same except for the colours of the shapes they sport; with three shapes and two colours, there are 8 possible cards in total.

Suppose you are told that some but not all of the 8 possible cards have the property of being a *dax* ("dax" is of course just a nonsense word). Specifically, of the 5 cards in figure 9.1, cards 2 and 4 are daxes, while cards 1, 3 and 5 are non-daxes. (This is indicated in figure 9.1 by the plus- and minus-signs next to the cards.) Your task is to devise, on the basis of the examples in figure 9.1, a general rule which determines whether any given card is a dax, including cards that you have not yet been shown.

If we ignore, for the moment, the probabilistic nature of medical diagnosis (we will return to this point in later sections), the similarities between the task of inferring diagnostic rules in medicine and that of inferring a rule to identify daxes in the abstract task of figure 9.1 are clear: the cards correspond to patients, the colours of the various shapes on the cards to the presence or absence of observable symptoms, and the property *dax* to a disease we want to diagnose. Many inductive reasoning problems have this form: a number of known positive and negative instances of some property are characterized in terms of a fixed list of observable

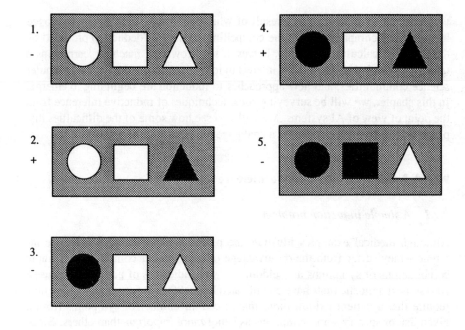

Figure 9.1   An abstract induction task

features, and the task is to infer a rule which predicts future instances of this property on the basis of the observable features.

Of course, one property of most serious induction tasks not shared by the example of figure 9.1 is that they normally involve a very large number of features, so that a casual glance at the data is not usually sufficient to infer any generalizations. It is in these cases that inductive reasoning procedures in AI can be practically useful. Probably the best-known application of inductive reasoning in AI concerns a rule-based system, PLANT/ds, developed to diagnose diseases in soybean plants. An induction procedure was used to infer diagnostic rules from numbers of past cases. It was found that the rules inferred by the induction procedure out-performed a set of rules explicitly devised in conjunction with experts in the area. (See further reading.)

Some terminology before we proceed. In the induction task of figure 9.1, the 5 presented cards are called the *training examples* or *data*, and the property for which we are supposed to find a rule is called the *target concept*. Cards 2 and 4, which we are told have this property, are called *positive examples*; cards 1, 3 and 5, which do not, are called *negative examples*. Thus, induction is the process of inferring a rule to predict instances of a target concept on the basis of positive and negative training examples.

	a	*b*	*c*	*C*
card 1	T	T	T	F
card 2	T	T	F	T
	T	F	T	-
	T	F	F	-
card 3	F	T	T	F
card 4	F	T	F	T
card 5	F	F	T	F
	F	F	F	-

Figure 9.2   Induction viewed as truth-table-completion.

9.2.2 Induction as formula-finding

For the purposes of analysis, it will help to view the problem a little more abstractly. First of all, there is nothing special about the particular target concept, *dax*, in this example: after all, "dax" is just a nonsense word. So we shall simply denote the target concept as C. Secondly, instead of drawing shapes on cards and colouring them black or white, we could just as easily take three proposition letters, a, b and c (corresponding to the shapes *circle*, *square* and *triangle*, respectively) and assign them the truth-values T or F (corresponding to the colours *white* and *black*, respectively). Thus, we can think of each of the 8 possible cards as a row of the truth-table involving the proposition-letters a, b and c. Figure 9.2 shows the truth-table for these proposition letters, with a column for the target concept, C. On the right-hand side (under the column marked C), we have put a T in those rows corresponding to the two positive training examples, and an F in those rows corresponding to the three negative training examples from figure 9.1.

Now, our task is to devise, on the basis of the training examples, a general rule which determines whether any new example has the target concept. That is: we would like some rule which enables us to fill in the missing entries, T or F, under the C-column of the truth-table of figure 9.2. Since a rule for filling in entries in a truth-table is just a *formula*, ψ, in the propositional calculus, we can view the induction problem as the problem of finding a formula involving a, b and c, given the truth-values it should have for *some* of the rows in the truth-table. This more abstract view of induction tasks will help us to get clear about some of the logical issues involved.

In particular, one aspect of induction becomes apparent. The task of completing the entries in a partially specified truth-table is *indeterminate*. *Any* way of completing the missing entries in the truth-table of figure 9.2 yields a perfectly sensible and properly defined truth-function; and there will certainly be formulae ψ which compute it. Thus, there are many rules for predicting a target concept C consistent with the five training examples presented in figure 9.1, and, logically, it is hard to see why there should be any reason for preferring any of these possibilities as the *correct* rule to infer. So it is generally with induction: the data underdetermine the choice of rule for predicting future cases, so that any rule suggested by an induction procedure will be, to some extent, a guess. Therefore, in understanding induction procedures in AI, we need to understand what is involved in assessing the quality of procedures which make different guesses from the same data. But the best way to get a feel for the general issues is to examine some specific induction procedures in detail. That is the task of the next section.

9.3   Monomial induction procedures

9.3.1   *Monomial rules*

We have seen how to view induction problems as a   matter of searching for a rule, in the guise of a propositional calculus formula, ψ, to predict positive and negative examples of a target concept, C. In general, ψ might be any formula of the propositional calculus; however, in many cases, we may want to restrict the form that ψ can take. This may either be because we have reason to believe that the correct rule obeys the restriction in question, or simply because we prefer to find a rule having a particularly simple form if possible. The space of possible formulae to which the induced rule ψ is assumed to be confined is known as the *concept space* of the induction problem.

One particularly simple concept space is the space of *monomials*. If $a_1, \ldots, a_n$ are proposition letters, then a *monomial* over $a_1, \ldots, a_n$ is defined to be a conjunction of literals involving $a_1, \ldots, a_n$ (remember: a *literal* is either a proposition letter, or a proposition letter preceded by a single negation). Thus, over the proposition letters a, b, c, the formulae a, $a \ \& \ b$ and $\neg a \ \& \ \neg b \ \& \ \neg c$ are all monomials, whereas, $\neg\neg a$, $a \lor b$ and $(\neg a \ \& \ \neg b) \rightarrow \neg c$ are not. In addition, the contradictory formula $\perp$ and the logically true formula $\top$ are counted as monomials. (See exercise 1.)

Figure 9.3 is a graphical representation of part of the concept space of monomials over the proposition-letters a, b and c. The lines joining monomials represent relations of implication. Thus, at the bottom is $\perp$, the logically contradictory formula which implies everything, while at the top is $\top$, the tautologous formula, which is implied by everything, with the other monomials coming in between. (Not all such monomials are shown, in order to avoid cluttering the diagram.)

Terminology: if ϕ and ψ are formulae such that $\phi \vdash \psi$, but not $\psi \vdash \phi$, we say that ϕ is *logically stronger than* ψ, and that ψ is *logically weaker than* ϕ. Notice that the logically stronger monomials are those with the greater numbers of conjuncts.

In most realistic domains, e.g. medicine, very few interesting conditions can be predicted by simple conjunctions of conditions. However, the concept space of monomials illustrates most of the fundamental issues in inductive inference. Accordingly, we will, for the time being, assume that the rule ψ which correctly predicts positive and negative instances of the target concept C takes the form of a monomial. Sections 9.3.2 and 9.3.3 discuss two procedures for inferring monomial

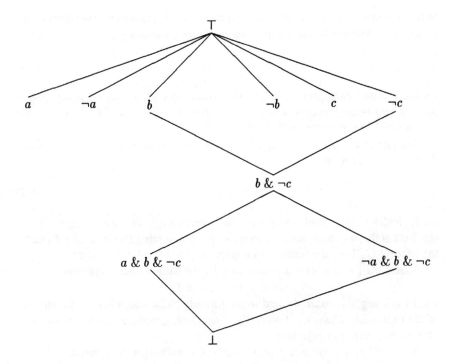

Figure 9.3   Part of the space of monomials over a, b and c.

rules from positive and negative examples. We return to other concept spaces in later sections.

9.3.2   A simple monomial induction procedure

In this section, we describe a procedure for inferring a monomial rule for a target concept on the basis of a collection of positive and negative training examples. We shall call this procedure grudge-induce, because it is as conservative as possible in admitting positive examples of the target concept. We present it here in order to help us understand the issues involved in induction, rather than as a practical proposal for performing inductive inferences.

Suppose that the *correct* rule for predicting the target concept is given by some formula ψ, which we assume to be a monomial. (Of course, it is the job of the induction algorithm to try to guess what ψ is.) The basic idea behind the procedure grudge-induce is to maintain a *current conjecture* ϕ as to the correct rule for C, on the basis of the training examples it has processed so far. This conjecture only ever errs on the side of conservatism, in that it never classifies an example as falling under C unless it is absolutely certain that this is correct. In terms of the relationship between ϕ and ψ, this amounts to the condition:

$$\phi \vdash \psi. \tag{9.1}$$

As the training examples are processed, the conjectured rule, ϕ, is updated to make it consistent with the data that have been presented so far. However, the condition (9.1) is maintained throughout.

The procedure can be illustrated by means of the example of figure 9.1. initially, the conjectured rule ϕ is set to

$$\phi = \bot, \tag{9.2}$$

the logically false formula (which implies everything). In terms of figure 9.3, ϕ starts off at the very bottom of the concept space, assuming that *nothing* falls under the concept C. Then the training examples are considered one at a time.

First, card 1 is considered, represented by the truth-value assignment:
$$a = \text{T}; b = \text{T}; c = \text{T}.$$
Card 1 is a negative example, and so the formula (9.2), which is false for all rows of the truth-table, classifies it correctly. Therefore, grudge-induce makes no change to its current conjecture.

Next card 2, is examined, represented by the truth-value assignment:
$$a = \text{T}; b = \text{T}; c = \text{F}.$$
Card 2 is a positive example, and so the formula (9.2), which is false for all rows of the truth-table, classifies it *incorrectly*. grudge-induce recognizes that its current conjecture must be weakened. More precisely, a new rule ϕ needs to be found which: (i) correctly classifies card 2, and (ii) still satisfies the condition (9.1). The solution is to move up the lattice of figure 9.3 one step at a time until a monomial is found which classifies this new example correctly. (There is a simple procedure for doing this, as we shall see below.) This will guarantee that we never produce a conjecture which is logically weaker than it need be.

In this case, where the previous conjecture was $\bot$, and the new example is card 2, the next monomial up in the lattice consistent with the new example is

$$\phi = a \ \& \ b \ \& \ \neg c. \tag{9.3}$$

This then becomes grudge-induce's new conjecture as to the rule for C. Clearly, ϕ is true under the assignment $a = \text{T}$, $b = \text{T}$, and $c = \text{F}$; so the new rule classifies card 2 correctly.

Next, card 3 is examined, represented by the truth-value assignment:
$$a = \text{F}; b = \text{T}; c = \text{T}$$
Card 3 is a negative example, and so the formula (9.3), which is false for the corresponding row of the truth-table, classifies it correctly. Therefore, grudge-induce makes no change to its current conjecture.

Next card 4, is examined, represented by the truth-value assignment:

$$a = \text{F}; b = \text{T}; c = \text{F}.$$

Card 4 is a positive example, and so the formula (9.3), which is false for the corresponding row of the truth-table, classifies it *incorrectly*. grudge-induce recognizes that its current conjecture must be weakened. Again, grudge-induce responds by moving up the lattice of figure 9.3 until a monomial is found which classifies this new example correctly. This time, the monomial found is

$$\phi = b \,\&\, \neg c. \tag{9.4}$$

This then becomes grudge-induce's new conjecture as to the rule for C. Clearly, ϕ is true under the assignment $a = \text{F}$, $b = \text{T}$, and $c = \text{F}$; so the new rule classifies card 4 correctly.

Finally, card 5 is examined, represented by the truth-value assignment:

$$a = \text{F}; b = \text{F}; c = \text{T}.$$

Card 5 is a negative example, and so the formula (9.4), which is false for the corresponding row of the truth-table, classifies it correctly. Therefore, grudge-induce makes no change to its current conjecture.

Since there are no more training examples to be processed, grudge-induce returns the monomial (9.4) as its result. In terms of the original problem, grudge-induce has inferred, on the basis of the 5 individual cases presented to it, that a card has the target concept if and only if it sports a white square and a black triangle. This rule succeeds in classifying the training examples correctly, and makes predictions about unseen cards.

More generally, the procedure grudge-induce, is as follows. Suppose we are presented with a list of m positive and negative training examples of a concept C, $x_1, \ldots, x_m$. Each example x_i is described as a *truth-value assignment* to the proposition letters $a_1, \ldots, a_n$, and, for each training example, we are told whether it has property C. The procedure returns a monomial for predicting whether any given example has C; this monomial gives the correct results for the training examples, and makes predictions about unseen examples.

The core of the procedure is move-up, which has, as arguments, ϕ, a monomial expressing the currently conjectured rule for C, and x, a new training example known to have the property C, expressed as a truth-value assignment to a collection of proposition-letters. It produces, as output, a monomial which (i) takes the truth-value T according to the truth-value assignment x, (ii) is logically weaker than (or equivalent to) ϕ, and (iii) is the logically strongest monomial satisfying conditions (i) and (ii). With a little thought, it can be seen that the following procedure does the job:

```
begin move-up (φ, x)
    if φ is ⊥ then
        let new-φ be the conjunction of all the
            literals that are true according to x
    else if φ contains literals that are false according to x then
        let new-φ be φ with all such literals deleted
    else
        let new-φ be φ
    end if
    return new-φ
end move-up
```

Applying the procedure move-up in response to new positive training examples ensures that all so-far-observed training examples are correctly classified, while maintaining the condition (9.1). The reader might like to verify that move-up produces the behaviour outlined above in response to the example of figure 9.1, where grudge-induce changes its current conjecture from (9.2) to (9.3) and thence to (9.4). But, to repeat, the best way to think of the procedure is in terms of the lattice in figure 9.3: the process is one of grudgingly moving up the lattice to the strongest monomial that classifies the so-far-processed training examples correctly. The whole procedure, grudge-induce, applied to training examples $x_1, \ldots, x_m$, is then simply as follows:

```
begin grudge-induce(x₁, . . . , xₘ)
    let φ be ⊥
    for each x in x₁, . . . , xₘ do
        if x is a positive example of C, then
            let φ be the result of move-up (φ, x)
        end if
    end until
end grudge-induce
```

(See exercise 2.)

The effect of the procedure grudge-induce is to induce a rule which classifies the given positive examples as falling under the target concept, and as few others as possible. This in-built conservatism makes grudge-induce an inappropriate procedure for induction in practical domains. But it is worth stressing that the induced rule by this procedure is always consistent with the data which it is given. As we have said, the task of inducing a general rule to account for observed cases is to some extent indeterminate; and, logically speaking, grudge-induce is a perfectly correct procedure for producing a rule which accounts correctly for training examples (assuming, of course, that the training examples can be accounted for by a monomial).

The manner in which an induction procedure extrapolates from the training examples it is given is called its *inductive bias*. Thus, the comments of the previous paragraph relate to the inductive bias of grudge-induce. In fact, viewing grudge-induce as working its way up a lattice of monomials as in figure 9.3 gives us a useful characterization of its inductive bias. It is now time to examine a more complicated induction procedure with a different inductive bias.

9.3.3 A more complex monomial induction procedure

The procedure grudge-induce works by starting at the bottom of the concept space and working its way up in response to positive examples. In this section, we present a monomial induction procedure, pincer-induce, which searches simultaneously from the top and bottom of the concept space and works its way to the middle in response to both positive and negative examples.

Suppose that the *correct* rule for predicting the target concept is given by some formula ψ, which we assume to be a monomial. (Again, it is the job of the induction algorithm to try to guess what ψ is.) The basic idea behind the procedure pincer-induce is as follows. Various conjectures as to the correct rule for C are maintained in the variables ϕ and Φ. The variable ϕ is familiar from grudge-induce: it is a conjectured rule which only ever errs on the side of conservatism. That is, it satisfies the condition

$$\phi \vdash \psi. \tag{9.5}$$

The variable Φ, however, contains a list of such conjectures, $[\phi_1, \ldots, \phi_k]$. These conjectures will always err, if at all, on the side of liberalism, in that they never classify an example as not falling under C unless it is absolutely certain that this is correct. In terms of the relationship between ψ and the ϕ_i, this amounts to the condition:

$$\psi \vdash \phi_i. \tag{9.6}$$

for all the ϕ_i in Φ. As the training examples are processed, ϕ and Φ are updated to make all the conjectures they contain consistent with the data that have been given so far. In particular, ϕ must be made weaker in response to positive examples (as in grudge-induce) while the conjectures in Φ must be made stronger in response to negative examples. However, the conditions (9.5) and (9.6) are maintained throughout. Thus the concept space is traversed simultaneously from top to bottom (by Φ) and from bottom to top (by ϕ), keeping the correct rule ψ pinned somewhere in between. The procedure stops when either the data run out or when the top-to-bottom and bottom-to-top processes meet.

The example of figure 9.1 illustrates how this idea works in detail. Initially, the variable Φ is set to the list of monomials $[\top]$, and the variable ϕ is set to the monomial $\bot$. This situation is shown in figure 9.4a, where the conjecture ϕ and the

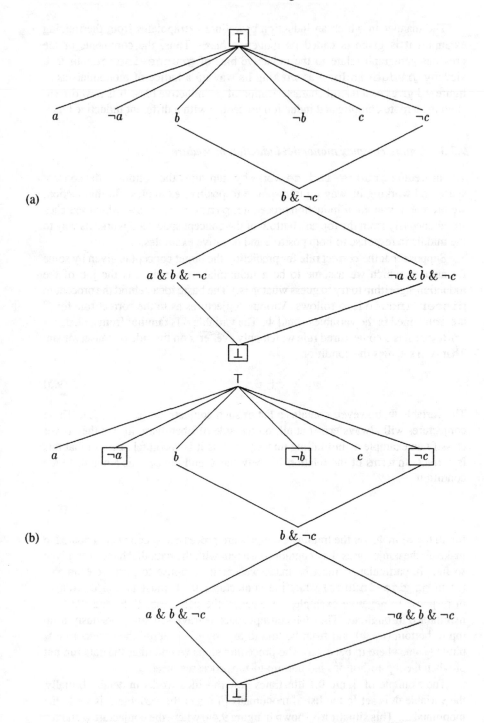

Figure 9.4 Example trace of pincer-induce *(part 1)*

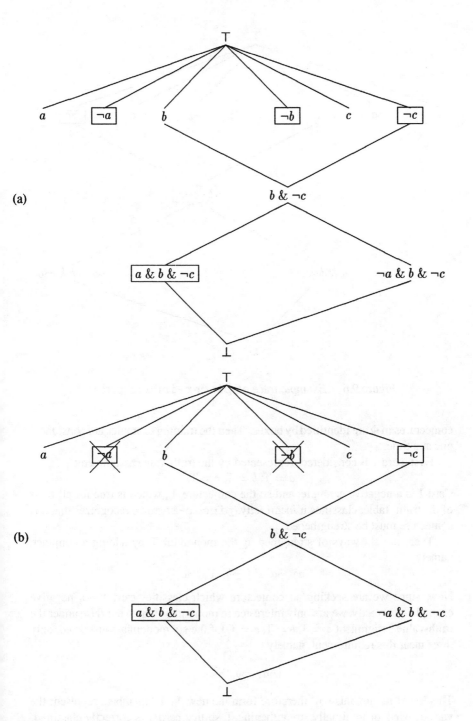

Figure 9.5   Example trace of pincer-induce *(part 2)*

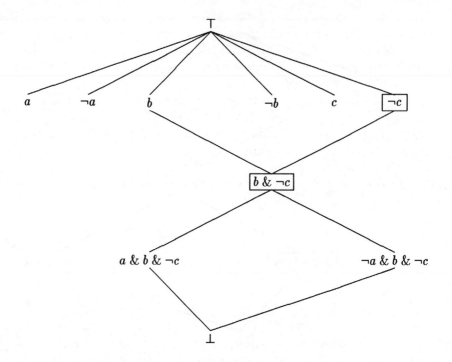

Figure 9.6   Example trace of `pincer-induce` *(part 3)*

conjectures in Φ are identified by boxes. Then the training examples are considered
one at a time.

First, card 1 is considered, represented by the truth-value assignment:

$$a = T; b = T; c = T.$$

Card 1 is a negative example, and so the conjecture T, which is true for all rows
of the truth- table, classifies it *in*correctly. `pincer-induce` recognizes that this
conjecture must be strengthened.

There are six ways of strengthening the monomial T by adding a conjunct,
namely:

$$a, \ \neg a, \ b, \ \neg b, \ c, \ \neg c.$$

Now, since we are seeking an conjecture which classifies card 1 – a negative
example – correctly, we are only interested in monomials which are *false* under the
truth-value assignment $a = T$, $b = T$, $c = T$. Of the six monomials just listed, only
three meet this requirement, namely

$$[\neg a, \ \neg b, \ \neg c].$$

This list of monomials will therefore form the new Φ. Its members represent the
various ways of minimally strengthening T so that card 1 is correctly classified.

This situation is shown in figure 9.4b, where, again, the conjecture ϕ and the conjectures in Φ are identified by boxes. Notice that, in general, as in this case, there is more than one way to strengthen a monomial so as to rule out a negative example; that is why a *list* of conjectures needs to be kept when working down from the top of the concept space.

Next, card 2, is examined, represented by the truth-value assignment:

$$a = \text{T}; b = \text{T}; c = \text{F}.$$

Card 2 is a positive example, and so the conjecture $\bot$, which is false for all rows of the truth-table, classifies it *incorrectly*, and so must be weakened. This is achieved in exactly the same way as with grudge-induce: the new conjecture is set to the strongest monomial which is made true under the truth-value assignment $a = \text{T}, b = \text{T}, c = \text{F}$, namely the monomial:

$$a \ \& \ b \ \& \ \neg c.$$

The situation is shown in figure 9.5a, where the conjecture ϕ can be seen to have moved up the lattice. Remember, conditions (9.5) and (9.6) ensure that the correct rule, ψ lies below each of the conjectures in Φ and above the conjecture ϕ.

At this point, however, pincer-induce is in a position to eliminate some of the conjectures in Φ. Consider the conjecture $\neg a$. This rule says that an example has the target concept C just in case it makes a false. Yet card 2 is a positive example, and makes a true, so the conjecture $\neg a$ classifies it incorrectly. Now, the members of Φ are supposed to be the most liberal (i.e. weakest possible) rules for C: they only get made stronger as pincer-induce proceeds. But if the monomial $\neg a$ classifies card 2 incorrectly as not falling under C, that means that the correct rule ψ cannot be logically stronger than $\neg a$. Therefore, having seen card 2, pincer-induce can throw away the conjecture $\neg a$, since ψ cannot lie below it in the lattice.

Similar remarks apply to the second conjecture in Φ, namely, $\neg b$. Again, it is false for card 2, and so cannot be weaker than the correct rule ψ. Therefore, it too can be discarded. Of the three conjectures in Φ, only $\neg c$ survives; notice that $\neg c$ is true for card 2, and so classifies it correctly. The resulting situation is shown in figure 9.5b, where the eliminated members of Φ have been crossed out.

The processing of the remaining cards is relatively uneventful. Card 3 is examined, represented by the truth-value assignment:

$$a = \text{F}; b = \text{T}; c = \text{T}.$$

Card 3 is a negative example, but is correctly classified by the only remaining member of Φ, $\neg c$, so no changes are made.

Next, card 4 is examined, represented by the truth-value assignment:

$$a = \text{F}; b = \text{T}; c = \text{F}.$$

Card 4 is a positive example, and so the current ϕ, namely, $a \ \& \ b \ \& \ \neg c$, which is false for the corresponding row of the truth-table, classifies it *incorrectly*. pincer-induce again responds by moving up the lattice of figure 9.3 until a monomial is found which classifies this new example correctly. Again, the monomial found is:

$$b \,\&\, \neg c.$$

leading to the situation is shown in figure 9.6.

Finally, card 5, is examined, represented by the truth-value assignment:

$$a = \text{F}; \, b = \text{F}; \, c = \text{T}.$$

Card 5 is a negative example, but is correctly classified by the only remaining member of Φ, $\neg c$, so no changes are made.

At the end of the training examples, `pincer-induce` chooses the first member of Φ, ϕ_1 as the rule for predicting C. In this case, the final rule is

$$\phi_1 = \neg c.$$

Notice that this is a different result from that returned by `grudge-induce` on the same training examples.

Formally, the procedure `pincer-induce` is as follows. There are three main sub-procedures: `move-up`, which is responsible for updating ϕ in response to positive examples, `move-down` which is responsible for updating Φ in response to negative examples, and `prune`, which deletes certain elements of Φ in response to positive examples.

The procedure `move-up` is exactly the same as for `grudge-induce`. The procedure `move-down` takes two arguments: Φ, a list of conjectures, and x, a new negative example specified as a truth-value assignment. It produces, as output, a list of monomials each of which (i) take the truth-value F according to the truth-value assignment x, (ii) are logically stronger than (or equivalent to) one of the monomials in Φ, and (iii) are the logically weakest monomials satisfying conditions (i) and (ii). With a little thought, it can be seen that the following procedure does the job:

begin `move-down` (Φ, x)
    let `new-`Φ be the empty list
    for each ϕ_i in Φ **do**
        if ϕ_i is true according to x **do**
            let `difference-list` be the list of all literals that are
            true according to x but do not occur in ϕ_i
            for each `literal` in `difference-list` (if any) **do**
                form monomial consisting of ϕ_i together with
                negation of `literal` (removing any double negations,
                and regarding $\top$ as a conjunction with zero literals)
            end for each
            add the list of all such monomials to the list `new-`Φ
            (deleting repetitions)
        end if
    end for each

remove any monomials from new-Φ which are logically
    stronger than any others
return new-Φ
end move-down

The procedure to prune Φ takes two arguments: Φ, a list of conjectures which are to be pruned, and ϕ, a monomial which is used to do the pruning. It produces, as output, a pruned version of Φ, in which only those elements compatible with ϕ remain. The procedure is as follows:

        begin prune(Φ, ϕ)
          let new-Φ be the empty list
          for each ϕ_i in Φ **do**
            if ϕ_i contains no literal whose negation
            is in ϕ **then**
              add ϕ_i to new-Φ
            end if
          end for each
          return new-Φ
        end prune

The complete procedure, pincer-induce, applied to training examples $x_1, \ldots, x_m$, is as follows.

        begin pincer-induce($x_1, \ldots, x_m$)
          let Φ be the 1-element list containing ⊤
          let ϕ be ⊥
          for each x in $x_1, \ldots, x_m$ **do**
          if ϕ is a member of Φ **do**
            halt and **return** ϕ
          end if
          if x is a positive example **then**
            let ϕ be result of move-up(ϕ, x)
          else
            let Φ be result of move-down(Φ, x)
            let Φ be result of prune(Φ, ϕ)
          end if
          end for each
          return first element of Φ
        end pincer-induce

(See exercise 3.)

9.3.4 *Inductive bias and sensitivity to the underlying representation*

Notice that pincer-induce and grudge-induce infer different rules on the basis of the same data: grudge-induce thinks that daxes are cards with white squares and black triangles on them, while pincer-induce thinks that daxes are simply cards with black triangles on them. These rules for predicting instances of C yield identical results on the training examples of figure 9.1, and differ only on the unseen cases. Thus, in the example of figure 9.1, pincer-induce and grudge-induce extrapolate from the data in different ways. As we say: pincer-induce and grudge-induce have different inductive biases.

By viewing pincer-induce and grudge-induce as searching through the space of monomials as represented in figure 9.3, we can get a good idea of how their inductive biases differ. First, pincer-induce is less conservative than grudge-induce in predicting instances of C among so-far-unobserved examples. Thus, while grudge-induce predicts that no unobserved cards will have the target concept, pincer-induce predicts that the unobserved cards characterized by the monomials a & $\neg b$ & $\neg c$ and $\neg a$ & $\neg b$ & $\neg c$ will both have the target-concept. Second, pincer-induce tends to produce syntactically simpler rules that grudge-induce. Thus, grudge-induce produced a rule with two conjuncts, while pincer-induce produced one with one conjunct. This is because grudge-induce starts with a monomial having many conjuncts, and progressively simplifies it, while pincer-induce starts from many monomials having one conjunct, and progressively complicates them. Nevertheless, both inductive biases represent *guesses* about future examples, both of which are consistent with the presented data.

A further, related fact about these induction algorithms deserves mention: it turns out that they are sensitive to the way in which the original induction task is described. For example, in the induction task of figure 9.1, we very naturally took the relevant features of the cards to be the colours (black or white) of the three shapes; and we denoted these features by the proposition-letters a, b and c. That is, we described the examples in terms of the features:

$$
\begin{aligned}
&a \qquad \text{card has a white circle} \\
&b \qquad \text{card has a white square} \\
&c \qquad \text{card has a white triangle.}
\end{aligned}
$$

Recall that the procedure pincer-induce, in response to the examples of figure 9.1 (described in terms of a, b and c), inferred the rule

$$\phi = \neg c$$

which is to say:

A card is a dax if and only if it has a black triangle   (9.7)

But there are alternative ways of describing the cards. Consider, for example, the following description:

a   card has a white circle
b   card has a white square
c^* card has either: (i) a white circle, black square and black triangle
                 or: (ii) a black circle and a white triangle
                 or: (iii) a white square and a white triangle.

This is a (to our sensibilities) bizarre set of features to be sure; but it is a set of features for all that, since each of the 8 possible cards can be described by a unique truth-value assignment to the proposition-letters *a*, *b* and c^*. (See exercise 4.)

Moreover, the five cards in figure 9.1 have the property that they are characterized by *the same* truth-value assignments to *a*, *b* and *c* as to *a*, *b*, and c^*. It follows, then, that if pincer-induce is executed using this bizarre description of the cards, everything will proceed in exactly the way described in section 9.3.3, but with *c* replaced throughout by c^*. Therefore, pincer-induce will infer the rule:

$$\phi = \neg c^*$$

which is to say:

> A card is a dax if and only if it (i) does not have a white circle, black square and black triangle and (ii) does not have a black circle and a white triangle and (iii) does not have a white square and a white triangle.   (9.8)

Rule (9.7) and rule (9.8) make *different* predictions about unseen cases. Thus: even for a fixed induction procedure, the predictions are sensitive to choices between different, equally adequate sets of describing features. We will return to this observation anon.

9.4   The choice of inductive bias and the justification of induction

The previous section described two induction procedures, grudge-induce and pincer-induce, which in general yield different results when presented with the same data. We said that these procedures differ in their *inductive bias*. We also pointed out that the rules inferred by a given induction procedure are typically sensitive to the choice of features with which to describe the presented examples.

Two related questions confront us, therefore, when programming a computer to make inductive inferences.

(i) Of all the possible inductive procedures, each with its own inductive bias, which, if any, is the correct one to use?

(ii) Suppose we choose one induction procedure as being superior to the others. What sort of validation process can we undertake to check that we have picked the right procedure?

It should be pointed out immediately that these are not purely theoretical questions, of no practical importance. As was remarked in the previous section, the example of figure 9.1 is nothing more than an abstract and somewhat simplified version of real induction tasks, in which the rules induced predict the occurrence of properties it is important to know about. If we are to build AI systems capable of inductive inference, we want to know which is the right induction procedure, and we would like to have some principled way of checking that whatever induction procedure we have chosen really is doing the job expected of it. Note that we should also bear in mind the possibility that different induction procedures might be successful in different domains.

Of course, for any given induction task, if we *know* the correct rule for the target concept in advance, then we hardly need an induction procedure. Yet, if we do not know the correct rule, any way we have of determining the effectiveness of any given induction procedure will itself involve inductive inference. That is: the process of determining how well an induction procedure performs ultimately reduces to the question of how well its predictions agree with our own predictions, given the evidence available. Unfortunately, human inductive practices are complex, and no one has written down a convincing account of what they are. Nor is there a corresponding account of the choice of basic features on which these algorithms should be run. These remain open questions. Moral: just because you see an induction procedure in AI, do not think that it necessarily tells us how to do inductive inference. There will always be alternatives to that procedure, and the principles for choosing between them are not at present well understood.

9.5   ID3

The algorithms examined in the previous section are capable only of inducing a monomial – that is, a conjunction of literals – from the given examples. (See exercise 5 and further reading.) In this section, we consider an influential learning algorithm which works on the full space of boolean functions: id3 .

9.5.1   Test-trees

The rules which id3 develops take the form of *test-trees*, as shown in figure 9.7. In a test-tree, the non-terminal nodes – i.e. the individual tests – are labelled by proposition letters, and have two branches, T and F. Such a test-tree classifies a given example x by asking a series of questions which lead sooner or later to a terminal node labelled *pass*, indicating that x has the property C, or *fail*, indicating that it does not.

The interpretation of the test-tree is straightforward. Consider a given training example x, specified as a truth-value-assignment to proposition-letters a, b and c. To subject x to the test-tree of figure 9.7, we simply start at the top, taking each branch, T or F, according to the truth-value which x determines for the proposition letter in question. Suppose, that, for example, x makes a true, b true and c false. In this case, the first test, on c, will give the result F. Following the F-branch, we next encounter the test b, which will give the result T. Following the T-branch, then, we

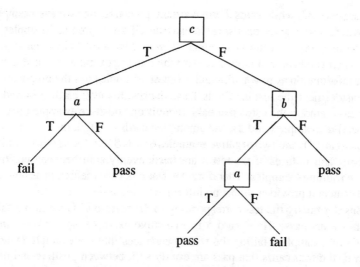

Figure 9.7   A test-tree involving a, b and c

encounter the test a, which also gives the result T. Finally, following the T-branch again, we arrive at the terminal node *pass*, indicating that x does have the concept C.

Note that a test-tree is just another way of writing a rule for predicting whether a given example has the target concept C. In fact, it is straightforward to translate between test-trees and formulae of the propositional calculus. However, for the purposes of this section it will be easier to think of rules as test-trees rather than as formulae. The function of the id3 induction procedure is to construct, on the basis of a sequence of positive and negative examples of a target concept C, a rule for predicting C in the form of a test-tree. The basic idea behind id3 is to construct a test-tree in which the *best* tests are carried out first. So, before describing how id3 works in detail, we need to explain the notion of an *efficient indicator* for a target concept.

9.5.2   Efficient indicators

Let us return again to the induction task of figure 9.1. Here, the training examples are described in terms of three features, a, b and c, which, as we have just seen, can be regarded as *tests* which the individual cards either pass or fail. In general, asking whether a card has any one of these features gives us information about whether that card has the target concept, C. Consider the test (i.e the feature) c. Three cards pass this test, namely, cards 1, 3 and 5; and two cards fail, namely, cards 2 and 4. But cards 1, 3 and 5 are precisely the negative examples of the target concept, C, while cards 2 and 4 are the precisely the positive examples. In other words, test c gives us a *sure-fire* way to tell those training examples which have the property C from those which do not. Or, as we might put it, c is the most efficient indicator of C possible (for the training examples) in that it gives us perfect information as to whether each of these examples has the property C.

Consider next the test a. Cards 1 and 2 pass this test; cards 3, 4 and 5 fail. In this case, among the cards that pass, there is one positive example (card 1) and one negative example (card 2); and among the cards that fail, there is one positive example (card 4), and two negative examples (cards 3 and 5). In other words, both the passes and failures of the test a are fairly evenly split between positive and negative training examples. Therefore, the test a is very inefficient as an indicator of C, because it provides almost no information about C.

Consider finally the test corresponding to the feature b. Only card 5 fails this test; the others pass. Here, card 5 is a negative example, so we know that (for the training examples) failing the test b guarantees that the example is negative. However, the four cards that pass are evenly split between positive and negative examples, so in this case, we have no information about C. Overall, then, the test b provides some information about C; but it is by no means as efficient an indicator as the test c.

Let us see if we can generalize these observations. Suppose that we are given m training examples, $x_1, \ldots, x_m$, for a target concept C, each characterized, in the familiar way, as a truth-value assignment to the proposition letters $a_1, \ldots, a_n$.

Let a be one of these proposition letters which divides the training examples into two classes: $y_1, \ldots, y_k$, which pass the test a (i.e. which make a true), and $z_1, \ldots, z_l$, which fail the test (i.e. which make a false). And let us concentrate, for the moment, on the $y_1, \ldots, y_k$. From the preceding discussion, we want to say that this set contains a lot of information about C if it contains either positive examples only, or negative examples only; by contrast, the set contains no information about C if there is a 50-50 mix of positive and negative examples. In other words, we want to say that the set contains a lot of information about C insofar as is it *homogeneous* with respect to C.

Let the proportion of positive examples among the $y_1, \ldots, y_k$ – that is, the examples which pass the test a – be p. And consider the quantity $\inf(C, a)$, defined as

$$\inf(C, a) = -p \log_2 p - (1 - p) \log_2 (1 - p). \tag{9.9}$$

Since p is always between 0 and 1, this quantity will also be between 0 and 1. Figure 9.8 shows how this function varies with p. There is one technical matter which needs to be sorted out before we proceed, and this concerns the behaviour of $\inf(C, a)$ where $p = 0$ or $p = 1$. In applying the expression (9.9) with $p = 0$, we have

$$\inf(C, a) = -0 \log_2 0 - 1 \log_2(1).$$

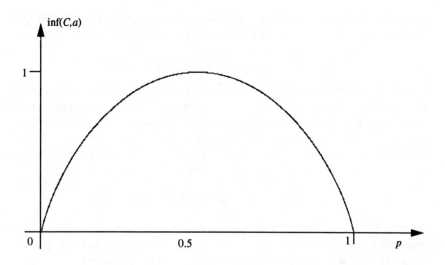

Figure 9.8   *The quantity* $\inf(C, a)$ *as a function of* p.

Now, the expression $\log_2(0)$ is not defined (it does not make sense to take the logarithm of 0), so strictly, the measure $\inf(C, a)$ is not defined in this case either. However, since the quantity $p \log_2(p)$ *tends* to zero as p tends to zero, we can safely assume that the term $0 \log_2(0)$ is equal to 0. So, if p is 0 – if, that is, the set of examples which pass the test a contains negative examples only – then we have

$$\begin{aligned} \inf(C, a) &= -0 \log_2 0 - 1 \log_2(1) \\ &= -0 - 0 = 0 \end{aligned}$$

Exactly the same points apply if p is 1 – that is, if the set of examples which pass the test a contains positive examples only: again we have $\inf(C, a) = 0$.

If, on the other hand, $p = 0.5$ – if, that is, the set of examples which pass the test a contains a 50-50 mix of positive and negative examples – then we have

$$\begin{aligned} \inf(C, a) &= -0.5 \log_2 0.5 - 0.5 \log_2(0.5) \\ &= -(0.5).(-1) - (0.5).(-1) = 1. \end{aligned}$$

As we can see from figure 9.8, this is the value of p for which $\inf(C, a)$ is at its maximum.

Thus, $\inf(C, a)$ is low when the $y_1, \ldots, y_k$ are either all positive examples or all negative examples; and it is high when this set contains a 50-50 mix of positive and negative examples. Therefore, $\inf(C, a)$ is a suitable measure of the *lack* of information which passing the test a conveys about C.

Let us turn our attention to the set of examples, $z_1, \ldots, z_l$ which *fail* the test a. Let the proportion of this set which are positive examples be q. Then, by similar reasoning to the above, we can measure the *lack* of information which failing the test a conveys about C using the quantity $\inf(C, \neg a)$, defined as:

$$\inf(C, \neg a) \;=\; -q\log_2 q - (1 - q)\log_2(1 - q).$$

Finally, we are in a position to define a measure of the overall lack of information which the test a conveys about C. We simply take the lack of information conveyed by passing the test together with the lack of information conveyed by failing the test, weighted according to the proportion of examples which pass and fail, respectively. Thus, if the proportion of the examples which pass the test a is r, the lack of information about C conveyed by the test a is given by the quantity

$$\mathrm{INF}(C, a) = r \,.\, \inf(C, a) + (1 - r) \,.\, \inf(C, \neg a).$$

We now have a measure which enables us to assess the effectiveness of any proposition-letter as a test for the target concept. The best test is the proposition-letter a for which the lack of information $\mathrm{INF}(C, a)$ is the smallest.

Remember the purpose of this measure: id3 needs it to decide how to construct a test-tree in response to its training data. We are now in a position to describe how this is done.

9.5.3   The procedure id3

Suppose we are presented with a list of m positive and negative training examples of a concept C, $x_1, \ldots, x_m$. Each example x_i is described as a *truth-value assignment* to the proposition letters $a_1, \ldots, a_n$, and, for each training example, we are told whether it has property C. The procedure id3 returns a test-tree for predicting whether any given example has C; this test-tree gives the correct results for the training examples, and makes predictions about unseen examples.

The basic idea behind id3 is as follows. Each of the proposition-letters is considered in turn, and the efficiency of that proposition letter as a test for C is computed, as described above, by finding $\mathrm{INF}(C, a_i)$, for $i = 1 \ldots n$. The proposition letter t_1 (where t_1 is one of the a_i) that provides the most efficient test for C is then chosen as the first test in the test-tree. At this stage, the test-tree is as shown in figure 9.9a. The training examples are then divided into two categories: those that pass the test t_1 and those that fail. Let the former group be $y_1, \ldots, y_k$ and the latter be $z_1, \ldots, z_l$. Now, it might be that passing or failing the test t_1 is a sure-fire indicator for C. Suppose, for example, that all the $y_1, \ldots, y_k$ have C: then we can terminate the T-branch of the test t_1 with the node pass; similarly, if none of the $z_1, \ldots, z_l$ have the property C, we terminate the F-branch of the test t_1 with the node fail. In general, however, even the most efficient test for C will produce classes $y_1, \ldots, y_k$ and $z_1, \ldots, z_l$ which contain both positive and negative examples. And in that case, further tests must be performed.

Consider first the $y_1, \ldots, y_k$; and assume that some of them have the property C and others do not. To distinguish between the C's and the non-C's, each of the

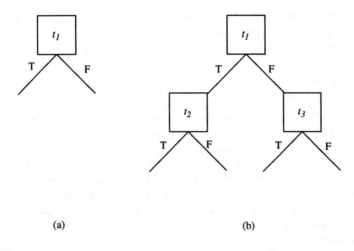

(a)   (b)

Figure 9.9   A test-tree being built

proposition letters is again considered in turn, and the efficiency of that proposition letter as a test for C among the $y_1, \ldots, y_k$ is computed. The proposition letter t_2 (where t_2 is one of the a_i) that provides the most efficient test for C is then chosen as the next test in the test-tree under the T-branch of the test t_1. Likewise for the $z_1, \ldots, z_l$: assume that some have the property C and others do not. Again, each of the proposition letters is considered in turn, and the proposition letter t_3 (where t_3 is one of the a_i) that provides the most efficient test for C among the $z_1, \ldots, z_l$ is chosen as the next test in the test-tree under the F-branch of the test t_1. At this point, the test-tree is as shown in figure 9.9b.

Clearly, we can proceed by adding new tests to the ends of the branches in the test-tree of figure 9.9b. Eventually, we will reach tests which constitute a sure-fire indicator for C, in that these tests divide the examples which are passed to them into perfectly homogeneous classes. At that point we will have a test-tree which classifies the training examples correctly; this test tree will then form the rule which we use to classify unseen cases.

The overall procedure, then, is as follows:

begin id3(training-examples, proposition-letters)
    if all examples in training-examples are positive **then**
        return the terminal test-tree pass
    else if all examples in training-examples are negative **then**
        return the terminal test-tree fail
    else
        let first-test be the test corresponding to that
        proposition letter in proposition-letters
        which is the most efficient indicator for C

    let new-proposition-letters be proposition-letters
    with first-test removed
    let pos-examples be those members of training-examples
    which pass the test first-test
    let neg-examples be those members of training-examples
    which fail the test first-test
    let true-tree be result of
    id3(pos-examples, new-proposition-letters)
    let false-tree be result of
    id3(neg-examples, new-proposition-letters)
    let test-tree be the tree formed by taking first-test
    as the first test, and by appending true-tree to the
    T-branch of that test, and false-tree to the F- branch
    return test-tree
    end if
end id3

As an example of ID3 in operation, consider the training data involving the three features a, b, c:

a	b	c	C
T	T	T	F
T	T	F	T
T	F	T	F
T	F	F	-
F	T	T	T
F	T	F	F
F	F	T	-
F	F	F	T

$$(9.10)$$

The tree produced will be that of figure 9.7. (See exercise 7.)

9.5.4 Approximate induction using id3

The procedure id3 has a further feature which deserves mention. So far in this chapter, we have been assuming that the set of features $a_1, \ldots, a_n$ in terms of which the training examples are characterized is *adequate* for predicting the target concept C. That is, we have assumed that, given two training examples, x_i and x_j, characterized by the *same* truth-value assignment to the $a_1, \ldots, a_n$, x_i and x_j must either be *both* positive examples or *both* negative examples. Clearly, if, say, x_i has C but x_j does not, then there is no possibility of devising a correct rule for predicting C in terms of the features $a_1, \ldots, a_n$.

In real life however, it is common to encounter induction problems where the features describing the data are not adequate for predicting the target concept.

Such cases can arise because the relevant features are not known, or because their determination is prohibitively expensive, or simply because errors creep in to the data-collection process. Nowhere is this more obviously true than in medicine: in inducing rules from individual case histories, we can expect that patients characterized as having the same list of symptoms can turn out to have been suffering from different diseases.

However, the id3 procedure can cope with induction over an inadequate set of features. To be sure, if the features really are inadequate, then no test-tree based on those features can correctly predict instances of C. However, the procedure used to construct test-trees based on choosing the most efficient indicators can be followed through as described in the previous section. In particular, the measure $\text{INF}(C, a)$ is perfectly well-defined even when there are many training examples with the same characterization in terms of truth-value assignments to the a_i, but differing on the property C.

There is one small amendment to be made. If the set of features is inadequate, the procedure id3 may run out of tests to perform. That is, one of the recursive calls

    id3(pos-examples,new-proposition-letters);

or

    id3(neg-examples,new-proposition-letters);

will be made, where new-proposition-letters is the empty list. In this case, then, a decision must be made as to how we are to terminate the test-tree at this point. A sensible policy seems to be to terminate the tree with the terminal node pass if most of the examples in question are positive, and with fail if most of the examples in question are negative. (See exercise 8.)

Thus, id3 constitutes a general induction procedure capable of inferring arbitrary rules based on Boolean combinations of features, for predicting a target concept from a set of training examples. The procedure works even if the connection between the target concept and the features in terms of which the examples are described is probabilistic in nature.

9.6 Induction and probability

Inductive inference is an inherently uncertain business. Whatever rule one induces from a limited collection of training examples, there is always the logical possibility that future cases will not conform to it. Thus, any method of inductive reasoning will have some degree of uncertainty associated with it. Moreover, the degree of uncertainty seems to depend in a systematic way on the nature of the evidence at our disposal. For example, rules induced on the basis of *many* training examples ought to lead to more confident predictions than rules induced on the basis of few training examples. How can we quantify and compare the certainty of various inductive inferences?

Since we argued in favour of probability theory as a means of representing uncertainty in chapter 8, we will take this as our point of departure. Viewing inductive inference in probabilistic terms gives us a good way of looking at inductive bias. Recall that, in probability theory, a reasoner's degrees of certainty are represented by a probability distribution, i.e. a function p mapping every proposition to a number, in accordance with certain axioms. The change of belief in response to new evidence is modelled by conditionalization: if b is a proposition (with $p(b) \neq 0$) representing new evidence, the reasoner's new probability distribution after accepting b as certain will be p_b, where, for any proposition a:

$$p_b(a) = p(a \mid b) = \frac{p(a \& b)}{p(b)}.$$

Now, this method of updating degrees of certainty is perfectly general, and can be applied to inductive reasoning just as well as to the sorts of diagnostic problems considered in chapter 8. To see how this works in detail, we will consider a particularly simple induction problem.

Consider what grounds we might have for believing that ravens are black. Ignoring books and other authorities as sources of evidence, it is reasonable to suppose that the observation of many black ravens and no (or very few) non-black ravens justifies confidence that the next raven observed will be black. Suppose, then, a reasoner observes a bird – call it *bird #1* – and sees that it is both a raven and black. Then we can assume the reasoner comes to accept the proposition b_1:

Bird #1 is a raven, and is black

as certain. Accordingly, the reasoner should update his initial probability distribution, p_0, by conditionalizing on b_1, to get the new probability distribution $p_1 = (p_0)_{b_1}$. Suppose that the reasoner then observes a second bird – call it *bird #2* – and sees that it is neither a raven nor black. Then we can assume the reasoner comes to accept the proposition b_2

Bird #2 is not a raven, and is not black

as certain. Again, the reasoner should update his old probability distribution p_1 by conditionalizing on b_2, to get the new probability distribution $p_2 = (p_1)_{b_2}$. More generally, we can model a sequence of n observations $b_1, \ldots, b_n$ by the reasoner as a sequence of conditionalization operations which take the reasoner's degrees of belief through a sequence $p_0, p_1, \ldots, p_n$ of probability distributions.

What does this way of looking at things tell us about induction? Well, consider the reasoner's expectation that the next raven he observes will be black. That expectation can be given by the conditional probability that the bird in question will be black given that it is a raven, namely,

$$p(\text{bird \#n+1 is black} \mid \text{bird \#n+1 is a raven}), \tag{9.11}$$

where bird #n+1 is a name for the next bird observed, and where p is the reasoner's current probability distribution. Thus, the change in the reasoner's expectation that the next raven he observes will be black can be modelled by the changes in the quantity (9.11), as p changes from p_0 to p_n.

What can we say in general about how (9.11) will change as the reasoner conditionalizes on observation propositions? Let us first consider what we would *like* to be able to say. Suppose that many ravens are observed, and all of them are black; we would like that fact to increase the quantity (9.11). Suppose, by contrast, that many ravens are observed, and few of them are observed to be black; we would like that fact to decrease the quantity (9.11). The question arises: does this ever turn out to be the case, and, if so, under what conditions?

The answer is that it all depends on the *initial* probability distribution p_0. It turns out that there do indeed exist some initial probability distributions with the desirable property that the observation of many black ravens (and few non-black ones) increases the conditional probability that the next thing observed will be black given that it is a raven. Unfortunately, however, it can be shown that there exist initial probability distributions with the undesirable property that the observation of many black ravens (and few non-black ones) *has no effect* on the conditional probability that the next thing observed will be black given that it is a raven! Thus, if a reasoner's response to evidence is modelled by conditionalization, then the reasoner will be able to learn from experience in intuitively plausible ways only if he has an appropriate initial probability distribution.

The technical details involved in constructing the initial probability distributions mentioned in the previous paragraph are too complex to describe here. However, the following overview should suffice to explain the key issues. (See also further reading.)

First, we must make some decisions about the language we are using. We shall adopt a predicate-calculus-based language in which there are N names, a_1, ..., a_N, denoting distinct individuals. We shall assume that these N individuals are the *only* individuals recognized by the domain of discourse. We suppose in addition that the language contains M 1-place predicates, $r_1(x)$, ..., $r_M(x)$ such as raven(x) and black(x) (we shall ignore 2- or more-place predicates for simplicity). It should be clear that such a language allows us to formulate simple inductive inferences such as the raven-example considered above.

Given such a language (and given the above assumptions about the domain of interpretation), the truth-value of every formula is decided by specifying, for each name a_i, and for each predicate $r_j(x)$, whether the atomic formula $r_j(a_i)$ is true. Thus, the complete state of the recognized universe can be specified by a formula of the form:

$$r_1^*(a_1) \ \& \ \ldots \ \& \ r_1^*(a_N) \ \& \ \ldots \ \& \ \ldots \ \& \ r_M^*(a_1) \ \& \ \ldots \ \& \ r_M^*(a_N). \qquad (9.12)$$

where, for $i = 1 \ldots N$ and $j = 1 \ldots M$, $r_j^*(a_i)$ is either $r_j(a_i)$ or $\neg r_j(a_i)$. Such a formula will be called a *state-description*. Since there are N names and M predicates, there must be 2^{NM} distinct state-descriptions. These 2^{NM} state-descriptions form a partition, in the sense of chapter 8. Thus, if we know the probability of each state-description, we can calculate the probability of any formula in the language. Hence, specifying the probability of each state-description amounts to specifying an entire probability distribution p.

Here, then, is a natural suggestion for constructing a reasoner's initial probability distribution: we shall take *all state-descriptions to have the same probability*, namely, $1/2^{NM}$. After all, the reasoner has, initially, no evidence to prefer one state-description to another, so they should be equiprobable.

Unfortunately, it can be shown that this probability distribution has the undesirable property that observation of past cases has no effect on probabilities concerning as-yet unseen individuals. In particular, the observation of many black ravens (and few non-black ones) has no effect on the conditional probability that the next thing observed will be black given that it is a raven. So this had better not be the reasoner's initial probability distribution if we want the reasoner to perform inductive inferences!

However, there are initial probability distributions that lead reasoners to react in more plausible ways to observation of past cases. One such distribution was suggested by Carnap [4]. To explain Carnap's idea, we need to introduce the notion of a *structure-description*. Consider any state-description σ of the form (9.12). What would happen if the names a_1 and a_2 were switched? Well, assuming a_1 and a_2 did not share all the same properties according to σ, a different state-description, σ' would result. But these two state-descriptions differ only in the switching of two names. Thus, we can think of σ and σ' as, to all intents and purposes, *describing the same state of affairs*. More generally, we say that state-descriptions σ and σ' are *isomorphic* if one can be obtained from the other permuting the names $a_1, \ldots, a_N$. If, then, σ is any state-description, we can collect together all the state-descriptions $\sigma'_1 \ldots, \sigma'_k$ isomorphic to σ, and form the formula τ:

$$\sigma \vee \sigma'_1 \vee \ldots \vee \sigma'_k. \tag{9.13}$$

A formula of the form (9.13) – that is, a disjunction of a complete set of isomorphic state-descriptions – is called a *structure-description*. It is, if you like, the result of taking a state-description, and abstracting away the choices we have made about the names for individuals.

Now for Carnap's proposal for an initial probability distribution. Instead of taking all the state-descriptions to be equiprobable, we take all the *structure-descriptions* to be equiprobable. Furthermore, if, τ is a structure-description involving the $k + 1$ state-descriptions $\sigma \vee \sigma'_1 \vee \ldots \vee \sigma'_k$, we shall assume that these $k + 1$ state-descriptions all have the same probability as each other. That is, whatever probability the structure-description τ has is divided up equally among the constituent state-descriptions. Since different structure-descriptions contain different numbers of state-descriptions, state-descriptions belonging to different structure-descriptions can, on this proposal, have different probabilities. In fact, the practice of assigning equal probabilities to structure-descriptions has the effect of making state-descriptions in which many of the N individuals have the same properties more probable than state-descriptions in which all the individuals have different properties. That is: the prior probability distribution is biased in favour of *homogeneous* state-descriptions and against *heterogeneous* ones. Let us call this initial probability distribution p_0^*.

The combinatorics involved in working out how many structure-descriptions there are, and how many state-descriptions the various structure-descriptions contain, are too complicated to describe here; so we shall have to content ourselves with stating one result without proof. Carnap showed that, given the initial probability distribution p_0^*, if s_1 individuals have been observed to have properties $r_1(x)$ and $\neg r_2(x)$, and s_2 individuals have been observed to have properties $r_1(x)$ and $r_2(x)$, then, after conditionalizing on this evidence, the conditional probability that the next individual observed will have property $r_2(x)$ given that it has property $r_1(x)$ can be shown to be

$$1 - \frac{s_1 + 2^{M-2}}{s_1 + s_2 + 2^{M-1}}. \tag{9.14}$$

(Remember, M is the number of predicates in the language).

To see why this rule gives us intuitively reasonable prescriptions for this particular inductive inference, let us assume that raven(x) and black(x) are the only predicates in the language, (so that $r_1(x)$ is raven(x), $r_2(x)$ is black(x), and M is 2). Then, if 10 black ravens have been observed and only 2 white ones, the probability that the next bird observed will be black given that it is a raven will be, from (9.14),

$$1 - \frac{2 + 2^{2-2}}{2 + 10 + 2^{2-1}} \quad = \quad 11/14$$
$$\approx \quad 0.786.$$

If 100 black ravens have been observed, and only 20 non-black ones, this quantity is

$$1 - \frac{20 + 2^{2-2}}{20 + 100 + 2^{2-1}} \quad = \quad 101/122$$
$$\approx \quad 0.828.$$

If 100 black ravens have been observed, and only 2 non-black ones, this quantity is

$$1 - \frac{2 + 2^{2-2}}{2 + 100 + 2^{2-1}} \quad = \quad 101/104$$
$$\approx \quad 0.971.$$

All this is very intuitive: the probability that the next observed raven will be black increases as the number and preponderance of confirming observations increases.

One slightly less intuitive feature is that the probability that the next observed raven will be black *decreases* as the number M of predicates in the language increases, even though these additional predicates may have nothing to do with ravens or blackness. For, instance, if there are 10 predicates in total, then observing 100 black ravens and 2 non-black ravens means that the probability that the next observed raven will be black is:

$$1 - \frac{2 + 2^{10-2}}{2 + 100 + 2^{10-1}} = 356/614$$
$$\approx 0.580,$$

a considerable reduction from 0.971! More generally, the results of this kind of inductive procedure can be seen to depend, often in quite bizarre ways, on the underlying language.

Let us step back to compare the results just given with those of previous sections. The results stated in this section establish that conditionalization can lead to apparently sensible inductive inferences (or at least, to their probabilistic analogues), but *only* when coupled with a suitable initial probability distribution. The initial probability distribution thus contains, in effect, the system's inductive bias, in that it controls how the reasoner will extrapolate from previous observations to unseen cases. Just as, when viewing induction in a non-probabilistic framework as truth-table completion, we found various induction procedures with different inductive biases, so too, in the probabilistic induction problems of this section, there are many possible initial probability assignments. In both cases, the problem is that these possibilities seem to be logically on a par with each other. Yet the choice of induction procedure has a radical effect on the inductive inferences licensed.

True, the initial probability assignment proposed by Carnap, which assigns equal probabilities to structure-descriptions, does combine (relative) simplicity with (some) intuitive consequences. But even if the results are intuitively correct, that still does not explain *why* they are any better than any of the logically possible alternatives. In fact, we are in the same position as we found ourselves when choosing between the different inductive biases exhibited by grudge-induce and pincer-induce.

9.7 Grue

The following problem, invented by the philosopher Nelson Goodman [5], illustrates, in an amusing way, how sensitive induction methods are to the underlying language: change the underlying language, and you change the inferences your induction procedure allows.

Consider the proposition that all emeralds are green. Fictionalizing somewhat, we might suppose that we believe this proposition because we have seen a large number of emeralds and they have so far all turned out to be green. Thus, the case is the same as the raven-example of section 9.6.

Now, as we have seen, the choice of initial probability distribution required to support this inference is problematical, and the details of the probability theory involved are complicated. But it seems at least intuitively reasonable that a good induction procedure should regard a large number of green emeralds (and no non-green ones) as evidence that the next emerald observed will be green.

But now define *grue* as follows:

x is grue if and only if x is green and is observed before the year 2000, or x is blue and is not observed before the year 2000.

True, grue is a made-up property, but a property nevertheless. Now, if all emeralds so far observed are green, then they are also (at the time of writing) grue, since they have been observed before the year 2000. But if a large number of *green* emeralds (and no non-green ones) is good evidence that the next emerald observed will be *green*, then, by the same token, a large number of *grue* emeralds (and no non-grue ones) ought to be good evidence that the next emerald observed will be *grue* too. If made just before the year 2000, this latter conclusion predicts that the next emerald observed will be blue.

It may be objected that *grue* does not count because it is a *defined* property. The reply is that the question of which properties are defined and which are not is to some extent a matter of choice. After all, we can define an equally odd predicate, *bleen*, as follows:

x is bleen if and only if x is blue and is observed before the year 2000, or x is green and is not observed before the year 2000.

And now, we can define *green* and *blue* in terms of *grue* and *bleen*:

x is green (blue) if and only if x is grue (bleen) and is observed before the year 2000, or x is bleen (grue) and is not observed before the year 2000.

In which case there is no obvious reason why an AI system could not start off with *grue* and *bleen* in its language, and regard *green* and *blue* as defined predicates. But if an AI system does that, then it will make some very odd predictions.

The question of which predicates are suitable for induction and which are not has spawned a huge literature, which we shall not review here. (See further reading.) We shall be content with the modest moral that for a system to exhibit good inductive inferences is a matter not only of its induction procedure proper, but also of the representation-language over which that procedure operates. Unfortunately, the general principles governing the choice of suitable languages are not at present well understood.

Exercises

1. With regard to the induction problem of figure 9.1, how many truth-functions involving the proposition letters a, b and c are there altogether? How many are consistent with the five examples given in figure 9.1? How many monomials involving these three proposition letters are there altogether? How many are consistent with the five examples given in figure 9.1?

2. (Programming) Implement the algorithm grudge-induce. Verify that it behaves as described on the example of figure 9.1.

3. (Programming) Implement the algorithm pincer-induce. Verify that it behaves as described on the example of figure 9.1.

4. In section 9.3.4, it was claimed that the set of features

   a card has a white circle

   b card has a white square

   c^* card has either: (i) a white circle, black square and black triangle

                         or: (ii) a black circle and a white triangle

                         or: (iii) a white square and a white triangle

   has the property that each of the eight possible cards in the induction task of figure 9.1 has a unique description as a truth-value assignment to the proposition-letters a, b and c^*. Verify this claim. Do you think there is anything objective we can say about this set of features that could provide a reason for not deploying it in an induction task?

5. Find a sequence of training examples for some target concept C (involving a collection of propositional variables) such that there is no monomial (in the relevant propositional variables) which classifies the examples correctly. What, *exactly*, happens when the procedures grudge-induce and pincer-induce are presented with such a sequence?

6. It is comparatively simple to read formulae off from test-trees, but what about the other way round? Construct test-trees corresponding to the following formulae.

   (a) $a \ \& \ \neg b \ \& \ c$

   (b) $a \ \lor \ \neg b \ \lor \ c$

   (c) $a \ \& \ (\neg b \ \lor \ c)$

   Can you think of alternative solutions?

7. (Programming) Implement the procedure id3. Show that the training examples (9.10) really do give rise to the test-tree of figure 9.7.

8. (Programming) Adapt the implementation of id3 to handle *inadequate* sets of features, i.e. features in terms of which some positive and negative training examples have the same description. You will need to insert a check to see whether new-proposition-letters is empty. If it is, then you must terminate the test-tree as described in section 9.5.4.

9. (To think about.) The probabilistic approach outlined in section 9.6 was applied to a particularly simple inductive inference: the inference that the next observed raven will be black given a collection of observations of birds. But can this same approach be used to make (probabilistic) predictions of more complex kinds? For instance, can we compute, given the cards in figure 9.1, the probability that a newly-observed card will be a dax, given that it has, say, a black circle, a black square and a black triangle on it? (Warning: if you are really determined to find a method to calculate this probability, be prepared to spend some time on the problem!)

Further reading

In AI, much work on induction is carried out under the banner of *machine learning*. However, machine learning includes aspects of reasoning, such as concept-acquisition, that are arguably unconnected with induction. For a good survey of progress in machine learning (including, but not confined to induction), see Buchanan and Wilkins [3]. The procedure pincer-induce is based on the work of Mitchell [7]. (In fact, the restriction of pincer-induce to monomial spaces is not really necessary and was only used here to simplify the exposition.) Michalski describes the soybean example in Michalski [6]. The procedure id3 was developed by Quinlan [8]. The statistical analysis of rule-induction procedures is investigated within the subdiscipline of *computational learning theory*. For an excellent and lucid introduction, see Anthony and Biggs [1]. Inductive logic is only just now making its way into AI. Carnap [4], though not the last word on the subject, provides a good introduction to the critical ideas. Goodman [5] is a classic in the philosophical literature on induction and still well worth reading.

Bibliography

[1] Anthony, M. and N. Biggs *Computational Learning Theory*, Cambridge: Cambridge University Press, 1992.

[2] Bruner, J.S., J. Goodnow and G.A. Austin *A Study of Thinking*, New York: Wiley, 1956.

[3] Buchanan, Bruce G. and David C. Wilkins *Readings in Knowledge Acquisition and Learning*, San Mateo: Morgan Kaufmann, 1993.

[4] Carnap, R. "On inductive Logic", *Philosophy of Science*, 12 (1945) pp. 72–97.

[5] Goodman, Nelson *Fact, Fiction and Forecast*, Indianapolis: Bobbs-Merrill, 1965.

[6] Michalski, R.S. and R.L. Chilauski "Learning by being told and learning from examples", *International Journal of Policy Analysis and Information Systems*, 4(2) (1980) pp. 125–160.

[7] Mitchell, Tom M. "Generalization as search", *Artificial Intelligence*, 18(2) (1982).

[8] Quinlan, J.R. "Induction of Decision Trees", *Machine Learning*, 1 (1986) pp. 81–106.

10 Neural Networks

Neural networks are computing architectures based on large numbers of relatively simple processors, called *units*, operating in parallel, and connected to each other by a system of *links*, along which relatively simple signals are passed. The motivation for such an architecture comes from the physiology of animal brains, which consist of a large number of relatively simple processors, called *neurons*, operating in parallel, and connected to each other by a system of *axons* and *dendrites*, along which relatively simple signals are passed. Neural networks are by no means a new idea in computing or psychological modelling, but in recent years, they have enjoyed a particularly strong revival.

It should be admitted at the outset that the artificial neural networks at present used in computing are at best a vast simplification of brain anatomy; and few such networks lay serious claim to anatomical veridicality. Neural networks do, however, offer us a different vision of knowledge representation from 'traditional' AI systems, and exhibit many effects reminiscent of human reasoning: forgetting seldom-used information, blurring of similar memories, accessing of memories from a large number of potential cues, graceful degradation (as opposed to crashing) following damage, and natural resilience to noisy and error-prone data. Whatever the ultimate outcome of the debate on the relative merits of traditional and neural approaches to AI, there is no doubt that the latter provide a striking and instructive contrast to the often rather alien character of the former.

The field of *connectionism*, or *neural computing*, or *neural networks* (it is all the same thing) is now so vast that it would be impossible to survey it in a single chapter. In the following pages, we content ourselves with introducing three of the most influential connectionist paradigms: the perceptron, feed-forward multi-layer networks and Hopfield nets. We conclude with some theoretical remarks on the significance of neural networks in AI and the cognitive sciences.

10.1 The perceptron

10.1.1 Computing functions with perceptrons

The perceptron is a simple neural network comprising n input units, $u_1, \ldots, u_n$, linked to a single output unit o, as shown in figure 10.1. Each link, from input unit u_i to the output unit, has a weight, w_i, where $w_1, \ldots, w_n$ are real numbers; in

216

output

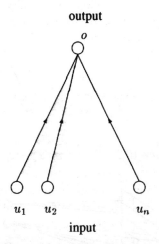

input

Figure 10.1   The perceptron

addition, the output unit has a *threshold*, θ, also a real number. Each of the units has an *activation level*, restricted to the binary values 1 and 0. The input to the perceptron is given by setting the activation levels $a_1, \ldots, a_n$ of the input units $u_1, \ldots, u_n$. The perceptron then computes the activation value of the output unit o according to the rule:

$$a = 1 \quad \text{if} \quad \sum_{i=1}^{n} w_i a_i \geq \theta$$
$$0 \quad \text{otherwise} \qquad\qquad (10.1)$$

The output of the perceptron is simply the activation level a of the output unit.

A unit having the activation function (10.1) is called a (linear) *threshold* unit: it has activation 1 just in case the weighted activation of the units feeding into it exceeds the threshold θ. Henceforth, we will sometimes speak of a unit as being *on* or *active* if its activation level is 1, respectively *off* or *inactive* if its activation level is 0.

To see how a perceptron works in practice, consider the perceptrons in figure 10.2(a) and (b), each of which has just two input units. Here, the weights w_1 and w_2 are shown next to the links to which they apply, and the threshold θ is shown next to the output unit. The perceptron of figure 10.2(a) will have its output unit on if and only if

$$a_1.1 + a_2.1 \geq 1.5$$

which will hold if and only if both input units are on, since activation levels are restricted to the values 1 and 0. Hence, interpreting the activation levels 1 and 0 as the truth-values T and F, respectively, we see that the perceptron of figure 10.2(a)

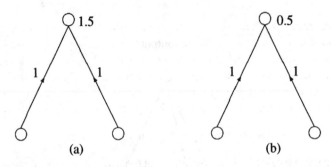

Figure 10.2   *Two simple perceptrons*

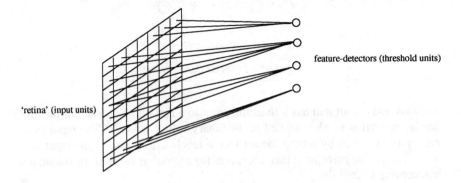

Figure 10.3   *Using perceptrons for feature-recognition (not all links shown)*

computes the Boolean function &. Similarly, the perceptron of figure 10.2(b) computes the Boolean function ∨.

In most serious applications however, perceptrons would be used not to compute truth-functions, but rather, and as their name implies, to recognize features in sensory (usually visual) input. Typically, each pixel in a digitized camera image would correspond to an input unit and would be turned on or off depending on whether that pixel was white or black in the image. These input units would feed their output to not just one, but a battery of perceptrons working in parallel, each recognizing some binary feature of the input. In this way, given the correct choice of weights and thresholds, certain visual recognition tasks can be performed. This architecture is shown schematically in figure 10.3. Of course, if we have the goal of distinguishing, say, visual presentations of apples from visual presentations of oranges, then choosing the weights and thresholds to perform this task, if it is possible at all, will not be easy. But the attraction of perceptrons – or rather, of neural networks generally – is that they admit of techniques for *learning* suitable weights (and thresholds) through repeated presentation of examples. We will describe a learning procedure for perceptrons shortly.

Before doing so, however, we conclude this section with a more abstract characterization of perceptrons. We may view the inputs $a_1, \ldots, a_n$ to a perceptron as a vector in n-dimensional space. (Since activation levels are restricted to 1 and 0, all input vectors will in fact lie at the corners of a hypercube in this space.) In addition, we may view the weights $w_1, \ldots, w_n$ and the threshold θ as defining a hyperplane in the same space – namely, the hyperplane satisfying the equation

$$w_1 x_1 + w_2 x_2 + \cdots + w_n x_n - \theta = 0.$$

In which case, the rule (10.1) for determining the activation level of the output unit has a simple geometric interpretation: an input vector $(a_1, \ldots, a_n)$ is classified according to which side of the hyperplane it falls on. This fact is sometimes expressed by calling the perceptron a *linear discriminator*.

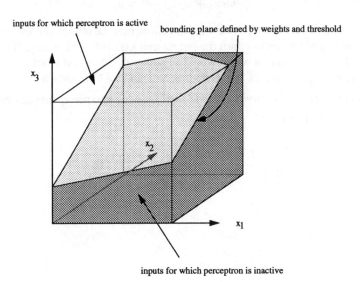

inputs for which perceptron is active

bounding plane defined by weights and threshold

x_3

x_2

x_1

inputs for which perceptron is inactive

Figure 10.4   Geometric interpretation of 3-input perceptron.

In the easily visualized case where $n = 3$, the eight possible input vectors correspond to the corners of a cube, and the weights w_1, w_2 and w_3 and threshold θ define a plane in space:

$$w_1 x_1 + w_2 x_2 + w_3 x_3 - \theta = 0.$$

Input vectors corresponding to a point on one side of this plane turn the output unit on; those corresponding to points on the other side turn the output unit off. This situation is shown in figure 10.4.

This geometric interpretation has the immediate consequence that there are functions which no perceptron, whatever its weights and threshold, can compute.

Consider the truth-function XOR (exclusive or), whose 'truth-table' (under the convention of using 1 for T and 0 for F) is:

x_1	x_2	x_1 XOR x_2
1	1	0
1	0	1
0	1	1
0	0	0

We can plot this function graphically as shown in fig 10.5, by placing, for each of the 4 points (x_1, x_2) in the plane, a white dot if the value XOR(x_1, x_2) is 1, and a black dot if XOR(x_1, x_2) is 0. Now, any perceptron computing the XOR-function would have weights w_1, w_2 and threshold θ corresponding to a line

$$w_1 x_1 + w_2 x_2 - \theta = 0.$$

such that all of the points on one side of the line turn the output unit on, and all of the points on the other side turn the output unit off. But we see from figure 10.5 that no line can be drawn which would separate the white and black dots. Hence no perceptron can compute the XOR-function, and we have shown

Theorem *There exist binary valued functions which no perceptron can compute.*

(See exercises 1 and 2.)

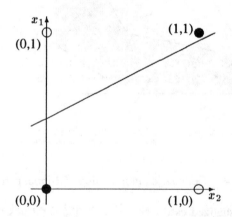

Figure 10.5   Plot of the XOR-function

It is worth remarking at this point that the above result applies only to perceptrons, and not to networks of threshold units comprising more than one layer. For example, the network of figure 10.6 does correctly compute the XOR-function. Here, the middle unit computes the AND-function (as in figure 10.2(a), whereas the input units and output unit (ignoring the middle unit) form a perceptron which computes the OR-function (as in figure 10.2(b)). The negative weight of -2 on the link from the middle unit to the output unit then ensures that the output unit is

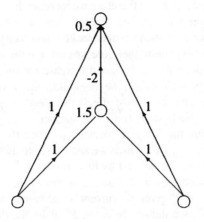

Figure 10.6   A network computing the XOR function

turned off when both of the input units are on. The critical middle unit is called a *hidden unit*, because it is neither an input unit nor an output unit. Thus, we need not concern ourselves with its activation level, so long as the network as a whole gives the correct results. We will investigate the behaviour of networks containing hidden units in section 10.2. (See exercise 3.)

10.1.2   Learning to compute functions with perceptrons

Any function that a perceptron can compute, a perceptron can learn. The learning procedure takes the form of presentations of the possible inputs to the function, together with the desired output. After each presentation, the weights and threshold are slightly adjusted, and the whole process is repeated until the perceptron finally computes the desired function. The purpose of this section is to describe this learning procedure in detail.

Suppose that we wish to teach a perceptron a function f which maps n input values $x_1, \ldots, x_n$ to an output value $f(x_1, \ldots, x_n)$. (Again, we assume that the inputs and output are restricted to the values 0 and 1.) For example, f could be the AND-function, so that $f(1, 1) = 1$, $f(1, 0) = 0$, $f(0, 1) = 0$ and $f(0, 0) = 0$. Starting off with weights and threshold randomly chosen, we take the first input pattern $x_1, \ldots, x_n$ and simply feed it through the perceptron; the output unit will respond with some activation level a – either 1 or 0. We then compare the *actual* output, a, with the *desired* output $f(x_1, \ldots, x_n) = t$ (t for "teaching"). If the two are the same, then we leave the weights and threshold alone. If, for some input pattern, $a = 0$ but $t = 1$, then we must make it more likely that the output unit is switched on by that input pattern; therefore we increase those weights w_i for which the corresponding input value x_i is 1, and we decrease the threshold θ. If, on the other hand, $a = 1$ but $t = 0$, then we must make it less likely that the output unit is switched on by that input pattern; therefore we decrease those weights w_i for which the corresponding input value x_i is 1, and increase the threshold θ. The amount by which we adjust the weights and the threshold, which we shall denote by η, is known as the *learning rate*, because it affects the speed of learning; normally, η is arbitrarily set to some fairly small (positive) number.

Let us suppose that the function we want to teach the perceptron is defined over r examples, $\mathbf{m}^1, \ldots, \mathbf{m}^r$, which we shall refer to as the *training examples*. Any training example $\mathbf{m}^p$ is defined by its n inputs, $(a_1^p, \ldots, a_n^p)$, and a *desired* output t^p. We will denote by a^p the *actual* output of the perceptron in response to the inputs $(a_1^p, \ldots, a_n^p)$, given its current weights and threshold. For a given training example, $\mathbf{m}^p$, we define the *error*, δ^p to be the difference between the desired output and the perceptron's actual output, i.e.

$$\delta^p = (t^p - a^p). \tag{10.2}$$

The adjustment of weights and thresholds proceeds as follows: the weights $w_1, \ldots w_n$ are adjusted according to the rule

$$w_i := w_i + \eta a_i^p \delta^p \tag{10.3}$$

and the threshold θ is adjusted according to the rule

$$\theta := \theta - \eta \delta^p. \tag{10.4}$$

These adjustments are then made for all the other possible input-output patterns. After having completed a sweep through all input-output patterns, the weights will have changed so as (hopefully) to classify more patterns correctly. By repeating the whole process over and over, the perceptron will eventually classify all patterns correctly. More formally, the procedure is as follows.

> **begin** `perceptron-learn`
>> **let** w_i $(i = 1 \ldots n)$ and θ be any real numbers;
>> **let** η be any positive real number
>> **until** all $a^p = t^p$ for each p $(1 \leq p \leq r)$ **do**
>>> **for** each training example $\mathbf{m}^p = (a_1^p, \ldots a_n^p)$ **do**
>>>> compute t^p using current weights and
>>>> threshold
>>>> **let** new weights and threshold be as follows:
>>>>> $w_i := w_i + \eta(t^p - a^p)a_i^p$
>>>>> $\theta := \theta - \eta(t^p - a^p)$
>>> **end for**
>> **end until**
> **end** `perceptron-learn`

Once the weights and threshold have adjusted themselves so that the correct output values are given for all possible inputs, then the perceptron can be said to have learned the function f. Once learning is completed, the weights are frozen at their current values, and the perceptron can thereafter be used to compute the function in question.

We have so far assumed that the weights and threshold will eventually stabilize as a result of applying the procedure `perceptron-learn`. But this fact is far from obvious: it is conceivable, for example, that the adjustment of weights to suit one input pattern will simply reverse the adjustments required by another so that a point is never reached in which all patterns are classified correctly. That this possibility is not realized is established by the so-called perceptron convergence theorem:

Theorem *If f is a function $f : \{0,1\}^n \rightarrow \{0,1\}$ and if there exist real numbers $w_1, \ldots, w_n$ and θ such that for each input pattern $(x_1^p, \ldots x_n^p)$*

$$\sum_{i=1}^{n} w_i x_i^p - \theta > 0 \ \text{ iff } \ f(x_1^p, \ldots, x_n^p) = 1$$

then the procedure `perceptron-learn` *will terminate.*

(For a proof of this theorem, see further reading.) Informally, the perceptron convergence theorem can be taken as establishing that if a perceptron can compute a function, it can learn to compute it. Of course, we know from the previous section that perceptrons cannot compute all binary-valued functions. (See exercise 4.)

10.1.3 Using perceptrons to perform induction

It is important that we be clear about the ways in which perceptrons – and indeed neural networks more generally – can be said to learn. The kind of learning we have discussed so far for perceptrons concerns merely the ability to recall information that has already been given (and many times at that!). That is: we can use the procedure `perceptron-learn` to make sure that an n-unit perceptron computes any perceptron-computable function f of our choosing; but we must, in general, train the perceptron on every one of the 2^n input-output patterns. That is, we must train the perceptron on every row of the truth-table for f.

Suppose, however, that we train a perceptron according to the procedure `perceptron-learn`, but using only a *subset* of the possible input vectors. We might then hope that the weights and threshold that the algorithm eventually yields will correctly classify not only the input patterns used for the training, but, in addition, those input patterns which the perceptron has not yet seen. That is, we may hope that the perceptron can perform induction, as discussed in chapter 9, inferring a general rule for classifying as-yet unseen patterns on the basis of a limited set of examples.

In one sense, it is obvious that the procedure `perceptron-learn` performs induction, since, after training on a subset of the possible inputs to a function f, the weights and threshold will stabilize at *some values or other*, and those values will then determine that the perceptron computes some function or other, say g, consistent with f over the set of training examples. But whether or not g is identical to f over all inputs (or at least agrees with f for most inputs) is another and less certain matter. As noted in chapter 9, the problem is that, logically speaking, there just is no single correct answer to the question "How do I extend this partially defined function to cover inputs I have not yet encountered?". Logically, all inductive biases are on a par.

In practice, however, such generalization can work surprisingly well. Suppose, for example, that we want to build a device for detecting the presence of a certain sort of object in its visual field. That is, we want a device to compute a function f mapping an array of n binary pixels to the output values 1 and 0 depending on whether the picture presented to it contains the object we would like to detect. Because of the large number of possible input patterns, it may be impractical to present every one in turn. However, by presenting a variety of representative pictures, some containing the object and others not, and by teaching the perceptron to give the correct responses in these cases, we may well end up with at least a reasonably reliable device for detecting objects of the requisite type. And, whilst such success is by no means assured, the utility of being able to train up such a detector from examples may be such as to make the enterprise worthwhile. So, to summarize: perceptrons have the potential not only to assimilate information they have been explicitly given, but also to perform induction on that information; however, the caveats from chapter 9 regarding inductive bias still apply.

10.2   Feed-forward, multi-layer networks

10.2.1   *Computing functions with feed-forward, multi-layer networks*

We saw above that networks with hidden units can be used to transcend the computational limitations of perceptrons. This leads us to turn our attention to extensions of the perceptron in which units are grouped into layers, with each unit in a given layer, other than the input layer, taking its inputs from each unit in the previous layer. Such networks are called *feed-forward, multi-layer* networks.

Feed-forward, multi-layer networks can contain any number of hidden layers, and any number of units within a layer. They are usually pictured with the layers arranged in a vertical stack, with the input units at the bottom and the output units at the top, as in figure 10.7. (Note: in this diagram, only the connections going from the left-most unit in each row have been drawn. This is simply to avoid clutter: each unit in any given layer other than the output layer is connected to each unit in the layer above.)   To compute a function using such a network, the activation levels of the input units (the bottom layer) are set as the input to the network. These input units send their activation values, via the network links, to all the units in the second layer, whose activation levels are thereby determined. These second-layer units then send their activation levels to all the units in the third layer, and so on,

output units

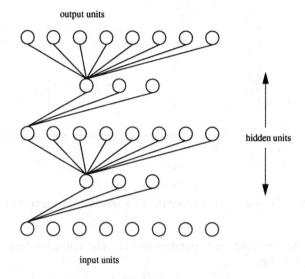

hidden units

input units

Figure 10.7   A multi-layer net (showing links only from left-most units)

until finally the activation levels of the output units are determined. The collection of activation levels of the output units constitutes the output of the whole network.

The units in multi-layer networks can in principle compute their outputs in any way. In practice, however, a continuous version of the linear threshold unit is normally employed for this purpose, as we shall now describe; the reason for this will emerge in section 10.2.2.

For the remainder of this section, then, we shall allow any unit u_j, other than those in the input layer, to have activation level a_j taking any real values (strictly) between 0 and 1. Such a unit is linked to all the units in the layer below, from which it receives input. If unit u_j receives input from unit u_i, the link from u_i to u_j has a weight, which we denote $w_{j,i}$; in addition, u_j has its own threshold, which we denote θ_j. As with the perceptron, the weights and threshold can take any real values. The units in the input layer will be treated somewhat differently. Their activation levels are set as the input to the network, and we shall still restrict these inputs to the values 0 and 1.

The activation level of each unit u_j (other than those in the input layer) is determined as follows. First, we take the *net input* to u_j to be the weighted sum

$$net_j = \sum_i w_{j,i} a_i - \theta_j. \tag{10.5}$$

Here, the summation runs over all the units u_i in the previous layer to u_j (remember: $w_{j,i}$ is the weight on the link from unit u_i to unit u_j, a_i the activation level of unit

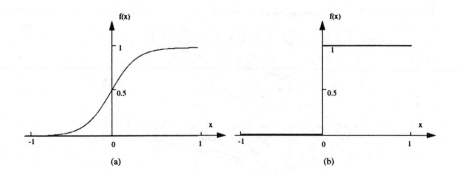

Figure 10.8   *Comparison between: (a) a sigmoid function and (b) a step function*

u_i, and θ_j the threshold corresponding to u_j). The activation level of unit u_j is then set as follows:

$$a_j = f(net_j)$$

where f is a so-called *sigmoid function*. The function normally used for this purpose is

$$f(x) = \frac{1}{1 + e^{-x/T}}$$

with T set to some small positive constant. This particular function is chosen largely because its shape is close to that of a step function, (see figure 10.8) and because of other mathematical properties which simplify certain calculations. The only really critical features of this function so far as its use in the network is concerned are: (i) $f(x)$ rises steeply near $x = 0$; (ii) when x is significantly greater than 0, $f(x)$ is close to 1; and (iii) when x is significantly less than 0, $f(x)$ is close to 0. Any smoothly varying (differentiable) function having these properties would do. Thus, the activation level a_j of unit u_j is

$$f(net_j) = \frac{1}{1 + e^{-(\sum_i w_{j,i} a_i - \theta_j)/T}}$$

where the summation runs over all the units u_i in the previous layer.

The units of these multi-layered networks can be viewed as approximations to threshold units. Suppose that the weighted inputs $\sum w_{j,i} a_i$ to unit u_j exceed the threshold θ_j. Then the net input to u_j will be positive, according to equation (10.5). Referring to figure 10.8, we see that the activation level a_j of u_j will be greater than 0.5 and will be close to 1 if net_j is significantly greater than 0 – i.e. if $\sum w_{j,i} a_i$ exceeds θ_j by a significant amount. Similar remarks apply when $\sum w_{j,i} a_i$ is significantly less than θ_j: then, a_j will be close to zero.

The problem with hidden units comes when we want to train the network by examples. With the perceptron, we could compare, for each input pattern, the actual value of the output unit with the desired value, and adjust the weights on the links (which all led to the output unit) if there was a discrepancy. But when there are hidden units, we do not know what their activation levels ought to be in response to a given input pattern, and so we do not know how we should adjust the weights on the links leading to those hidden units, if there is an error in the output units. The recent resurgence of interest in neural networks was due in part to the development of a learning procedure for use with hidden units. Just such a learning procedure, known as *backpropagation*, is described in section 10.2.2. The idea is to find a way of trickling the error down from the output units to the hidden units below them.

10.2.2 *Learning to compute functions with multi-layer networks*

The basic training regime is the same as with perceptrons. The input patterns are fed one at a time into the network's input units, and the actual responses of the output units (which this time, remember, are real numbers between 0 and 1) are compared with the desired outputs (which, we shall assume, are always either 0 or 1). For each input pattern, adjustments are made to the weights in response to discrepancies between the desired and actual outputs. After all input patterns have been given, the whole process is repeated over and over until the actual activation levels of the output units are tolerably close to the desired activation levels. (The two will never be exactly the same since the activation level of a unit lies strictly between 0 and 1.)

We now examine the procedure for adjusting the weights after presentation of a given input pattern $\mathbf{m}^p = (x_1^p, \ldots, x_n^p)$. If u_j is an output unit, then the error δ_j^p at u_j in response to presentation of input pattern p can simply be taken to be the discrepancy between u_j's desired response t_j^p and its actual response a_j^p. We write

$$\delta_j^p = (t_j^p - a_j^p), \tag{10.6}$$

just as we did for the perceptron in equation (10.2). The weights leading to u_j and the threshold for u_j are again modified in much the same way as for the perceptron. For all units u_i which feed into u_j the weights $w_{j,i}$ are adjusted according to the rule

$$w_{j,i} := w_{j,i} + \eta a_k^p \delta_j^p f'(net_j^p) \tag{10.7}$$

and the threshold θ_j is adjusted according to the rule

$$\theta_j := \theta_j - \eta \delta_j^p f'(net_j^p). \tag{10.8}$$

The rules (10.7) and (10.8) are the same as the corresponding rules (10.3) and (10.4) for the perceptron, except for the inclusion of the factor $f'(net_j^p)$, where $f'(x)$ is the function obtained by differentiating the sigmoid function $f(x)$ with respect to x. (But see exercise 5.) The reasons for this difference are technical in nature and will not be discussed here. (See further reading.)

The rules (10.7) and (10.8) make reference to the quantity δ_j^p, the error at unit u_j for input-pattern $\mathbf{m}^p$. But equation (10.6) only makes sense for output units, for these are the only units for which a desired response t_j^p is available. So we need a method for calculating the error for hidden units. We proceed as follows. The error at u_j is taken to be the weighted sum of all the errors at the units u_k such that there is a link from u_j to u_k:

$$\delta_j^p = \sum_k w_{k,j} \delta_k^p . \tag{10.9}$$

Equation (10.6) tells us how to calculate errors for output units; and equation (10.9) tells how to calculate errors for hidden units in terms of the errors in the layer above. In this way, we can compute errors for all the units in the network, starting at the output layer and proceeding layer by layer until we reach the layer immediately above the input units. Thus, equation (10.9) gives us a way of trickling the error down from the output units to the hidden units below them. Once we have the errors for all units in the network, we can then adjust the weights and thresholds using rules (10.7) and (10.8). (See exercise 6.)

The exact rationale for applying this particular learning method involves technical considerations beyond the scope of this book; however, the general outlines can be easily explained. Given a particular assignment of values to the weights and thresholds of a network, we can construct a goodness-of-fit measure, which determines how close the network is to computing the function we are trying to teach it.

A sensible goodness-of-fit measure for the particular training example $\mathbf{m}^p$ is:

$$E_p = \frac{1}{2} \sum_j (t_j^p - a_j^p)^2,$$

where the sum ranges over all output units u_j. Clearly, the closer the actual output is to the desired output, the smaller this quantity. A sensible overall goodness-of-fit measure for all training examples is therefore

$$E = \sum_{p=1}^r E_p$$

where the sum ranges over all possible input patterns $\mathbf{m}^1, \ldots, \mathbf{m}^r$. Thus, E is effectively a *total* error function.

Now, the quantity E depends on the weights and thresholds of the network, since it is these that determine how well or how badly the network will do at computing the desired function. The space of weights and thresholds in the network is usually referred to as *weight space*. What we wish to do, in teaching the network the function, is to move in this space to a point where the quantity E is as small as possible.

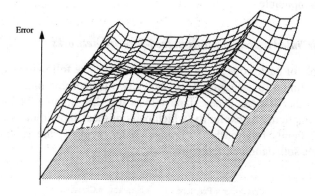

Figure 10.9   A schematic representation of the error measure for a neural network

The situation is represented schematically in figure 10.9: the points in the plane represent the possible combinations of values for the weights and thresholds of the network, and the height of the surface above gives the error-measure E for each of these combinations: making a small adjustment to the weights and thresholds of the network is seen as a matter of moving from one point in the plane to a nearby point. (Actually figure 10.9 is a misleading representation of how the error E depends on the weights and thresholds, since, in reality, the weight space is multi-dimensional, with 1 dimension for every weight and threshold. It is merely for purposes of visualization that we pretend in figure 10.9 that weight space is 2-dimensional.) In terms of figure 10.9, the goal of learning the function translates into the goal of getting to the lowest point in the landscape.

Simplifying somewhat, it can be shown that rules (10.7) and (10.8) prescribe a small move in weight space in the direction which will cause E to *decrease most rapidly*. In other words, adjusting the weights and thresholds according to these rules represents the strategy of taking many small steps in whatever direction leads downhill, on the error surface of figure 10.9, as quickly as possible. We sometimes say that this learning procedure performs *gradient descent* in the weight space.

Of course, this strategy is fallible. For if the 'landscape' incorporates local minima which are greater than the global minimum, and if the weights should chance to wander into the vicinity of such a local minimum, backpropagation will home in on the local minimum, and the weights and thresholds will stabilize at the wrong values. Hence, just because a network *can* compute a function, in the sense that there are possible assignments of values to the weights and thresholds such that the activations of the outputs are very close to the desired activations, the application of the backpropagation method is by no means guaranteed to get the network to learn the function in question. Note the contrast with the perceptron learning algorithm, which always succeeds in learning a function, provided it is perceptron-computable.

10.2.3 Distributed representations in feed-forward networks

As an example of backpropagation in action, consider the following experiment, described in Hinton [3]. Figure 10.10 shows two isomorphic family trees, one English, the other Italian. These family trees together involve 24 individuals, and specify, implicitly or explicitly, which pairs of these individuals stand in the following 12 family relationships: *brother, sister, nephew, niece, uncle, aunt, husband, wife, son, daughter, father, mother.*

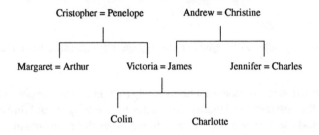

Figure 10.10   Two isomorphic family trees

Figure 10.11 shows a feed-forward network with units gathered into groups as shown. There are two groups of input units: group 1, consisting of 24 units, with each unit labelled by one of the 24 individuals in the two family trees; and group 2, consisting of 12 units, with each unit labelled by one of the above 12 family relationships. These two input groups feed into groups 3 and 4, in the second layer of the network; these two groups feed in turn to a middle layer of 12 units, which feeds into a penultimate layer of 6 units and thence into the final output layer containing one unit corresponding to each of the 24 individuals. The

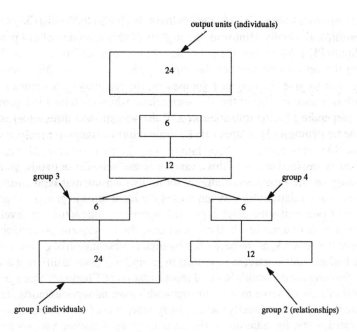

Figure 10.11   A feed-forward network for encoding family relationships.

connectivity between the units in connected groups is total. Thus, each of the units in group 1 has a link to each of the units in group 3; each of the units in group 2 has a link to each of the units in group 4; and so on. (We will see the motivation for this pattern of connectivity presently.)

Now, we would like this network to encode the information in the family trees of figure 10.10 in a way which makes that information easy to retrieve by activating the appropriate input units and reading off the answer from the output units. Suppose, for example, we want to know who Colin's aunts are. Then we set two input units to 1: the unit in group 1 labelled *Colin*, and the unit in group 2 labelled *aunt;* all other input units are set to 0. Activation will feed through the network as described in section 10.2.1, so that some of the output units become active (have activation near to 1), while the others become inactive (have activation near to 0). Now, what we would like to happen is that the output units labelled *Margaret* and *Jennifer* will become active (because these are Colin's aunts), while the other output units become inactive. Similarly for the other individuals and relations: we would like to specify a person a (by activating one of the group 1 units) and a relation R (by activating one of the group 2 units), and then to be able to read off from the output units who stands in relation R to a.

Hinton showed that such a network could be made to learn the entire family trees of figure 10.10, by training it, using the backpropagation method, to give the correct responses to every possible query involving the 24 individuals and 12 family relationships. (Actually, Hinton used a slightly modified version of this procedure. See Hinton [3].) Moreover, the network exhibits some ability to generalize. By training the network on *most* of the triples ⟨ person₁, *relationship*, person₂ ⟩, it can be seen to give the correct responses on the remainder. Specifically, if the network is trained on 100 of the 104 such relationships contained in figure 10.10, it can (depending on the initial settings of the weights and thresholds) correctly infer the remaining 4. This amounts to a limited form of inductive reasoning. (See exercise 8.)

What is instructive about this example is the way the network, as a result of training on the inputs and outputs, forms its own internal representations of individuals and relationships. When one of the input units in group 1 is activated – say, the *Colin*-unit – the units in group 3 assume various activation levels. This collection of activation levels then functions, for subsequent processing in the middle of the network, as the network's internal representation of Colin. Likewise, if the *Charlotte*-unit is activated, the units in group 3 will assume different activation levels, forming the network's internal representation of Charlotte. More generally, the units in group 3 serve to store the network's internal representations of the 24 possible individuals. In exactly the same way, when one of the input units in group 2 is activated – say, the *aunt*-unit – the units in group 4 assume various activation levels. And this collection of activation levels then functions, for subsequent processing in the middle of the network, as the network's internal representation of the aunt-relationship. More generally: the units in group 4 serve to store the network's internal representations of the 12 possible relationships.

Note that these individuals and relationships are represented in groups 3 and 4 in a way which is *distributed* across the activation levels of the units in question. The activation level of a given unit in group 3 or 4 does not represent any single individual or relationship; and a given individual or relationship is not represented by any single unit's activation level. Rather, each individual or relationship is represented by a pattern of activation levels in group 3 or 4; and the activation level of each unit in those groups features in the representation of every individual or relationship. Such internal representations – known as *distributed representations* – are the source of much of the excitement that has surrounded the subject of neural networks.

Thus the network operates by first translating its given inputs into its own internal (distributed) representations, then combining these representations to produce its own internal (distributed) representation of the output, and then finally decoding that representation to produce the desired pattern of activations among the output units. That is the motivation behind the particular pattern of connectivity used here.

Surprisingly, Hinton found that the units in groups 3 and 4 tended to respond to *significant*, but *implicit* features of the individuals and relationships. For example, after training on one occasion, one of the six units of group 3 was very active for the English inputs and inactive for the Italian inputs: thus, this unit encoded individuals' *nationality*. Another unit in that group was very active for individuals in the first row of the family trees, moderately active for individuals in the second row, and very inactive for individuals in the third row: thus, this unit encoded individuals' *generation*. Similar observations were made concerning the units of group 4, encoding the family relationships. For example, one unit was found to encode sex by becoming active in response to female relations like *sister* and *aunt*, while becoming very inactive for male relations like *brother and uncle*. Features such as nationality, generation and sex are clearly significant in determining family relationships. However, these features were 'discovered' by the network as a result of the backpropagation process: the training the network received made no explicit mention of them.

It should be pointed out, however, that the correspondence between the way in which units of groups 3 and 4 respond to inputs, and the (for us) meaningful characteristics of those inputs such as nationality, generation, sex, etc. is only approximate. It may turn out that, for example, some of the units respond *somewhat* to sex, and *somewhat* to generation; other units may respond overwhelmingly to nationality but with some exceptions; yet other units may not be obviously correlated with any significant features at all. So the units in groups 3 and 4 do not have 'clean' meanings: the most we can say is that there is a rough (but nevertheless surprising) correlation between some of these units and certain significant features of the individuals and relations that they collectively represent.

One final observation concerning this example. We have said that, as a result of training by backpropagation, the network comes to encode the information in the family trees of figure 10.10. Thus, in particular, it encodes the fact that Jennifer is Colin's aunt. (We know the network encodes this, and the other facts, because it gives the correct answers in response to our queries.) But if we were to ask *where* the network stores this fact, the answer must be: all over! The network encodes this fact because the backpropagation process has set the weights and thresholds to the appropriate values, but there is no particular weight or threshold that represents the fact that Jennifer is Colin's aunt: it just emerges, along with all the other stored facts, from the total set of weights and thresholds. The knowledge is, as we say, *distributed* over the weights and thresholds in the network. The weight on a given link does not encode any single fact; and a given fact is not encoded by any single weight. Rather, each fact is encoded by the entire pattern of weights and thresholds, and each weight and threshold participates in the representation of all the facts.

This form of representation is quite unlike the data-structures which we have examined so far in this book, where lists of facts are stored as collections of separate, isolatable symbols. For example, in chapter 3, we represented knowledge about a house as a list of separate facts

```
[in(bob,hall),in(bookcase,hall),in(table,study)]
```

where each of the three encoded facts has a separate and isolatable bit of the data-structure encoding it. Or again, in chapter 7, we represented (primitive) knowledge of restaurants using a script

```
script(
  name(restaurant-script)
  variables(Customers,Restaurant,Table,Waiter,Food,
            Money),
  events(
    [enters(Customers,Restaurant),
     sits-at(Customers,Table),
     waits(Customers),goes(Waiter,Table),
     orders(Customers, Food),waits(Customers),
     places(Waiter,Food,Table),
     eats(Customers,Food),
     gives(Waiter, Customers, bill(Money)),
     gives(Customers,Waiter,Money),
     leaves(Customers,Restaurant)]))
```

where each of the component event-types has a separate and isolatable bit of the data-structure encoding it. This sort of representation is sometimes called a *symbolic* representation, to contrast it with the *distributed* representations in the network of figure 10.11. Some researchers speculate that distributed representations are more likely to be useful in producing intelligent behaviour than the more traditional symbolic representations. We will return to the subject of distributed representations below.

10.3 Hopfield Nets

In perceptrons and multi-layer, feed-forward nets, the flow of information through the system is all one-way, from inputs to outputs. However, other sorts of neural architectures exists in which there is no such inherent directionality. One example of such a network is the *Hopfield net*.

10.3.1 Retrieving information from Hopfield nets

A Hopfield net consists of n binary-valued units $u_1, \ldots, u_n$ with *total connectivity*: every unit is connected to every other unit (but not to itself). As before, we denote the activation level of unit u_i by a_i, and the weight on the link from unit u_i to unit u_j by $w_{j,i}$. We assume that the connection between u_i and u_j is symmetric: that is, $w_{j,i} = w_{i,j}$. Furthermore, since we assume that units are not connected to themselves, we insist that $w_{i,i} = 0$ for $i = 1 \ldots n$. Finally, each unit u_i has its own threshold-value, θ_i, just as in feed-forward networks.

Hopfield nets were originally used by physicists to model not neural activity, but rather, the magnetic properties of materials known as spin-glasses. The units of the network represent individual electrons in the material, the weights on the links represent magnetic couplings between the electrons, and the thresholds at the units represent an external magnetic field. However, we will not be concerned here with the original motivation behind the development of Hopfield nets, and we will concentrate exclusively on their computational properties. The similarity between these simplified models of the magnetic properties of materials and neural processing is a mere coincidence. It is common, when discussing Hopfield nets, to take the possible values of the activations a_j to be -1 and 1, rather than 0 and 1. This is the convention we shall adopt here.

The units in a Hopfield net are linear threshold units. That is, the activation level a_j of a unit u_j is given by:

$$
\begin{aligned}
a_j &= 1 \quad \text{if } \sum_{i=1}^{n} w_{j,i} a_j \geq \theta_j \\
a_j &= -1 \quad \text{otherwise.}
\end{aligned}
\tag{10.10}
$$

where the sum ranges over all units in the network. (Remember, $w_{i,i} = 0$ for $i = 1 \ldots n$.)

The way a Hopfield net is run is as follows. All the units are first set to some initial value as input (always either 1 or -1). Then, a unit u_{r_0} is chosen at random. Rule (10.10) is used to calculate what the activation level of u_{r_0} should be given the activation levels of all the other units. The activation value of u_{r_0} will be updated, if necessary, accordingly. Then a second unit, u_{r_1}, is chosen at random, and rule (10.10) is used to calculate what its activation level should be given the activation levels of all the other units (note: the activation level of unit u_{r_0} used in this calculation is the *new* one). Again, the activation value of u_{r_1} will be updated, if necessary, accordingly. The process is repeated with new units u_{r_2}, u_{r_3}, $\ldots$, being chosen at random and updated, if necessary, as prescribed by rule (10.10), given the activation levels of all the other units. The process stops when the activation levels of all units in the network are in agreement with rule (10.10), so that no more updating is possible.

Thus, when a Hopfield net is run, there are no special input units from which information flows, and no special output units to which information flows. Rather, the input is the initial state of the network and influences flow around the network. Each unit may be updated several times before the network finally settles and the run terminates. Formally, the procedure is as follows.

begin hopfield-run
    set initial activation levels a_i ($i = 1 \ldots n$) as input;
    until all units have activation values in agreement with rule (10.10) **do**
        select a unit u_r at random such that a_r is not equal to the
            activation prescribed by rule (10.10);
        update a_r according to rule (10.10);
    end until
end hopfield-run

The procedure hopfield-run is guaranteed to terminate. To see this, define the *energy*, E, of a Hopfield net as follows:

$$E = -\frac{1}{2}\sum_{j=1}^{n}\sum_{i=1}^{n} a_j a_i w_{j,i} + \sum_{j=1}^{n} a_j \theta_j. \tag{10.11}$$

It is important to understand what this quantity is a function of: for a given set of weights and thresholds (which we will regard as fixed for the time being), the energy E is a function of the activation values a_i of the units in the network. Thus: change the activations in the network and you change the energy.

Now, a little calculation suffices to show that, if a unit u_r has its activation level changed according to the updating rule (10.10), the energy of the network must *decrease*. Suppose, for example, that the activation level of u_r is changed from 1 to -1. Then we have

$$\text{old } a_r = 1$$
$$\text{new } a_r = -1.$$

For this change to have occurred in accordance with rule (10.10), we must have

$$\sum_{i=1}^{n} a_i w_{r,i} - \theta_r < 0. \tag{10.12}$$

Now, the change in energy of the network, from equation (10.11), is

$$\text{new } E \quad - \quad \text{old } E =$$

$$\left(-\sum_{i=1}^{n}(\text{new } a_r)a_i w_{r,i} + (\text{new } a_r)\theta_r \right) \quad - \quad \left(-\sum_{i=1}^{n}(\text{old } a_r)a_i w_{r,i} + (\text{old } a_r)\theta_r \right)$$

since the terms not involving a_r cancel out. So the change in energy is

$$\left(-\sum_{i=1}^{n}(-1)a_i w_{r,i} + (-1)\theta_r \right) \quad - \quad \left(-\sum_{i=1}^{n}(1)a_i w_{r,i} + (1)\theta_r \right)$$

$$= \quad 2\left(\sum_{i=1}^{n} a_i w_{r,i} - \theta_r \right)$$

which is negative by (10.12), indicating a *decrease* in energy. (See exercise 9.)

Thus, as the algorithm hopfield-run flips units, it always does so in such a way that the total energy E decreases. Since the energy must have a global minimum (there are only a finite number of binary-valued units), the algorithm is guaranteed to reach a point where the energy cannot be reduced by flipping any single unit – that is, the network will reach a quiescent state in which no more flips can be performed. Thus we can see the process of running a Hopfield net as one of gradually reducing the energy until a minimum is reached.

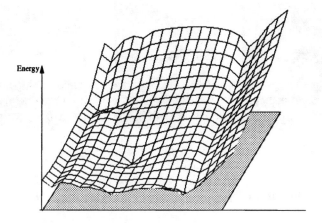

Figure 10.12   A schematic representation of an energy landscape

We can picture the process schematically with the diagram of figure 10.12. Points in the horizontal plane correspond to a set of the activation levels of the units in the network, while the height of the surface above represents the energy for any given set of activation levels. This surface is often called the *energy landscape* of the network. When the Hopfield net is run, we start from an initial set of activation levels and flip the activation levels of units in such a way as always to reduce the energy, much as a ball will always roll downhill on a bumpy surface (if we ignore inertia). Notice that the process will halt when we reach a *local* energy minimum; this may or may not be the smallest value of the energy function.

Warning: the diagrams of figures 10.9 and 10.12 may look similar; but they represent very different things! In figure 10.9, the base plane represents the *weight*-space of the network, and movements in this plane correspond to the adjustments to the weights and thresholds that occur during *learning*. In figure 10.12, by contrast, the base plane represents the *activation*-space of the network, and movements in this plane correspond to changes in the activation levels of units that take place while *running* the network. Note that the same caveats apply to interpreting both diagrams, however. In particular, figure 10.12 is misleading as a representation of the way in which energy depends on the activation levels of the units, since the activation space is multi-dimensional (1 dimension for every unit). It is merely for purposes of visualization that we pretend in figure 10.12 that activation space is 2-dimensional. Remember, when running a Hopfield nets, only the activation levels are changed in order to minimize the energy: the weights and thresholds remain constant. However, it is the weights and thresholds that determine the *shape* of the energy landscape – and in particular, where the local minima are.

The tendency of Hopfield nets, when run, to drop into the nearest local energy

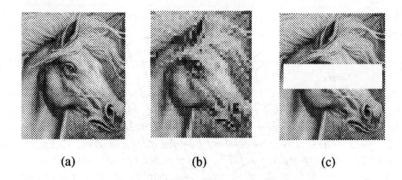

(a)   (b)   (c)

Figure 10.13   Retrieval of memories using Hopfield nets

minimum makes these networks useful for retrieving specific pieces of information
from partial or noisy cues. That is, we think of the local energy minima – more
exactly, the sets of activation levels at which there is a local energy minimum –
as being specific *memories*; we think of the initial activation state into which the
network is put as a *cue* (this may be a partial or corrupted version of the memory),
and we think of the process of finding a local energy-minimum as the *retrieval* of
a memory from the cue (usually the most similar memory).

Figure 10.13 shows an example where the remembered information is a picture,
and the cue for the memory is a corrupted version of that picture. We can represent
a picture using a Hopfield net by taking each unit in the network to correspond
to a pixel, where an activation of 1 encodes a white dot, and an activation of
−1 a black dot. (Thus, the network required would be very large.) The total
activation state of the network thus encodes an entire picture. Let us now imagine
that the weights and thresholds of the network have been so set up that the energy
landscape has a *minimum* at the set of activation levels corresponding to the picture
in figure 10.13(a). (We will discuss presently how this is achieved.) If the network
is then put into an initial activation state corresponding to the slightly corrupted
version of the picture, perhaps the version shown in figure 10.13(b), then the
algorithm hopfield-run, in finding a nearby energy minimum, can produce a
final activation state corresponding exactly to the original picture. Figure 10.13(c)
shows a partial version of the picture, which can also (provided the energy landscape
is set up properly) fall into the minimum corresponding to figure 10.13(a), and will
thus reconstruct the picture exactly. These examples illustrate how the Hopfield
net can be used to retrieve memories from corrupted or partial cues. Accordingly,
a Hopfield net is said to provide a *content-addressable memory* – that is, we can
retrieve a piece of remembered information on the basis of what the relevant
memory contains, rather than on the basis of its *location*. Moreover, there is
nothing special about pictures here: Hopfield nets could be use to store other kinds

of information, appropriately coded as strings of 1's and −1's. Thus, for example, a Hopfield net could in principle be made to remember a list of facts describing the locations of objects in a house, or a restaurant script.

10.3.2 Storing information in Hopfield nets

In the previous section, we saw how to retrieve information from Hopfield nets, where that information is stored in the form of activation-patterns corresponding to local minima in the energy landscape of the network. The question therefore arises: given some pieces of information (e.g. the picture of figure 10.13(a)) which we want the network to remember as a set of unit-activations, how do we set up the weights and thresholds so that the energy landscape has the local minima required to store that information? This is the question we address in this section.

Suppose m^1, ..., m^r are patterns that we want the network to store. Each pattern m^p is simply a specification of the activation levels for all the units in the network:

$$m^p = (a_1^p, \ldots, a_n^p)$$

where the a_i^p are all either 1 or −1. Our problem is to choose weights and thresholds so that the activation-patterns m^1, ..., m^r are at local minima of the network's energy landscape – that is, so that these activation patterns are stable states into which the network will settle, via the process hopfield-run, if started off in a similar state.

It can be shown that, *under certain conditions*, the following weights and thresholds suffice for this purpose:

$$w_{i,j} = \sum_{p=1}^{r} a_i^p a_j^p$$

$$\theta_j = 0 \tag{10.13}$$

(Thus, in this case, we are in effect ignoring the thresholds.) When, given these weights and thresholds, the activations of the units are set to a perturbed version of one of the m^p, the procedure hopfield-run will terminate with the activation levels of the original m^p.

Notice, incidentally, that we can think of the weights and thresholds specified by equations (10.13) as being produced by the following learning procedure:

```
begin hopfield-ortho-learn
    let w_i (i = 1...n) and θ be zero;
    let η be 1/n;
    for each input pattern m^p = (a_1^p, ... a_n^p) do
        let new weights be as follows:
            w_{j,i} := w_i + η a_i^p a_j^p
    end for each
end hopfield-ortho-learn
```

The similarity with the learning procedures for other networks should be clear. However, this kind of learning does not involve any error term, unlike perceptron learning or backpropagation. Moreover, the storage process is, in this case, *one-shot*: it is not necessary to present the r training examples over and over again.

To explain the conditions under which the equations (10.13) lead to successful recall, we must introduce the notion of *orthogonality*. Two activation patterns

$$\mathbf{m}^p = (a_1^p, \ldots, a_n^p)$$
$$\mathbf{m}^q = (a_1^q, \ldots, a_n^q)$$

are *orthogonal* just in case:

$$\sum_{i=1}^{n} a_i^p a_i^q = 0.$$

We then have the following theorem, which, again, we state without proof.

Theorem *Let* $\mathbf{m}_1, \ldots, \mathbf{m}_r$ *be pairwise orthogonal activation patterns*

$$\mathbf{m}^p = (a_1^p, \ldots, a_n^p),$$

for $p = 1 \ldots r$, *and let the weights and thresholds of a Hopfield net be as specified by equations (10.13). Then the patterns* $\mathbf{m}_1, \ldots, \mathbf{m}_r$ *are stable states of the network: the network's energy cannot be reduced by flipping any unit.*

If the activation levels of the network are set to a pattern:

$$\mathbf{m} = (a_1, \ldots, a_n)$$

close to one of the original patterns $\mathbf{m}^p$, and the procedure hopfield-run is executed, then it will terminate with activation levels in the state $\mathbf{m}^p$.

When the memories stored in a Hopfield net are not orthogonal, then they start interfering with each other. That is, the attempt to store one memory will distort the memories already stored in the network. The more similar the memories being stored, the greater the degree of interference (or *crosstalk*, as it is sometimes called) between them. Indeed, the situation may arise in which the attempt to store similar patterns results in a 'compromise' local minimum which blends together features of each of the patterns. Actually, it is possible to modify the procedure hopfield-ortho-learn to deal with the case where the patterns to be stored are not orthogonal. In this case, recall will not be perfect, because of crosstalk, but it may still be good enough to be practically useful. The procedure is to repeat hopfield-ortho-learn using many sweeps through the set of patterns to be stored, and to update the weights only by a small amount. Thus, in this case, the storage process ceases to be one-shot. (See further reading.)

Now, since two vectors which are very similar (differ only with respect to a small number of their components) will be far from orthogonal, we can see how it is easier and more reliable to store several very different memories in a Hopfield net than several very similar ones. This fact is suggestive, firstly because it is reminiscent of human memory, where it is a matter of everyday experience that similar things are more easily mixed up than different things, and secondly because it is so very different from what we observe with the knowledge representation techniques found in traditional AI systems, where data-structures that differ even by the tiniest amount are effortlessly distinguished.

10.3.3 Distributed representations in Hopfield nets

As, we have seen, then, a Hopfield net can contain many memories, because its energy landscape can incorporate many local minima. Because the minima of the energy landscape are properties of the whole network, rather than of any specific unit, there is no one place in which any given memory is stored; and there is no one memory which is stored at any given place. Rather, each memory is distributed over all weights and thresholds, and each weight and threshold participates in the storage of all memories. (This is also the way in which the feed-forward network considered in section 10.2.3 encodes the family trees.) Thus, Hopfield nets encode information in the form of distributed representations.

For example, if a Hopfield net remembers a hundred pictures like that of figure 10.13(a), there need be no easily identifiable parts of the network to which we can point and say "This bit encodes the picture of the *horse*", "That bit encodes the picture of the *elephant*", and so on. Rather, each of the memories of a picture is spread out over the whole collection of weights and thresholds. Or again, if such a network is trained to recall the sequence of actions that normally take place in restaurants – the entering, the sitting, the ordering, etc. – there is no reason why these significant constituents need be identifiable as isolatable parts of the network: the representation of each of these constituents will be spread out over the whole collection of weights and thresholds. Again, this is quite different from the scripts used to encode this information in chapter 8. There, the restaurant script was stored as a structured object, with identifiable components of the representation corresponding one-to-one with the component events.

10.4 Distributed representations

In this chapter, we have met two kinds of neural network in which information is stored in a distributed fashion, and we have contrasted *distributed* representations with *symbolic* representations. Let us finish by making this distinction a little clearer.

Given any representation – be it a neural network or a script encoded using a conventional data-structure, or a matrix of 1's and 0's – we have two ways of describing that representation. On the one hand, we can describe it in terms of the *information it contains*. Thus, for example, we might say of a network that it has stored the picture of figure 10.13(a) (and perhaps other pictures besides), or we might say of a conventional data-structure that it represents facts about what normally happens in restaurants. Let us call this kind of description of a representation a *semantic* description, because it is couched in terms of the *meanings* of the representations involved.

On the other hand, we can describe the representation in terms of its *constituent parts and their properties*. Thus, for example, we can give the magnitudes of the weights and thresholds of the network. Or we can list the patterns of symbols (i.e. primitive objects of the programming language in question) used to implement the restaurant-script. Let us call this kind of description an *intrinsic* description, because it makes reference to the constituents of the representation and their properties, independent of what, if anything, those constituents may mean.

Now, the feature that distinguishes distributed from symbolic representations seems to be just this. In a traditional, symbolic representation of the restaurant script, we can point at certain, isolatable parts of the structure – i.e. at collections of symbols contained within it – and say: "*That bit* represents the sitting-down event; *that bit* represents the paying event; ...." That is, we can put certain intrinsically describable parts of the representation into some correspondence with the semantically significant components of the representation. But if the same information were stored in a distributed form in a Hopfield net, we could not do this – all the significant components of the network's total content would be distributed over all the weights and thresholds; and no isolated part of the network would have any recognizable meaning. We might say, then, that the critical feature of distributed representations concerns the way in which states of the system characterized in terms of their *meaning* relate to states of the system characterized in terms of their *intrinsic properties*. With distributed representations, there is no *simple* correspondence between the semantic and intrinsic descriptions – between what the network represents and the weights and thresholds that, ultimately, are responsible for the representing.

Of course, even for distributed representations, there must be *some* correspondence between the semantic and intrinsic descriptions. For example, let W be any assignment of values to the weights and thresholds of some Hopfield net, and let m be an assignment of activation levels to the units of the network corresponding to some piece of information to be remembered – for example, the picture of figure 10.13(a) or an event in the restaurant-script. Now, the energy landscape defined by W will either have a local minimum at m or it will not. (We assume that borderline cases involving very shallow local minima do not affect the argument here.) Now imagine assembling the set S of all and only those weight-threshold assignments W such that W has a local minimum at m. Then we can regard a specification of S as an intrinsic description corresponding, in general, to the storing of the memory m. However – and this is the crux of the matter – there is no obvious reason why S should be specifiable in any *simple* way. In particular, there might be no practical possibility of ever writing out the set of weights and thresholds in a network that are correlated in this way with a given memory.

Thus, with symbolic representations, the *semantic* components of what the representation represents – e.g. the individual pictures in a knowledge-base of many pictures, or the individual events in a representation of what happens in restaurants – correspond to intrinsic components of the representation which are *relatively easy to identify* – e.g. the occurrence of a certain pattern of symbols at a certain memory location. With distributed representations, by contrast, the *semantic* components of what the representation (i.e. the network) represents do not correspond to any such easily identifiable intrinsic components of the representation: they are, as it were, spread out over the whole network. To be sure, the meaningful states of the a connectionist system are correlated with *some* intrinsic states of the network, but these states will be complicated and messy-to-describe, and not easily identifiable in terms of, for example, specifications of weights and thresholds.

The above account has gone some way towards characterizing the distinction between symbolic and distributed representations. Unfortunately, however, matters are more complicated than this simple discussion suggests. We mention here just one important observation. So-called symbolic knowledge-representation systems, involving such data-structures as scripts or frames or predicate-calculus formulae, are standardly implemented in a *high-level* programming language such as LISP or Prolog, and are mapped down by the compiler onto complicated machine states with which, for most purposes, programmers need not concern themselves. Now there is no reason, in principle, why the physical states of the machine corresponding to these data-structures need not be very complicated and messy-to-describe states of affairs. Therefore, there is no reason, in principle, why these high-level, symbolic data-structures need correspond to states which have any simple description in terms of the physical characteristics of the computer in which they reside. Thus, the process of compilation blurs the distinction between symbolic and distributed knowledge-representation techniques. In fact, it is a matter of current philosophical debate how fundamental or theoretically interesting this distinction is. (See further reading.)

Exercises

1. Find all of the Boolean functions of 2 variables (under the usual encoding of 1 for T and 0 for F) which no perceptron can compute.
2. By generalizing the argument of figure 10.5 to three dimensions, find all the Boolean functions of 3 variables which no perceptron can compute.
3. Find a 1-input perceptron which will compute the Boolean function ¬. Using this perceptron, together with the perceptrons of figure 10.2, show that any Boolean function can be computed using a network of threshold units (with hidden units). How many layers of hidden units do you think are needed, at most?
4. What would happen if the procedure `perceptron-learn` were used to try to teach a perceptron the XOR function?

5. (Mathematics) Verify that, if $f(x)$ is the standard sigmoid activation function

$$f(x) = \frac{1}{1 + e^{-x/T}},$$

then

$$\frac{df(x)}{dx} = (1 - f(x))f(x).$$

Why is this useful when it comes to implementing the backpropagation learning algorithm?

6. In section 10.2.2, we described how the weights and thresholds on a multi-layer, feed-forward network can be modified in such a way that the network comes to compute a function of our choice. Rewrite this description in terms of an algorithm, in the same style as the procedure perceptron-learn of section 10.1.2.

7. (Programming) Implement the algorithm developed in exercise 6.

8. (Programming) Using the implementation described in exercise 7, reproduce Hinton's family tree experiment as described in section 10.2.3. How well do you find the network generalizes (inductively) from partial specifications of the family tree?

9. We showed in section 10.3 that the energy of a Hopfield net decreases when a unit flips in accordance with rule (10.10) from activation level 1 to activation level -1. Show that the energy also decreases when a unit flips in accordance with rule (10.10) from activation level -1 to activation level 1.

Further reading

A comprehensive and general introduction to neural networks is to be found in the two-volume survey by Rumelhart, McClelland and the PDP research group [5] and [6]. Readers interested in the technical details of the backpropagation algorithm are referred to this work. A shorter, and older, but still very useful survey is Arbib [1]; Arbib's book contains a proof of the perceptron convergence theorem. An even better, even shorter overview of connectionist learning procedures is Hinton [4].

One of the most striking and best-known applications of backpropagation is the NETtalk program of Sejnowski and Rosenberg [8]. This network, which has just one hidden layer of units, learns a mapping from groups of letters to phonemes that allows it to pronounce English text. After substantial training, the program is able to perform well on new examples.

The philosophical implications of connectionism – particularly the status and significance of the distinction between symbolic and distributed representations – has provoked considerable debate. For an introduction and discussion, see Clark [2]. A useful collection of papers of this topic is Ramsey, Stich and Garon [7].

Bibliography

[1] Arbib, Michael A: *Brains, Machines and Mathematics*, 2nd ed., New York: Springer-Verlag, 1987.

[2] Clark, Andy *Microcognition: Philosophy, Cognitive Science and Parallel Distributed Processing*, Cambridge, MA: MIT Press, 1989.

[3] Hinton, G. "Learning distributed representations of concepts", *Proceedings of the Eighth Annual Conference of the Cognitive Science Society*, Hillsdale, NJ: Lawrence Erlbaum, 1986.

[4] Hinton, G. "Connectionist Learning Procedures", *Artificial Intelligence*, vol 40, 1–3 (1989) pp. 185–234.

[5] McClelland, James L., David E. Rumelhart and the PDP Research Group *Parallel Distributed Processing: Explorations in the Microstructure of Cognition*, vol. 2, Cambridge MA: MIT Press, 1986.

[6] Rumelhart, David E., James L. McClelland and the PDP Research Group *Parallel Distributed Processing: Explorations in the Microstructure of Cognition*, vol. 1, Cambridge MA: MIT Press, 1986.

[7] Ramsey, William, Stephen P. Stich and Joseph Garon (eds.) *Philosophy and Connectionist Theory*, Hillsdale, NJ: Lawrence Erlbaum, 1991.

[8] Sejnowski, T. and C. Rosenberg " Parallel networks that learn to pronounce English text", *Complex Systems*, 1 (1987) pp. 145–168.

Appendix: The Predicate Calculus

The purpose of this appendix is to provide a tutorial introduction to the predicate calculus. The emphasis throughout is on presenting the essential material as simply and briefly as possible. For more thorough and systematic treatments, see further reading.

A.1 Introduction

Logics standardly have three components: a *syntax*, a *semantics* and a *proof theory*. In the sequel, we shall describe the syntax, semantics and proof theory of the predicate calculus. However, since the details are a little complicated to grasp in one go, we introduce the essential ideas by describing a simpler and more restricted language – the propositional calculus. We shall then see how these ideas can be extended to the predicate calculus.

A.2 The propositional calculus: syntax, semantics and proof theory

A.2.1 Syntax

The *syntax* of a logic is a system of rules specifying which formulae belong to the language under consideration. In the propositional calculus, formulae are built up by combining *proposition-letters* by means of *Boolean connectives*. We give the formal presentation of the syntax first, and then explain the intended interpretation. Formally, then, the set of formulae in the propositional calculus is generated by the following two rules.

1. All proposition-letters,

$$p, q, r, \ldots, p_1, q_1, r_1, \ldots, p_2, q_2, r_2, \ldots,$$

are formulae.

2. Any two formulae ϕ and ψ can be combined by means of the Boolean connectives &, $\vee$, $\neg$ and $\rightarrow$ to produce the more complex formulae:

$$(\phi \& \psi), \quad (\phi \vee \psi), \quad (\neg \phi) \quad \text{and} \quad (\phi \rightarrow \psi).$$

246

Intuitively, proposition-letters stand for actual or possible states of affairs, much as variables in applied mathematics problems stand for physical quantities. For example, the proposition-letters p, q and r might have the following readings:

p	Block a is on block b	
q	Block b is on block c	(A.1)
r	Block a is on the table.	

The crucial thing about a proposition-letter is that it can be *true* or *false*, according to whether the state of affairs it stands for obtains or not. Thus, we take proposition letters to have *truth-values* – either T (for *truth*) or F (for *falsity*) – much as variables in applied mathematics problems have numerical values. The propositional calculus is the calculus of the truth-values of propositions.

The Boolean connectives, by means of which proposition letters are combined into complex formulae, have the standard natural language readings:

&	and
∨	either ... or ... (or both)
→	if ... then
¬	not.

To see these connectives in action, suppose that the proposition letters p, q and r have the readings given in (A.1) above. Then we can form the following more complex formulae:

$(p \ \& \ q)$	Block a is on block b *and* block b is on block c
$(p \lor q)$	Block a is on block b *or* block b is on block c (or both)
$(\neg p)$	Block a is *not* on block b
$(p \to q)$	*If* block a is on block b, *then* block b is on block c.

Iterating these connectives allows us to construct yet more complex formulae. For example, we can construct the formula

$$(r \lor (p \ \& \ q)) \tag{A.2}$$

with the reading

Either block a is on the table *or*, otherwise, block a is on block b *and* block b is on block c (*or both*).

Using a formal language such as the propositional calculus allows us to keep track of complicated states of affairs in a way that would be difficult if we had to use English. It is important to develop some facility in translating between formulae in the propositional calculus and English (See exercises 1 and 2.)

One technical point before we move on. So far, we have been careful to include parentheses (...) whenever we apply a Boolean connective to create a more complex formula. This has the advantage of making it clear exactly which things the different connectives apply to. For example, we must be careful to distinguish between formula (A.2) above and the differently bracketed

$$((r \lor p) \ \& \ q).$$

However, too many parentheses make formulae ugly and difficult to read. So a convention is adopted whereby some Boolean connectives are assumed to take priority over others. For example, ¬ is assumed to have higher priority than &; and this means that the formula

$$\neg p \,\&\, q$$

is interpreted as $((\neg p) \,\&\, q)$ rather than as $(\neg(p \,\&\, q))$. Similarly, & is assumed to have higher priority than →, which means that the formula

$$p \,\&\, q \rightarrow r$$

is interpreted as $((p \,\&\, q) \rightarrow r)$ rather than as $(p \,\&\, (q \rightarrow r))$. In this book we follow this convention of leaving parentheses out where the priority of connectives is clear. In particular, the outer pair of parentheses will always be omitted.

Furthermore, it turns out that when several formulae are joined together by ∨, it does not make any difference how the parentheses are arranged. Thus, for example, the formulae

$$(p \vee (q \vee r)) \quad \text{and} \quad ((p \vee q) \vee r)$$

denote the same state of affairs and can simply be written, without ambiguity, as

$$p \vee q \vee r.$$

A corresponding point applies to &. The formulae

$$(p \,\&\, (q \,\&\, r)) \quad \text{and} \quad ((p \,\&\, q) \,\&\, r)$$

can both be written

$$p \,\&\, q \,\&\, r.$$

Again, this is a convention we adopt in this book.

In this section, we have introduced the basic language of the propositional calculus, and have indicated, informally, how propositional calculus formula can be used to represent various states of affairs. We now proceed to a more technical characterization of the meanings of these formulae.

A.2.2 Semantics

The *semantics* of a logic is a system of rules which determine how the interpretations of complex expressions depend on the interpretations of their constituents. In the case of the propositional calculus, these rules are standardly given in terms of *truth-tables*, which are simply instructions for computing truth-values of complex formulae in term of the truth-values of their simpler constituents. Formally, the truth-tables are as follows:

ϕ	ψ	$\phi \& \psi$
T	T	T
T	F	F
F	T	F
F	F	F

ϕ	ψ	$\phi \vee \psi$
T	T	T
T	F	T
F	T	T
F	F	F

ϕ	ψ	$\phi \rightarrow \psi$
T	T	T
T	F	F
F	T	T
F	F	T

ϕ	$\neg\phi$
T	F
F	T

In these truth-tables, T and F are the truth-values, *truth* and *falsity*, and ϕ and ψ are any formulae. To understand the way these truth-tables are supposed to work, consider the truth-table for $\&$. Each row in this truth-table concerns a different possible combination of truth-values for formulae ϕ and ψ, and specifies the corresponding truth-value of the more complex formula $\phi \& \psi$. For example, the first row states that, if ϕ and ψ are both true, then the formula $\phi \& \psi$ is true; the second row states that, if ϕ is true and ψ is false, then $\phi \& \psi$ is false; the third row states that, if ϕ is false and ψ is true, then $\phi \& \psi$ is false; and the fourth row states that, if ϕ is false and ψ is false, then $\phi \& \psi$ is false. This is what one would expect given the reading of the symbol $\&$ as "and". The other truth-tables are interpreted similarly; notice that the truth-table for $\neg$ is especially simple: the first row says that if the formula ϕ is true, then the formula $\neg\phi$ is false; the second row says that if the formula ϕ is false, then the formula $\neg\phi$ is true. Again, this is what one would expect given the reading of the symbol $\neg$ as "not".

By repeated application of these tables, the truth-value for any formula in the language can be computed, provided we know the truth-values of the constituent proposition letters. As an illustration, suppose that p and q are true and that r is false: we shall work out the truth-value of the complex formula

$$p \rightarrow (\neg q \vee (p \& r)). \tag{A.3}$$

First, if p is true and r false, we see from the truth-table for $\&$ (second row) that $p \& r$ is false. Secondly, given that q is true, we see from the truth-table for $\neg$ (first row) that $\neg q$ is false. Now, since $p \& r$ and $\neg q$ are both false, we can then apply the truth-table for $\vee$ (fourth row), whence we see that $\neg q \vee (p \& r)$ is also false. Finally, since p is true, and $\neg q \vee (p \& r)$ is false, the truth-table for $\rightarrow$ (second row) tells us that the formula (A.3) is false.

A corresponding procedure can be used to determine the truth-value of any formula, given the truth-values of its constituent proposition-letters. The idea is to work out the truth-values of successively more complex constituent formulae by applying the appropriate rows of the truth-tables. It is sometimes useful to look at the truth-values of a given formula such as (A.3) given *all* possible combinations of truth-values of its constituent proposition letters. For the three proposition letters, p, q and r, there are eight possible combinations of truth-values, arranged in the table below. The truth-value of formula (A.3) is given for each of the eight cases. The example just worked out above corresponds to the second row. (See exercise 3.)

p	q	r	$p \rightarrow (\neg q \vee (p \;\&\; r))$
T	T	T	T
T	T	F	F
T	F	T	T
T	F	F	T
F	T	T	T
F	T	F	T
F	F	T	T
F	F	F	T

The above truth-tables for the Boolean connectives &, $\vee$, $\rightarrow$ and $\neg$ can be thought of as specifying the meanings of these symbols; they specify how these connectives determine the truth-conditions of sentences in which they occur.

The following semantic properties and relations are important for the application of logic to reasoning.

Definition *A formula which is true in every case (for every row in the truth-table) is called a tautology.*
A formula which is false in every case (for every row in the truth-table) is called a contradiction.
If two formulae have the same truth-tables (the same entry in every row) then they are said to be (logically) equivalent.

As a simple example of a tautology, consider the formula $p \vee \neg p$: its truth-table is as follows:

p	$p \vee \neg p$
T	T
F	T

Similarly, the formula $p \;\&\; \neg p$ is seen to be a contradiction, for its truth-table is:

p	$p \;\&\; \neg p$
T	F
F	F

The reader is invited to check these facts. (See also exercises 4 and 5.)

As an example of logically equivalent formulae, consider $\neg(p \vee q)$ and $\neg p \;\&\; \neg q$. Their truth-tables can easily be computed:

p	q	$\neg(p \vee q)$	$\neg p \;\&\; \neg q$
T	T	F	F
T	F	T	T
F	T	T	T
F	F	T	T

Perhaps the simplest example of logically equivalent formulae is provided by the pair p and $\neg\neg p$ – it is easy to see that both of these are true if p is true and false if p is false.

If ϕ and ψ are equivalent, we write:

$$\phi \Longleftrightarrow \psi.$$

Let ϕ, ψ and π be any formulae (not necessarily proposition letters). The following equivalences can be verified by constructing the appropriate truth-tables:

$$\phi \rightarrow \psi \iff \neg\phi \vee \psi$$
$$(\phi \mathbin{\&} \neg\psi) \rightarrow \pi \iff \neg\phi \vee \psi \vee \pi \qquad \text{(A.4)}$$

These particular equivalences will prove useful later. (See exercise 6.)

So much, then, for the semantic notions of *tautology*, *contradiction* and *logical equivalence*. We now proceed to introduce a further semantic notion, which should make clear the relevance of the technical apparatus presented in this section to the problem of guiding inferences in a computer program:

Definition *An argument with premises* $\{\phi_1 \ldots \phi_n\}$ *and conclusion* ψ *is said to be valid just in case any interpretation which makes each of the* $\{\phi_1 \ldots \phi_n\}$ *true also makes* ψ *true.*

In short: an argument is valid just in case, whenever the premises are all true, the conclusion is also true. Thus, *valid arguments* show us patterns of inference which, in some sense, we know it is alright to follow, because, as long as the premises with which we start are true, we will never thereby be led into falsity.

By way of illustration, consider the following example. Let the proposition-letters p, q, r, s stand for the following states of affairs:

p	Country I invades country K
q	Country A bombs city B
r	Country I sabotages oil installations in country K
s	Country I immediately withdraws from country K.

Now consider the following argument:

If Country I invades country K, then country A will bomb city B. If country A bombs city B, and if country I does not immediately withdraw from country K, then country I will sabotage the oil installations in country K. But country I will invade country K, and will not immediately withdraw. Therefore country I will sabotage the oil installations in country K.

Taking some liberties with the verb tenses in the above (which are not really crucial here), we may formalize the argument in the propositional calculus as:

$$p \rightarrow q$$
$$q \& \neg s \rightarrow r$$
$$p$$
$$\neg s$$

$$\overline{}$$

$$r$$

(Note: in this book, we sometimes use a horizontal line in this way to separate the premises of an argument from its conclusion.)

With a little thought, it can be seen that the above argument is (intuitively) valid. To see that it is formally valid, we need only examine all the possible truth-value assignments to the relevant proposition-letters, p, q, r, s, computing the truth-values of the premises and the conclusion, for each assignment. Then it is a simple matter to check that, for each such assignment, *if* all the premises are true, *then* the conclusion is also true.

p	q	r	s	$p \rightarrow q$	$(q \& \neg s) \rightarrow \neg r$	p	$\neg s$	r
T	T	T	T	T	T	T	F	
T	T	T	F	T	T	T	T	T
T	T	F	T	T	T	T	F	
T	T	F	F	T	F	T	T	
T	F	T	T	F	T	T	F	
T	F	T	F	F	T	T	T	
T	F	F	T	F	T	T	F	
T	F	F	F	F	T	T	T	
F	T	T	T	T	T	F	F	
F	T	T	F	T	T	F	T	
F	T	F	T	T	T	F	F	
F	T	F	F	T	F	F	T	
F	F	T	T	T	T	F	F	
F	F	T	F	T	T	F	T	
F	F	F	T	T	T	F	F	
F	F	F	F	T	T	F	T	

In fact, only one row – the second – has all the premises true, and the conclusion is true in that row. Therefore the argument is indeed valid. (See exercise 7.)

There is an important relationship between the notions of *validity* and *tautology*. A tautology is an unconditionally true formula, one that is true in all interpretations. This means that we can think of a tautology as the conclusion of a valid argument with *no* premises. In fact, the following result can be established.

Theorem *Consider an argument with premises* $\phi_1, \ldots, \phi_n$ *and conclusion* ψ. *Then this argument is valid just in case the formula*

$$\phi_1 \& \ldots \& \phi_n \rightarrow \psi.$$

is a tautology.

One final point of notation. If an argument with premises $\phi_1, \ldots, \phi_n$ and conclusion ψ is valid, then we write

$$\{\phi_1, \ldots, \phi_n\} \models \psi.$$

Likewise, if ψ is a tautology, we write

$$\models \psi.$$

We often use this notation in this book.

A.2.3 Proof theory

We proceed now to the third component of logic: the proof theory. A proof theory is a technique for establishing the validity of arguments. Of course, we can do this by truth-tables, but a truth-table with n proposition letters has 2^n rows. And checking truth-tables is sometimes unnecessarily inefficient.

By way of preparation, we must explain the notion of *clause form*. We introduce the following definitions:

Definition *A literal is a proposition letter or a proposition letter prefixed by $\neg$.*

Thus, b, c, $\neg d$ are all literals; $a \vee a$, $a \,\&\, b$ and $\neg\neg a$ are not literals.

Definition *A formula is in clause form if it is a literal or a collection of literals all joined by $\vee$.*

Thus $\neg p$, $p \vee q$, $\neg p \vee \neg q \vee r$ are all in clause form; $p \,\&\, q$, $p \to q$ and $\neg\neg p$ are not. The following result can easily be established:

Theorem *Let ϕ be a formula. Then there exist formulae $c_1, \ldots, c_n$ in clause form, such that*

$$\phi \iff c_1 \,\&\, c_2 \,\&\, \ldots \,\&\, c_n.$$

In other words, any formula is logically equivalent to a conjunction of formulae in clause form.

Moreover, it turns out that there is a completely mechanical process which, given any formula ϕ, will produce a suitable collection of clause form formulae $c_1, \ldots c_n$ such that ϕ is equivalent to their conjunction, $c_1 \,\&\, c_2 \,\&\, \ldots \,\&\, c_n$. We illustrate this process with an example (the generalization is straightforward). Suppose ϕ is the formula,

$$r \vee (p \,\&\, q)$$

The truth-table for ϕ is:

p	q	r	$(r \lor (p \,\&\, q))$
T	T	T	T
T	T	F	T
T	F	T	T
T	F	F	F
F	T	T	T
F	T	F	F
F	F	T	T
F	F	F	F

The first step is to look at each row in this truth-table where ϕ has the value F: that is, rows 4, 6 and 8. Each of these rows will contribute a c_i, in clause form. To see how this works, let us start with row 4. Here p is T, q is F and r is F. Accordingly, we form the clause form formula:

$$\neg p \lor q \lor r$$

where proposition letters having the truth-value T appear *negated* and those having the truth-value F appear *unnegated*. Let us call this formula c_1. Next, we look at row 6. Here, p is F, q is T and r is F. Accordingly, we form the clause form formula:

$$p \lor \neg q \lor r$$

according to the same principle. Let us call this formula c_2. Finally, and similarly, from row 8, we form the clause form formula

$$p \lor q \lor r.$$

Let us call this formula c_3. Now, it turns out that we have the equivalence:

$$\phi \Longleftrightarrow c_1 \,\&\, c_2 \,\&\, c_3$$

where the c_1, c_2 and c_3 are the formulae we just constructed. That is:

$$\neg p \lor q \lor r \Longleftrightarrow (\neg p \lor q \lor r) \,\&\, (p \lor \neg q \lor r) \,\&\, (p \lor q \lor r).$$

The reader might like to check that this equivalence does indeed hold.

We introduce one final semantic relation:

Definition   *A set of formulae* $\{\phi_1 \ldots \phi_n\}$ *is said to be contradictory just in case there is no row in the truth-table which makes them all true.*

Notice that an argument with premises $\{\phi_1 \ldots \phi_n\}$ and conclusion ψ is valid just in case the set of formulae

$$\{\phi_1, \ldots, \phi_n, \neg\psi\}$$

is contradictory. Henceforth, we shall refer to this collection of formulae as the *conflict set*; it will play a significant role in our discussion of proof theory.

Now for the proof theory proper. Our task is to find a way of determining whether a given argument is valid. Our strategy will be as follows:

1. Form the conflict set (premises + negation of conclusion).
2. Convert the conflict set to a set of formulae in clause form.
3. Repeatedly apply the "resolution rule" (described below) to try to derive a contradiction.
4. If a contradiction is found, then the argument is valid.

The resolution rule is just a rule of inference which is guaranteed never to lead from truth to falsity. We begin by presenting a special case. Let p, q, r be proposition letters. Then we have the rule of inference:

$$\frac{p \lor q \qquad\qquad \neg q \lor r}{p \lor r}$$

which says that, from $p \lor q$ and $\neg q \lor r$, we can infer $p \lor r$. The justification for this inference can be seen by looking at the truth-table of the formulae concerned:

p	q	r	$p \lor q$	$\neg q \lor r$	$p \lor r$
T	T	T	T	T	T
T	T	F	T	F	T
T	F	T	T	T	T
T	F	F	T	T	T
F	T	T	T	T	T
F	T	F	T	F	F
F	F	T	F	T	T
F	F	F	F	T	F

Here, we can see that, whenever both $p \lor q$ and $\neg q \lor r$ are true, $p \lor r$ is true.

Other special cases of the resolution rule are:

$$\frac{p \lor q \qquad\qquad \neg p}{q} \qquad \text{and} \qquad \frac{\neg p \lor q \qquad\qquad p}{q} \ .$$

Again, it can be seen from truth-tables that these rules lead from truths only to truths.

The general version of the resolution rule looks fierce, but is in fact quite straightforward. Suppose we have two formulae in clause form:

$$\phi_1 \lor \ldots \phi_{i-1} \lor p \lor \phi_{i+1} \ldots \lor \phi_n$$

and

$$\psi_1 \lor \ldots \psi_{j-1} \lor \neg p \lor \psi_{j+1} \ldots \lor \psi_m$$

where the ϕ's and the ψ's are literals, and where the first formula contains a literal p and the other contains its negation, $\neg p$. The resolution rule says that if both of these formulae are true, then so is a third formula,

$$\phi_1 \lor \ldots \lor \phi_{i-1} \lor \phi_{i+1} \ldots \lor \phi_n \lor \psi_1 \lor \ldots \lor \psi_{j-1} \lor \psi_{j+1} \ldots \lor \psi_m$$

formed by sticking the two formulae together (with a disjunction), missing out the p and the $\neg p$. The rule can be more succinctly written as follows:

$$\frac{(\phi_1 \vee \ldots \phi_{i-1} \vee p \vee \phi_{i+1} \ldots \vee \phi_n) \qquad (\psi_1 \vee \ldots \psi_{j-1} \vee \neg p \vee \psi_{j+1} \ldots \vee \psi_m)}{\phi_1 \vee \ldots \vee \phi_{i-1} \vee \phi_{i+1} \ldots \vee \phi_n \vee \psi_1 \vee \ldots \vee \psi_{j-1} \vee \psi_{j+1} \ldots \vee \psi_m}$$

The reader should check to see how the special cases given above fit into the general case.

As an example of how the above proof procedure can be used to show that an argument is valid, consider the argument used above:

$$p \rightarrow q$$
$$q \& \neg s \rightarrow r$$
$$p$$
$$\neg s$$
$$\overline{}$$
$$r.$$

We now follow the four-stage proof-strategy just outlined.

1. The conflict set of this argument is:

$$\{p \rightarrow q, \quad q \,\&\, \neg s \rightarrow r, \quad \neg s, \quad p, \quad \neg r\}$$

2. The equivalences in (A.4) show that $p \rightarrow q \Longleftrightarrow \neg p \vee q$, and that $q \,\&\, \neg s \rightarrow \neg r \Longleftrightarrow \neg q \vee s \vee r$. Applying these equivalences allows us to transform the conflict set into clause form:

$$\{\neg p \vee q, \quad \neg q \vee s \vee r, \quad p, \quad \neg s, \quad \neg r\}$$

3. We then apply resolution to derive a contradiction:

1.	$\neg p \vee q$	
2.	$\neg q \vee s \vee r$	
3.	p	conflict set
4.	$\neg s$	
5.	$\neg r$	
6.	$\neg q \vee s$	from 2 and 5 by resolution
7.	$\neg q$	from 4 and 6 by resolution
8.	$\neg p$	from 1 and 7 by resolution
9.	contradiction	from 3 and 8.

4. We have found a contradiction in the conflict set, and so the argument is valid.

It is important to understand the overall strategy in this proof method. We started off with the premises of the argument and the negation of the conclusion. We converted these into clause form, thus obtaining propositions which said exactly the same things as the originals, but which were in the appropriate form to apply the resolution rule. Then the resolution rule was applied repeatedly to derive a contradiction. Now, since a contradiction can never be true, and since the resolution rule never leads from truth to falsity, we know that the formulae in the conflict set cannot possibly be true together: that is, they are contradictory. It follows that, if ever all the premises are true, the negation of the conclusion must be false, and so the conclusion is true. Thus, if all the premises of the argument are true, so is the conclusion.

Notice that all the manipulations involved in this process are completely mechanical, and can easily be performed by a computer. There is no special "intuition" required to "see" the correctness of the argument. Distinguishing valid from invalid arguments in the propositional calculus is straightforwardly mechanizable. (See exercises 8 and 9.)

One special case arises when the argument in question has *no* premises. (Thus the conflict set consists solely of the negation of the conclusion.) Applying the above proof strategy in this case enables us to establish tautologies. If a formula ψ is shown by a proof strategy to be a tautology, ψ is said to be a *theorem*.

One final point of notation. If an argument with premises $\phi_1, \ldots, \phi_n$ and conclusion ψ can be shown to be valid by our proof strategy, we write:

$$\{\phi_1, \ldots, \phi_n\} \vdash \psi.$$

Likewise, if ψ is a theorem, we write

$$\vdash \psi.$$

Again, we often use this notation in this book.

A.2.4 Heuristics, correctness and completeness

It is important to notice that, in the above proof, certain choices were made about what to resolve with what. We chose to resolve proposition 2 with proposition 5, then 4 with 6, then 1 with 7, because such a sequence of resolutions led swiftly to the goal of deriving a direct contradiction. Other sequences of resolution steps would have been equally admissible, some more efficient than others. Thus, seeking a proof for the validity of a proposed argument involves searching through a space of possible sequences of resolutions. If one finds a resolution sequence leading to a contradiction, then one knows the argument is valid. But if one has not found such a resolution sequence, one does not in general know that the argument is invalid until one has tried all the possibilities.

This point is of crucial importance. The propositions we accept, together with the rules of inference we employ (in this case, resolution theorem proving), license certain arguments as valid by laying down criteria for a proof of their validity. But they do not tell us how to find such a proof. Whatever rules we use to guide us in our choice of resolutions must lie outside logic. Such rules, which guide us in our search for a proof within some formal reasoning system, are known as *heuristics*, and form an important part of artificial intelligence. Good heuristics are what make a knowledgeable reasoner intelligent.

The above proof procedure was presented as a means of checking the validity of arguments in the propositional calculus, where, recall, an argument was said to be valid if the conclusion is true whenever all the premises are true. The question arises as to whether the given procedure really does this job. Specifically, we have two questions:

- o If the above proof procedure *says* that an argument is valid, is the argument therefore really valid?
- o If an argument really is valid, does the above proof procedure, given a suitable choice of resolution steps, *say* that the argument is valid?

The answers to both these questions is yes. That is: the above proof procedure never tells us that an argument is valid when it is not, and, provided we choose the right resolution sequence, never fails to tell us an argument is valid when it is. Thus the above proof procedure says, in some sense, all there is to say about the validity of arguments.

The above two questions about the relationship between a proposed proof procedure to the semantics of the logic are so obviously important that they lead to the following definitions:

Definition *A proof procedure which does not say of any invalid arguments that they are valid is said to be correct (otherwise incorrect).*
A proof procedure which, for any valid argument, can show that argument to be valid by some appropriate sequence of inference steps, is said to be complete.

It is in the existence of theorems such as this that the advantage of logic, as a paradigm of reasoning in AI, is often said by its proponents to lie. The semantics of the logic tells us what we really mean by the symbols involved; and a correct and complete proof procedure then constitutes a method of reasoning within that logic which we know to be right.

Now we can state an important theorem about the relationship between the semantics and proof theory of the propositional calculus.

Theorem *The proof procedure described in section A.2.3 is correct and complete, given the semantics described in section A.2.2.*

Note that, with the aid of the symbols $\models$ and $\vdash$, we can write this theorem more succinctly as:
Let $\phi_1, \ldots, \phi_n, \psi$ be any formulae in the propositional calculus. Then

$$\{\phi_1, \ldots, \phi_n\} \vdash \psi \quad \text{if and only if} \quad \{\phi_1, \ldots, \phi_n\} \models \psi.$$

A.3 Predicate calculus: syntax, semantics and proof theory

The predicate calculus is more complex than the propositional calculus, but still consists of the trio of syntax–semantics–proof-theory, all standing in much the same relationship as for the propositional calculus.

A.3.1 Syntax

The basic terms of the language are as follows:

o An infinite stock of *names*:
socrates, parthenon, mount_olympus, block_a, block_b ...
o An infinite stock of *predicates*:
philosopher(x), building(x), mountain(x), is_a_block(x) ...
is_a_teacher_of(x, y), sees(x, y), is_on(x, y) ...
...

In the predicate calculus, names are used, as one might expect, to denote entities of all sorts, including people, material objects, places, times, and more abstract things such as numbers or situations. *Predicates*, by contrast, are used to denote properties which those entities can have, or relations in which they can stand to one another. From these names and predicates we can construct *atomic formulae* standing for states of affairs, for example:

man(socrates)
mortal(socrates)
mountain(olympus)
is_a_teacher_of(plato, socrates)
is_on(block_a, block_b)

with the obvious intuitive readings. These atomic formulae can be combined using the standard Boolean connectives as in the propositional calculus, thus:

man(socrates) → mortal(socrates)
man(socrates) & philosopher(socrates)

and so on.

In addition to names, predicates and Boolean connectives, the language of the predicate calculus includes:

o an infinite stock of *variables*:
$x, y, z, \ldots, x_1, y_1, z_1, \ldots, x_2, y_2, z_2, \ldots,$
o the *quantifiers*:
∀ (the *universal* quantifier)
∃ (the *existential* quantifier).

Quantifiers and variables can be used to construct formulae denoting general states of affairs. For example, the following formula can be constructed with the universal quantifier:

$$(\forall x)(\text{man}(x) \rightarrow \text{mortal}(x)).$$

It is read as

For all x, if x is a man, then x is mortal

or, in plainer English: all men are mortal. Similarly, the sentence

$$(\exists x)(\text{man}(x) \ \& \ \text{philosopher}(x))$$

is read as:

For some x, x is a man and x is a philosopher

or, in plainer English: some men are philosophers.

By using two quantifiers, we can construct the formula:

$$(\forall x)(\forall y)(\text{parent}(x,y) \ \& \ \text{male}(x) \rightarrow \text{father}(x,y)),$$

which is read as:

For all x, for all y, if x is a parent of y and x is male then x is a father of y,

or, in plainer English: anyone's male parent is his father. A more tricky example of a two-quantifier formula is

$$(\exists x)(\forall y)(\text{loves } (x,y)),$$

read as:

For some x, for all y, x loves y

which is to say: there's someone who loves everyone. By reversing the order of the quantifiers, we get a different state of affairs. The formula

$$(\forall y)(\exists x)(\text{loves } (x,y)),$$

says:

For all y, for some x, x loves y

which is to say: everyone is loved by someone or other (but not necessarily the same person!).

Finally, in addition to denoting objects by names, we shall make use of function-symbols, such as $\text{father}(x)$, $\text{president}(x)$, $+(x,y)$, ... Thus, if the name socrates denotes a person, Socrates, then the complex term $\text{father}(\text{socrates})$ denotes another person – namely, Socrates' father; if the name usa denotes a country, the United States, then the complex term $\text{president}(\text{usa})$ denotes a person – namely, the president of the United States; if the names 5 and 11 denote numbers (in the obvious way), the complex term $+(5,11)$ denotes another number, namely 16. And so on. Function symbols allow the formation of such formulae as

$$\forall x \ \text{loves}(x, \text{father}(x))$$

with the intuitive interpretation that everyone loves his father. Do not confuse predicates with functions: predicates combine with names to makes statements; functions combine with names to refer to individuals.

The foregoing paragraphs have presented, in an informal way, the language of the predicate calculus. A precise statement of predicate calculus syntax will not be given here, because it would involve us in technical details of marginal relevance to AI. (See exercises 10 and 11.)

A.3.2 Semantics

Recall that the semantics of a logic is a system of rules which determine how the interpretations of complex expressions depend on the interpretations of their constituents. In the case of the predicate calculus, the most fundamental constituents are names, predicates and function symbols; and their interpretations are given by means of a *structure*, as we shall now describe.

A *structure* M consists of a set D of elements called the *domain of interpretation* (or just *domain*) together with an *interpretation function*, I, which relates the names, predicates and function symbols to elements of D. It may help to visualize D as a 'bag' of dots, as in figure A.1, where each dot represents an individual recognized by M.

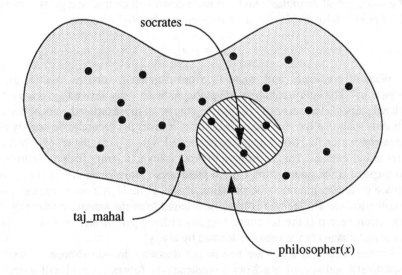

Figure A.1   Visualization of a structure M

The interpretation of a name – say, socrates – in M is simply an element of D (intuitively, the individual Socrates). So we say that the interpretation function I maps the name socrates to that individual. This is represented in figure A.1 by an arrow from the name socrates to one of the individuals in D.

The interpretation of a 1-place predicate, on the other hand – say, philosopher(x) – is a set of elements of D (intuitively, the set of elements of D which happen to be philosophers). So we say that the interpretation function I maps the predicate philosopher(x) to that set of individuals. This is represented in figure A.1 by an arrow from the predicate philosopher(x) to a set of the individuals in D. More generally, if $p(x)$ is a 1-place predicate, then $I(p(x))$ is a subset of D. This set is sometimes referred to as *the extension* of $p(x)$ in M: intuitively, it is the set containing any element α in the domain such that α has the property denoted by $p(x)$.

Now, if a is a name and $p(x)$ a 1-place predicate, we say that a structure M makes the formula $p(a)$ true just in case the interpretation of a (which is just an element of D) is a member of the interpretation of $p(x)$ (which is just a subset of D). This is intuitively correct: the formula $p(a)$ has the intuitive reading "*a* has the property p", so this formula should count as true in a structure M just in case the individual denoted by a is in the extension of the predicate $p(x)$. If $p(a)$ is true in M we say that M *models* the formula $p(a)$, or that M *is a model for* $p(x)$; we write

$$M \models p(a).$$

Of course, not all formulae which we write down will be true in a given structure M. If $p(a)$ is false in M – i.e. if M does not model $p(a)$ – we write:

$$M \not\models p(a).$$

What of predicates with more than one argument, such as is_on(x, y), or loves(x, y)? The interpretation of a 2-place predicate – say, loves(x, y) – is a set of ordered pairs of elements of D (intuitively, the set of those ordered pairs of domain elements such that the first member of the pair loves the second). So we say that the interpretation function I maps the predicate loves(x, y) to that set of of ordered pairs of individuals. This is difficult to draw using a diagram such as figure A.1; but the idea is the same as for 1-place predicates. More generally, if $r(x, y)$ is a 2-place predicate, then the interpretation of $r(x, y)$ in M is a set of ordered pairs of individuals in D. This set is likewise referred to as *the extension* of $r(x, y)$ (in M): intuitively, it is the set containing any ordered pair of elements $\langle \alpha, \beta \rangle$ such that α and β stand in the relation denoted by $r(x, y)$.

Furthermore, if a and b are two names denoting domain elements α and β, respectively, and $r(x, y)$ is a 2-place predicate, the formula $r(a, b)$ will be true in M just in case the ordered pair $\langle \alpha, \beta \rangle$ is a member of the interpretation of $r(x, y)$. Again, this is intuitively correct: the formula $r(a, b)$ has the intuitive reading "*a* stands in the relation r to b", so this formula should count as true in a structure M just in case the pair of individuals denoted by a and b is in the extension of the predicate $r(x)$. Again, in this case we write

$$M \models r(a, b).$$

Exactly the same principle applies in determining the truth-values of such formulae with three or more arguments.

Once we have rules for determining the truth-values of atomic formulae (i.e. formulae involving no Boolean connectives or quantifiers), the truth-values of Boolean combinations thereof are determined via the standard truth-tables. Expressing these somewhat more succinctly, we may write:

$M \models \phi \,\&\, \psi$ iff $M \models \phi$ and $M \models \psi$

$M \models \phi \vee \psi$ iff $M \models \phi$ or $M \models \psi$ (or both)

$M \models \neg\phi$ iff $M \not\models \phi$

$M \models \phi \rightarrow \psi$ iff $M \not\models \phi$ or $M \models \psi$ (or both)

The reader should check that these really are just the rules encapsulated in the truth-tables given for $\&$, $\vee$, $\neg$ and $\rightarrow$ in section A.2.2.

The rules for determining the truth-vales of quantified formulae are complicated to state here, and would involve us in too much irrelevant detail. But we can get an idea of their flavour by giving the following special cases:

If $p(x)$ is a 1-place predicate, then the formula $(\exists x)p(x)$ is true in structure M, i.e.

$$M \models (\exists x)p(x),$$

just in case there is (at least) one domain element in the interpretation of $p(x)$ in M.

Similarly, the formula $(\forall x)p(x)$ is true in structure M, i.e.

$$M \models (\forall x)p(x),$$

just in case every domain element is in the interpretation of $p(x)$ in M.

As they stand, these rules are not quite adequate, because they do not enable us to state the truth-conditions for formulae such as

$$(\exists x)(\mathrm{man}(x) \,\&\, \mathrm{philosopher}(x)) \quad \text{or} \quad (\forall x)(\mathrm{man}(x) \rightarrow \mathrm{mortal}(x)),$$

where the quantifiers are applied to complex expressions. The reader interested in a full statement of the semantics of the predicate calculus, including a proper treatment of those aspects we have skipped here, is referred to any introduction to formal logic. (See further reading.) But it should not be difficult to see, in outline, how rules can be given which enable us to decide, for a given structure M, the truth-value of every formula in the predicate calculus, just as the truth-tables of section A.2.2 enable us to decide, for a given assignment of truth-values to proposition letters, the truth-value of any formula in the propositional calculus.

As with the propositional calculus, so also with the predicate calculus, certain semantic notions present themselves as salient:

Definition *A formula which is true in every possible structure M is called a tautology.*

A formula which is false in every possible structure M is called a contradiction.

For example, the formula $\mathrm{philosopher}(\mathrm{socrates}) \vee \neg\mathrm{philosopher}(\mathrm{socrates})$ is a tautology. To see this, note that, in any model M, the individual represented by socrates either is or is not in the extension of $\mathrm{philosopher}(x)$. In the former case, we have $M \models$ philosopher(socrates); in the latter, $M \models$ ¬philosopher(socrates). Either way, the truth-table for $\vee$ guarantees that

$$M \models \text{philosopher(socrates)} \vee \neg\text{philosopher(socrates)}.$$

That is, the formula is true in all models. Likewise, it is easy to see that, the formula philosopher(socrates) & ¬philosopher(socrates) is a contradiction. (See exercises 12 and 13.)

Definition *If two formulae are true in exactly the same structures, then they are said to be logically equivalent.*

Again, if ϕ and ψ are equivalent, we write:

$$\phi \iff \psi$$

Definition *An argument with premises $\{\phi_1 \ldots \phi_n\}$ and conclusion ψ is said to be valid just in case all structures which make all the $\{\phi_1 \ldots \phi_n\}$ true also make ψ true.*

In short: an argument is valid just in case, whenever the premises are all true, the conclusion is also true. Notice that we can rephrase the definition of validity as follows:

Definition *An argument with premises $\{\phi_1 \ldots \phi_n\}$ and conclusion ψ is said to be valid just in case ψ is true in all structures which are models of all the formulae $\{\phi_1 \ldots \phi_n\}$.*

One final semantic notion:

Definition *A collection of formulae $\{\phi_1 \ldots \phi_n\}$ is said to be contradictory just in case there is no structure which makes them all true together.*

Notice that an argument with premises $\{\phi_1 \ldots \phi_n\}$ and conclusion ψ will be valid just in case the *conflict set* $\{\phi_1 \ldots \phi_n, \neg\psi\}$ is contradictory.

Again, our interest in these properties from the point of view of formalizing reasoning should be obvious. In particular, we are interested in valid arguments, because they represent patterns of reasoning which are guaranteed never to lead from truth to falsity.

A point of notation. As with the propositional calculus, so too with the predicate calculus, if an argument with premises $\phi_1, \ldots, \phi_n$ and conclusion ψ is valid, then we write

$$\{\phi_1, \ldots, \phi_n\} \models \psi.$$

Likewise, if ψ is a tautology, we write

$$\models \psi.$$

Notice that the symbol $\models$ is being used slightly differently to when we write

$$M \models \psi$$

where M is an interpretation. However, both these uses of $\models$ are common in practice, and no confusion will arise.

A.3.3 Proof theory

In section A.2.2, we saw that it was possible to check the validity of an argument in the propositional calculus by means of a truth-table. Effectively, this procedure amounted to exhaustively enumerating the possible interpretations of the argument's premises and checking to see that those interpretations which make all of the premises true also make the conclusion true. In the predicate calculus, however, this strategy is not open to us, because, in general, sets of predicate-calculus formulae have infinitely many models, so that we could not exhaustively enumerate them. For the predicate calculus, then, an alternative way of determining the validity of arguments – that is to say – a proof theory, is particularly important.

The proof theory of the predicate calculus proceeds much as for the propositional calculus. Again, the stages are:

1. Form the conflict set (premises + negation of conclusion).
2. Convert the conflict set to a set of formulae into clause form.
3. Repeatedly apply the "resolution rule" (described below) to try to derive a contradiction.
4. If a contradiction is found, then the argument is valid.

There are two major differences from the propositional calculus:

1. The process of getting quantified formulae into clause form involves an extra stage, called *Skolemization*.
2. The resolution rule, when modified to handle clause-form formulae containing variables, requires an extra operation, called *unification*.

We shall digress briefly to describe each of these differences in turn.

First digression

Transforming predicate calculus formulae into clause form involves a number of stages. The process is completely mechanical, and we give here only a rough outline. (See further reading.)

Stage 1: Convert to prenex form.

A formula in the predicate calculus in which all the quantifiers are at the front (i.e. have the whole formula within their scope) is said to be in *prenex form*. For example,

$$(\forall x)(\text{man}(x) \rightarrow \text{mortal}(x))$$
$$(\forall x)(\exists y)(\text{loves}(x, y))$$

are in prenex form; by contrast

$$(\forall x)(\text{boy}(x) \rightarrow (\exists y)(\text{girl}(y) \ \& \ \text{loves}(x, y)))$$
$$(\forall x)((\text{boy}(x) \ \& \ (\exists y)(\text{girl}(y) \ \& \ \text{loves}(x, y))) \rightarrow \text{happy}(x)) \quad \text{(A.5)}$$

are not. There is a procedure whereby any formula in the predicate calculus can be converted into a logically equivalent formula in prenex form. For instance, it can be shown that the formulae (A.5) are equivalent to

$$(\forall x)(\exists y)(\text{boy}(x) \rightarrow (\text{girl}(y) \ \& \ \text{loves}(x, y)))$$
$$(\forall x)(\forall y)((\text{boy}(x) \ \& \ \text{girl}(y) \ \& \ \text{loves}(x, y)) \rightarrow \text{happy}(x)), \qquad \text{(A.6)}$$

respectively.

Stage 2: Purge existential quantifiers.

Consider the formula

$$(\exists x)(\text{man}(x) \ \& \ \text{philosopher}(x))$$

This says that some man is a philosopher. So we might as well introduce a name, say a, to stand for such an object, thus:

$$\text{man}(a) \ \& \ \text{philosopher}(a).$$

(This name must be *new*: i.e. not occurring in any other formulae.) Similarly, the formula

$$(\exists y)(\forall x)(\text{loves}(x, y))$$

can be transformed into

$$(\forall x)(\text{loves}(x, b))$$

where b is our new name for that most fortunate of people who is loved by everyone. Things are different however, for:

$$(\forall x)(\exists y)(\text{loves}(x, y)).$$

This formula must be transformed into:

$$(\forall x)(\text{loves}(x, f(x)))$$

where f is a function (called a *Skolem function*). Note the use of a function (rather than a constant): the formula says that everyone loves someone or other – *but not necessarily the same person*. So we need a function whose value depends on x. More generally, the process of removing any existential quantifier $(\exists z)$ involves replacing all occurrences of its variable z by a term of the form $f(x_1, ... x_n)$, where f is a *new* function symbol (i.e. one not occurring anywhere else in the premises), and $x_1, ..., x_n$ are the variables occurring in the universal quantifiers which precede the existential quantifier being removed. If there are no preceding universal quantifiers, we replace z with a new constant symbol a. This whole process is known as *Skolemization*.

As an example, consider the formulae (A.6), which have been put in prenex normal form. Skolemizing gives:

$$(\forall x)(\text{boy}(x) \rightarrow (\text{girl}(f(x)) \ \& \ \text{loves}(x, f(x))))$$
$$(\forall x)(\forall y)((\text{boy}(x) \ \& \ \text{girl}(y) \ \& \ \text{loves}(x, y)) \rightarrow \text{happy}(x)), \qquad \text{(A.7)}$$

respectively.

Stage 3: Once we have removed all the existential quantifiers in this way, we are left with a formula having only universal quantifiers at the front. Since all quantifiers are universal, these carry no information, and can simply be dropped. (That is, we will henceforth take all variables to be implicitly universally quantified.) For example, removing the universal quantifiers from the Skolemized formulae (A.7) gives:

$$\text{boy}(x) \rightarrow (\text{girl}(f(x)) \ \& \ \text{loves}(x, f(x)))$$
$$(\text{boy}(x) \ \& \ \text{girl}(y) \ \& \ \text{loves}(x, y)) \rightarrow \text{happy}(x), \qquad \text{(A.8)}$$

respectively.

Stage 4: Finally, we put the remaining quantifier-free formula into clause form. This process proceeds exactly as for the propositional calculus. For example, putting the quantifier-free formulae (A.8) into clause form gives:

$$\neg\text{boy}(x) \lor \text{girl}(f(x)), \qquad \neg\text{boy}(x) \lor \text{loves}(x, f(x))$$

$$\neg\text{boy}(x) \lor \neg\text{girl}(y) \lor \neg\text{loves}(x, y) \lor \text{happy}(x), \qquad \text{(A.9)}$$

respectively. Notice that the first formula actually translates into two clauses. End of first digression.

Second digression

Resolution in the predicate calculus proceeds just like resolution for the propositional calculus, except that now we may have to substitute various expressions for variables in order to make resolution possible.

Consider, for example, the two premises:

$$(\forall x)(\text{man}(x) \rightarrow \text{mortal}(x)) \qquad\qquad \text{man}(\text{socrates}).$$

In clause form, these become:

$$\neg\text{man}(x) \lor \text{mortal}(x) \qquad\qquad \text{man}(\text{socrates}).$$

Remember: the variable x here is (implicitly) universally quantified. This means that, if the original formulae are true, we can substitute any name for x, and still get a true formula. Suppose, then, we substitute the name socrates for x. We then obtain:

¬man(socrates) ∨ mortal(socrates)   man(socrates).

At this point, we can apply the special case of the resolution rule

$$\frac{\neg\phi \lor \psi \qquad\qquad \phi}{\psi}$$

which, in this case, is

$$\frac{\neg\ \text{man(socrates)} \lor \text{mortal(socrates)} \qquad \text{man(socrates)}}{\text{mortal(socrates)}}\ .$$

   Thus, in predicate calculus resolution, we choose assignments of expressions to variables in the formulae so as to produce instances to which we can apply the normal (propositional calculus) resolution rule. In the previous example, we chose the assignment:

$$x \longleftarrow \text{socrates}$$

in order to 'match' man(x) in ¬man(x) ∨ mortal(x) with man(socrates). Notice that, when an expression is assigned to a variable, *all* instances of the variable in the formula in question must be replaced. This process of choosing assignments to variables in order to make two formulae match is called *unification*. Deciding under what substitutions, if any, two formulae unify can be achieved by a straightforward algorithm. Again, the details are not particularly important for our purposes, and we omit them. End of second digression.

   We now have all the components required for our proof procedure. To see how they all fit together, consider the following simple argument:

All men are mortal

<u>Socrates is a man</u>

Socrates is mortal

This argument gets formalized as:

$$\frac{(\forall x)(\text{man}(x) \to \text{mortal}(x))}{\frac{\text{man(socrates)}}{\text{mortal(socrates)}}}.$$

Now for the proof procedure. We follow the four-stage strategy outlined above.

   1. The conflict set of the argument is:

$$\{(\forall x)(\text{man}(x) \to \text{mortal}(x)),\ \text{man(socrates)},\ \neg\text{mortal(socrates)}\}$$

2. Getting this conflict set into clause form simply involves removing one quantifier and applying a standard propositional calculus equivalence. The result is

$$\{\neg\text{man}(x) \vee \text{mortal}(x), \quad \text{man}(\text{socrates}), \quad \neg\text{mortal}(\text{socrates})\}$$

3. We then apply resolution to derive a contradiction:

1. $\neg\text{man}(x) \vee \text{mortal}(x)$ ⎫
2. $\text{man}(\text{socrates})$ ⎬ conflict set
3. $\neg\text{mortal}(\text{socrates})$ ⎭

4. $\neg\text{man}(\text{socrates})$ from 1 and 3
5. contradiction   from 2 and 4

4. Since we have derived from the conflict set (by truth-preserving rules), a direct contradiction, we know that the propositions in the conflict set are contradictory, and hence that the original argument is valid.

A more complex example is provided by the argument:

> Any parent of someone is that person's ancestor
> Any ancestor of someone's parent is that person's ancestor
> Pam is a parent of Bob
> Bob is a parent of Ann
> Ann is a parent of George
> _____
> Pam is an ancestor of George

This argument gets formalized as:

$(\forall x)(\forall y)(\text{parent}(x, y) \rightarrow \text{ancestor}(x, y))$
$(\forall x)(\forall y)(\forall z)(\text{parent}(z, y) \,\&\, \text{ancestor}(x, z) \rightarrow \text{ancestor}(x, y))$
$\text{parent}(\text{pam}, \text{bob})$
$\text{parent}(\text{bob}, \text{ann})$
$\text{parent}(\text{ann}, \text{george})$
_____
$\text{ancestor}(\text{pam}, \text{george})$

Putting the conflict set into clause form, and applying the indicated sequence of resolution steps gives us a direct contradiction:

1. $\neg\text{parent}(x, y) \vee \text{ancestor}(x, y)$ ⎫
2. $\neg\text{parent}(z, y) \vee \neg\text{ancestor}(x, z) \vee \text{ancestor}(x, y)$ ⎪
3. $\text{parent}(\text{pam}, \text{bob})$ ⎪
4. $\text{parent}(\text{bob}, \text{ann})$ ⎬ conflict set
5. $\text{parent}(\text{ann}, \text{george})$ ⎪
6. $\neg\text{ancestor}(\text{pam}, \text{george})$ ⎭

7. $\neg\text{parent}(z, \text{george}) \vee \neg\text{ancestor}(\text{pam}, z)$ from 2 and 6
8. $\neg\text{ancestor}(\text{pam}, \text{ann})$ from 5 and 7

9. ¬parent(z, ann) ∨ ¬ancestor(pam, z)   from 2 and 8
10. ¬ancestor(pam, bob)   from 4 and 9
11. ¬parent(pam, bob)   from 1 and 10
12. contradiction   from 3 and 11

Hence, the argument is shown to be valid.

One final point of notation. As with the proof procedure for the propositional calculus, so with the proof procedure for the predicate calculus, if an argument with premises $\phi_1, \ldots, \phi_n$ and conclusion ψ can be shown to be valid by our proof strategy, we write:

$$\{\phi_1, \ldots, \phi_n\} \vdash \psi.$$

And again, if ψ is a theorem, we write

$$\vdash \psi.$$

A.3.4 Heuristics, correctness and completeness

As with the propositional calculus, it is important to consider whether the properties of correctness and completeness apply to the proof procedure we have just introduced. Recall that the validity of arguments is defined with reference to the semantics of the predicate calculus: (an argument is valid if its conclusion is true in all structures in which all of its premises are true.) Recall also that a proof procedure which does not say of any invalid arguments that they are valid is *correct* (otherwise *incorrect*). And a proof procedure which, given a suitable sequence of resolution steps, says of any valid argument that it is valid is *complete*. We have the following theorem:

Theorem *The proof procedure described in section A.3.3 is correct and complete with respect to the standard semantics for the predicate calculus.*

The proof is rather complicated for beginners in logic, and will not be given here. (See further reading.)

Note that, with the aid of the symbols $\models$ and $\vdash$, we can write this theorem more succinctly as:

Let $\phi_1, \ldots, \phi_n, \psi$ be any formulae in the predicate calculus. Then

$$\{\phi_1, \ldots, \phi_n\} \vdash \psi \quad \text{if and only if} \quad \{\phi_1, \ldots, \phi_n\} \models \psi.$$

Again, it should be stressed that logic is, first and foremost, a theory of *validity*. It tells us *whether* a given argument, broken down into its elementary steps, is valid. What logic is not is a theory which tells us *how to find* an argument for a given conclusion, on the basis of given premises. As with the propositional calculus, guiding the choice of reasoning steps from among the many possible ones is the job of heuristics. For the predicate calculus, reliance on good heuristics is, in a well-defined sense, crucial. For it turns out that the predicate calculus, unlike the propositional calculus, is *undecidable*. That is, there is no procedure – i.e. no computer program – which, when given an argument in the predicate calculus as input, can be guaranteed to say of that argument whether it is valid or not. But a full discussion of this topic would take us well beyond the logic required in this book.

Exercises

1. Let the proposition-letters p, q and r stand for the following states of affairs:

p	Block a is on block b
r	Block a is on the table
s	Block a is on block c.

   What states of affairs do the following formulae stand for?

   (a) $(\neg p)$ & q
   (b) $\neg(p$ & $q)$
   (c) $p \to (\neg q)$
   (d) $p \to \neg(q \lor r)$

2. Given the intuitive interpretations of p, q and r in exercise 1, write down formulae standing for the following states of affairs:

   (a) Block a is either on block b or on the table
   (b) Block a is neither on the table nor on block b nor on block c
   (c) If block a is not on block b and not on block c, then it is on the table.

3. Verify the truth-table given in section A.2.2 for the formula (A.3). Calculate a similar table for the formulae

   (a) $p \to (\neg p \lor q)$
   (b) p & $\neg q \to r$
   (c) $(q \to \neg p)$ & $(\neg p \to q)$
   (d) $p \to (q \to r)$
   (e) $(p \to q) \to r$

4. Verify that the following formulae are tautologies by constructing their truth-tables:

   (a) p & $q \to p$
   (b) $p \to p \lor q$
   (c) $((p \lor q)$ & $(\neg q \lor r)) \to (p \lor r)$

5. Verify that the following formulae are contradictions by constructing their truth-tables:

   (a) $(p \to \neg p)$ & $(\neg p \to p)$
   (b) $\neg(p$ & $q \to p)$
   (c) $\neg((p$ & $q) \lor (p$ & $\neg q) \lor (\neg p$ & $q) \lor (\neg p$ & $\neg q))$

6. Verify the logical equivalences (A.4) by filling in the appropriate truth-tables.

7. Consider the following argument, concerning the robot, Bob, of chapter 1:

> If the table is in the bedroom, Bob cannot be in the sitting room. Bob is either in the sitting room or in the study. The table is in the bedroom. Therefore, Bob is in study.

Choose proposition letters, p, q and r to represent appropriate states of affairs, so that this argument can be formalized using the propositional calculus. Use the method of truth-tables illustrated at the end of section A.2.2 to demonstrate that this argument is valid.

8. Use the refutation proof-procedure of section A.2.3 to establish the validity of the argument in exercise 7. Remember the sequence of steps:

   (a) Form the conflict set (premises + negation of conclusion).
   (b) Convert the conflict set to a set of formulae in clause form.
   (c) Repeatedly apply the resolution rule to derive a contradiction.
   (d) If a contradiction is found, then the argument is valid.

   (Hint: in step b, you may need to use the logical equivalence $p \rightarrow \neg q \Longleftrightarrow \neg p \vee \neg q$.)

9. The argument

> If the table is in the bedroom, Bob cannot be in the hall. Bob is either in the sitting room or in the study. The table is in the bedroom. Therefore, Bob is in study.

is not valid: that is to say, the premises could all be true and the conclusion false. How would you establish this fact, using the techniques explained here?

10. Let the intuitive interpretation of the predicates $block(x)$, $clear(x)$, $on(x, y)$ be as follows:

$block(x)$	x is a block
$clear(x)$	the top of x is clear
$on(x, y)$	x is on the top of y,

and let a, b, c be names of blocks, and let table denote a particular table on which blocks a, b and c are stacked.
What states of affairs do the following formulae express?

   (a) $clear(a) \& on(a, table)$
   (b) $(\forall x)(block(x) \& clear(x) \rightarrow \neg(\exists y)on(y, x))$
   (c) $(\forall x)(block(x) \rightarrow (on(x, table) \vee (\exists y)(block(y) \& on(x, y))))$
   (d) $(\forall x)(\forall y)(\forall z)((on(x, y) \& on(x, z)) \rightarrow y = z$

11. Given the intuitive interpretations of the names and predicates in exercise 10, write down formulae denoting the states of affairs:

   (a) The table is not a block and is clear
   (b) Block a is either on block b or on the table

(c) Every block has at most one block on it
(d) No block is on itself
(e) If nothing is on a block, then that block is clear.

12. Argue informally that the following formulae are tautologies

(a) philosopher(socrates) $\rightarrow \exists x(\text{philosopher}(x))$
(b) $\forall x(\text{philosopher}(x)) \rightarrow$ philosopher(socrates)
(c) $\exists x \forall y(\text{loves}(x, y)) \rightarrow \forall y \exists x(\text{loves}(x, y))$

(Remember: you must show that they are true in all models)

13. Argue informally that the following formulae are contradictions

(a) $\neg$philosopher(socrates) & $\forall x(\text{philosopher}(x))$
(b) $\neg\exists x(\text{happy}(x))$ & happy(socrates)

(Remember: you must show that they are false in all models)

14. Consider the following argument.

If one block, x, is on another block, y, then block x is above block y
If one block, x, is above another block, y, which is on a third block, z,
   then block x is above block z.
Block a is on block b
Block b is on block c
Block c is on block d
Block a is above block d

Formalize this argument in the predicate calculus, using the predicates on(x, y) and above(x, y). (If you assume that all the elements in the domain are blocks, there is no need for a predicate block(x).) Use the proof procedure explained in section A.3.3 to show that it is valid.
(Hint: compare this argument with the the argument concerning Pam, Bob, Ann and George.)

Further reading

There are many good introductions to logic. One of the most gentle is Hodges [3]. More challenging and mathematical treatments, which cover correctness and completeness results, Skolemization and decidability – topics which we have merely touched on in this introduction – are those by Boolos and Jeffrey [1] and Mendelson [4].

The programming language Prolog is closely related to the predicate calculus. A good introduction to this language, with a clear explanation of its relationship to the predicate calculus, is to be found in Clocksin and Mellish [2].

Bibliography

[1] Boolos, George S. and Richard C. Jeffrey *Computability and logic*, 3rd ed., Cambridge: Cambridge University Press, 1989.

[2] Clocksin, W. and C. Mellish *Programming in Prolog*, 2nd ed., Berlin: Springer, 1984.
[3] Hodges, W. *Logic*, Harmondsworth, Middlesex: Penguin Books, 1977.
[4] Mendelson, Elliott *Introduction to Mathematical Logic*, 2nd ed., New York: D. Van Nostrand, 1979.

Index